RANDOM
HOUSE

LARGE
PRINT

UNITED

CORY BOOKER

UNITED

THOUGHTS ON FINDING COMMON GROUND
AND ADVANCING THE COMMON GOOD

RANDOM HOUSE
LARGE PRINT

To the people of **Harrington Park**
and the surrounding small towns of
New Jersey's Northern Valley
and
to the people of New Jersey's largest city, **Newark:**
These two communities gave me gifts of wisdom,
love, and support
that I can never repay.
I am who I am because of you.
And together you both gave me greater clarity
to see that though there are many lines that
divide and separate us,
they are feeble compared to the powerful ties
that bind and unite us one to another.

CONTENTS

UNITED

INTRODUCTION
EMPATHY, RESPONSIBILITY, ACTION

Mama exhorted her children at every opportunity to "jump at the sun." We might not land on the sun, but at least we would get off the ground.

—ZORA NEALE HURSTON

THIS BOOK IS ABOUT MY POLITICAL AND PERsonal awakening, but it is my hope that the stories within it speak to us all. My official bio—as is so often the case—fails to capture the most meaningful aspects of my life. It marks public and professional achievements, yes, but it ignores the personal journey; the private difficulties and breakthroughs; the low moments and highlights I experienced along the way, where I found true growth and learned hard lessons. Résumé milestones may sound good, but they scarcely begin to account for what gives life real substance and meaning.

Over the past two decades, I have tried to take on some of the thorniest issues of our day, and I have been humbled and inspired, time and again, in the search for solutions. In the following pages I will introduce you to many of the people—family and friends, teachers and mentors, grassroots leaders and determined citizens—who influenced, shaped, and guided me at the moments I needed it most: people who didn't necessarily have fancy résumés but who, in the face of staggering challenges, managed to bring about substantive change and make profound contributions to their communities. They are people I try to honor every day. To honor someone is not just about venerating them; it's about learning from them. And one of the most valuable things I've learned since moving to Newark almost twenty years ago is the need for a deeper awareness of our human connection.

I've learned that we must be more courageous in the empathy we extend to one another; we must shoulder a deeper responsibility for one another, and we must act in greater concert with one another. This is the wisdom that has been imparted to me by so many of the people I have met on my life's journey. It is a refrain I have heard, time and again, and come to revere: the lines that divide us are nowhere near as strong as the ties that bind us; despite our very real differences, we share common interests, a common cause, and, incontrovertibly, a common destiny. And it is this spirit, this ideal, that is at the core of this book.

E pluribus unum—out of many, one. I am proud of this virtue, so evident in the people I've met in my life, and find myself returning to it as one of our most consequential values. Our nation speaks of individual rights and freedoms, personal responsibility and self-reliance, and yet we have consistently demonstrated, in spirit and sacrifice, the idea that we are better together—that while our differences matter, our nation matters more.

We make a grave mistake when we assume this spirit of connectedness is automatic or inevitable. It is not a birthright. A united country is an enduring struggle. It takes collective work and individual sacrifice. It is not enough to call on others or wait for a leader to emerge who will exalt our national values. I believe this is the question we face, as citizens of this nation: what will we do to affirm this most critical American virtue? When too many are despairing over a nation that seems mired in partisanship, divisions, and petty grievances, and a society that still struggles to address enduring injustices, it is imperative that we recognize the power we have to transform the reality we criticize or condemn. As Alice Walker wrote, "The most common way people give up their power is by thinking they don't have any."

We have a choice to make: accept things as they

are or—like so many before us, from the patriots of Lexington and Concord to the Freedom Riders of the modern civil rights movement—take responsibility for changing things. We must push ourselves out of our comfort zones, and realize that the world will not change unless we do. It is not enough to seek modest improvement; we must reach beyond such meager measures and find the breakthroughs that come from working together. We must begin to **see** and understand one another, and to realize that we are one another's best hope to fulfill our nation's bold promise.

In the end, it is up to us to instruct, inspire, and encourage one another by what we do and how we live. We must all, in this sense, be activists. If we want more connection, we must work harder to connect with others. If we want more unity, we must work to be uniters. If we want more leadership, then we must lead. The most profound changes in our country have come when individuals joined with other individuals in the stubborn belief that they could make change. This is a phenomenon I have been blessed to witness throughout my life and career, and it is a lesson I have learned the hard way, through trial and error, and through the grace and generosity of those I have met on my journey.

What we need now, more than anything else, are people who are willing to do the difficult work of bridging gaps and healing wounds, people in our communities who can rally others together, across lines of division, for the greater good, people who reject cynicism and winner-take-all politics, and instead embrace the more difficult work this generation now faces: to unite our country in common cause.

I celebrate ideals of individual excellence, self-reliance, and personal responsibility. These are values that were instilled in me by my mother and father, and modeled for me by a loving community of elders. I hold these values deeply. But rugged individualism alone did not get us to the moon. It did not end slavery, win World War II, pass the Voting Rights Act, or bring down the Berlin Wall. It didn't build our dams, bridges, and highways, or map the human genome. Our most lasting accomplishments require mutual effort and shared sacrifice; this is an idea that is woven into the very fabric of this country. You need look no further than the Declaration of Independence, in which the Founders set forth the essential notion that we must, above all, be committed to one another: "And for the support of this Declaration," they wrote, "with a firm reliance on the protection of divine Providence, we mutually pledge to each other our Lives, our Fortunes and our sacred Honor." Or to George Washington, who reminded our young nation in his farewell address: "You have in a common cause fought and triumphed together; the independence and liberty you possess are the work of joint counsels and joint efforts—of common dangers, sufferings, and successes."

This book is my attempt to honor the best of our history and the truth of my mentors, and to share some of the ideals they instilled in me: empathy and connection, responsibility and obligation—and, perhaps most of all, the urgent need to act. It is my hope that the people in the chapters that follow form a chorus of conviction, a clarion call to our country: to find common ground, and to advance the common good by joining together in common cause. Or, put simply, to be united.

1

A CONSPIRACY
OF LOVE

Know from whence you came. If you know whence you came, there are absolutely no limitations to where you can go.

—James Baldwin

I HATE Henry Louis Gates Jr.

Okay, I don't, I love him. But can I at least say that he is guilty of assault and battery on my ego? That he has a talent for inflating the egos of others only to deftly and without warning pop them . . . and then to sport a rascally grin, as if to say, **What, did I do something?**

And what was the transgression committed by this public intellectual, this Harvard professor of African American studies, this award-winning filmmaker and author and editor of dozens of books? It was calling me up and offering me a dream, saying something like, **Cory, hey, man, I've got this show called** Finding Your Roots **where we trace the ancestry of two individuals** . . .

I knew about these shows, of course. The premise was to select well-known personalities—Oprah, Chris Rock, Barbara Walters, John Legend, Martha Stewart—and through research, DNA testing, and more, unearth their genealogical roots. The stories were fascinating and often shocking, complete with reveals in which guests lit up with joy or were struck with astonishment at the realization of who they are and where they come from. Many guests wept at the revelation. I think the good professor likes to make people cry on TV.

I figured he was calling me to invite me to a premiere.

Well, we decided to do a special about two elected leaders, he said, **and I want you to be one of them. Interested?**

I almost dropped the phone. **Interested?** Are you kidding? I'd love that. But are you sure?

He responded with something like, **Absolutely. I thought it would be good to get someone from your generation, an up-and-comer** . . . He went on saying such nice things about me. I didn't care whether or not they were true—they were compliments from a man I looked up to. As we talked, I was full of excitement at the prospect of having my genealogy traced. Then I thought of something.

"Can I ask who you're pairing me with on the show?"

John Lewis, he said.

I said nothing. I might have stopped breathing. He repeated the name deliberately, perhaps to fill the silence, or maybe to stick it to me a bit more.

John Lewis.

Congressman John Lewis is a living legend, and a hero of mine and to many. He was born a son of sharecroppers outside of Troy, Alabama. Inspired by Dr. Martin Luther King Jr., Lewis left Fisk University to go to the front lines of the civil rights movement in America. He helped found and was eventually named chairman of one of the most important civil rights organizations of the time: the Student Nonviolent Coordinating Committee (SNCC). Lewis organized voter registration drives and sit-ins; he led the Freedom Rides; he was a keynote speaker at the March on Washington. More than once he was beaten during his nonviolent protests. He was renowned for his humility, self-sacrifice, and leadership, and was seen by many as one of the most courageous people in the civil rights movement. Today Lewis serves in the House of Representatives; thanks to his moral stature, his grace, and his statesmanship, he is considered the conscience of the Congress.

All of which is to say that Henry Louis Gates Jr. had envisioned a show in which he would partner Jimmy Olsen with Superman.

I did the show, and—this is a phrase I don't throw around lightly—it was life-changing. I'm profoundly grateful to Professor Gates for the opportunity. But of course any viewer could detect the difference between our introductions. In my head, I heard the announcer in a deep TV-ready voice:

John Lewis, hero of the civil rights movement, marching with grace and determination from Selma, Alabama, to the Edmund Pettus Bridge on what would become forever known as Bloody Sunday. He stood at the front lines of history, leading peaceful protestors, courageously standing and praying before Alabama state troopers. The troopers fired tear gas, then swarmed into the crowd, wearing gas masks and swinging billy clubs, hitting marchers, striking John Lewis in the skull. This righteous and courageous man literally bled the southern soil red for freedom. . . .

And then, in that same splendiferous voice:

And Cory Booker, of suburban New Jersey, riding his Big Wheel toward his family's five-bedroom, four-and-a-half-bathroom house. He takes a turn too sharply . . . oh no! He falls off, skins his knee, and runs home screaming for his mother. He literally bled the northeastern soil red for . . . Big Wheel riders everywhere.

Like I said, I don't hate Henry Louis Gates Jr., because he managed to put my life in perspective, in light of what came before, in light of where I came from, in light of our collective American heritage. Perhaps he didn't know it (or perhaps he did), but this invitation and his revelations about my family gave me my first full glimpse of the beautiful, seemingly infinite lattice that connects us all. It compelled me to look closer, to see how my family's journey intersected with and almost immediately benefited from John Lewis and all the others who marched onto that bridge. Their collective courage, leadership, and love helped to unlock a literal door for me and my family—they helped to secure for my family and me a New Jersey home.

I've said many times of my generation that we drink deeply from wells of freedom and opportunity that we did not dig, that we eat from tables prepared for us by our ancestors, that we sit comfortably in the shade of trees that we did not cultivate. We stand on the shoulders of giants.

My family worked to have me understand that there are two interrelated ethics critical for citizenship. One is that we all must take responsibility for ourselves, invest in our own development, strive for personal excellence. My family taught me that we are all responsible for our own well-being, our growth, and most of all our attitude: **The most**

consequential daily decision you make, I was told, **is the attitude you choose as you engage in your day.**

If I was doing a shoddy job of cleaning out the garage, my mother would give it to me about working with the right attitude, about a commitment to excellence. I would hear echoes of the civil rights movement in her lectures about personal accountability, complete with Dr. Martin Luther King Jr. quotes tailored to the chore: "If it falls your lot to be a street sweeper, sweep streets like Michelangelo painted pictures. Sweep streets like Shakespeare wrote poetry. Sweep streets so well that all the hosts of heaven and earth will have to pause and say, 'Here lived a great street sweeper who swept his job well.'"

But my family also insisted that personal ethic must be seamlessly bound with a larger communal ethic, a sense of connectedness: a recognition that we are all a part of something and have reaped the benefits of the struggles waged by those who had an unwavering commitment to the common good. From my earliest days, I was informed that I was the result of a conspiracy spanning space and time—that billions of meritorious actions past and present yielded the abundance I enjoy.

These twin ethics—responsibility and connection—reverberated throughout my young life, especially when I started to enjoy personal success. In my last years under my parents' roof, my father would watch me walking around the house with a particular degree of teenage swagger, and he'd make a crack: "Son, don't you dare walk around this house like you hit a triple, 'cause you were born on third base." Then I would inevitably hear stories about my father's childhood: born poor, to a single mother, in the segregated South. He would detail the many people whose acts of kindness, decency, and love had enabled him to escape poverty and dislocation. He made it clear to me that I was—that we in this generation are—the physical manifestation of a conspiracy of love. The conspiracy of love wasn't conducted with grand gestures or expansive deeds; it was powered by people who practiced consistent acts of decency that, when combined over time and with the acts of others, carried a transformational power. My father made it clear to me as a child that I was alive because of the relentless actions of humble people who will never make it into a history book but define the character of this country. He called on me to be such a person, to always remember that the biggest thing you can offer on any given day is a small act of kindness.

My maternal grandparents also embodied this ethic of kindness. They helped raise my brother, my five cousins, and me; they were ever present in our lives. I savor memories of grandparent getaways in their big green mobile home, which my grandfather called **The Green Dream**. My grandparents drove us across America in it, all the while modeling for us the virtues of kindness, generosity, and compassion. And they were fun! As we crisscrossed the country, my grandfather was a font of family lore, American history, and bad jokes.

"Do you know why they call this town Yuma, Arizona?" he'd ask. "Well, it's because it was founded on the site of a famous gunfight. One man shot the other, and the dying man's last words as he grabbed his chest was to yell at the shooter, 'You mo . . . !' " My grandfather feigned grabbing his chest and mouthed the rest of the sentence, **you motherf——**, to the delight of his grandchildren.

My grandparents showed up at every one of my graduations from eighth grade through law school. For them education was paramount, and I think my graduations were more emotionally significant for them than they were for me. And on those days my grandfather's humor was once again present. When I graduated from Stanford it was: "So, I see you aren't graduating magna cum laude or summa cum laude—you are just 'Thank ya, Lawdie, I'm outta here.' " But after the jokes, my grandfather would get serious, grabbing my arm to get my attention and make his point. His lectures would go something like this:

Son, what you are doing now, the doors you are opening and that are opening to you; this, this all would have been a dangerous dream for me even to say out loud

when I was growing up. Saying out loud in front of some folks that one day my grandson, my blood, would graduate from a school like this could have come with consequences.

This degree you hold, you earned it through your hard work; be proud of that. But you can't forget—don't you ever forget—that it was also paid for by the blood, sweat, and tears of your ancestors.

My grandfather talked often of ancestors, and I imagined them, but I could not name them and knew little of their lives. But then came Henry Louis Gates Jr., and he finally gave me a measure of insight into my history—the history I wished my grandfather had lived to know.

After Gates and his team did their research, they kept it from me. Gates was saving it for the cameras—the big reveal. But he did tell me one thing over the phone: "Cory, you hit the lottery."

Gates explained that for most blacks it is hard to trace their history beyond 1870. With slavery officially abolished by the Thirteenth Amendment in 1865, and with the Fourteenth Amendment in 1868 more firmly establishing the citizenship of all blacks, the 1870 census was the first that sought to include all blacks. Before this, the recording of black lives and documentation of black history in America was often consciously omitted, obscured, and overlooked. As Gates's team examined my family tree, they were able to find a wealth of records that helped them trace much of my background well beyond 1870. He was genuinely surprised by how much he found.

On the day of the filming Gates walked me through my ancestry, including an analysis of my chromosomes. The expanding research on DNA shows how truly interconnected we are, if not actually related to one another. Gates informed me that most American blacks—save those who immigrated recently and directly from nations in Africa—have a significant amount of European blood, usually far more than they would guess. His team tested my DNA and found that my ancestry was 47 percent African, 45 percent European, and 7 percent Native American.

In constructing my actual family tree, Gates's team was able to trace many of my black ancestors, giving me invaluable peeks into their lives. He also answered some questions with regard to the white Americans from whom I descend.

As names and histories were revealed, I saw the intersecting cords of American history—and learned the deeds and experiences of my ancestors. I am descended from slaves and slave owners. I have Native American blood and am also the great-great-great-grandson of a white man who fought in the Creek War of 1836, in which Native Americans were forcibly removed from their land.

I am the great-great-grandson of many slaves, and I am also the great-great-grandson of a corporal who fought in the Confederate Army and was captured by Union troops.

Gates and his team solved an enduring family mystery: the identity of my grandfather's father. My grandfather was born in 1916 in Columbia, Louisiana. He describes his birth in his journal:

> I was told later that a lot of hell was raised when I was born. A 14 lb baby boy, white with red hair and freckles. Needless [to say] I was different from my brothers and my mother's husband. There was a lot of white blood in my ancestors and this sort of quieted some of the gossip.

My grandfather's mother, Alzenia, whom I knew as a boy—we all called her "Big Mamma"—spoke of people who were "passing." This is a practice that was more common than many people know, by which biracial black Americans with certain European features would go into white communities, conceal their black identity, and live as whites, marrying and having families of their own. In this time of legal segregation—and of laws such as the "one-drop rule," which determined that people with even one ancestor who was black faced fierce denials of opportunity and vicious hate—some chose to escape. As Gates would tell me, more white folks in our nation have black ancestry than would ever realize it, not just because of relatively common interracial sex—voluntary and forced—but also because of people who were passing. As my grandfather wrote in his journal:

> Mama said her folks came from Raleigh, North Carolina and that they had half sisters that were passing for white that resided in Raleigh, NC.

My grandfather told me that, as a kid, he endured considerable abuse because of questions about who his father was. Many didn't believe he was the biological son of his father. He told me later that he carried the stigma throughout his childhood of being a "bastard."

When he was thirteen years old, on a visit to a white doctor in Columbia, Louisiana, my grandfather's mother turned to him as they were leaving the office and told him that the doctor they had just visited was his father. She made no more mention of it—yet it suggested to him that the stigma he was enduring was in fact correct.

When I told Henry Louis Gates Jr.'s team this story, they set out to test it to see if it was true. They researched all of the doctors in the Louisiana parish at the time who could have impregnated my great-grandmother. Looking at the age of my great-grandmother and the age of the doctors in that

Louisiana parish, they centered on a man named Dr. Stephen Henry Brown. They found one of Stephen Brown's descendants—a man named Michael Hislop—and asked if they could test his DNA.

Sitting with me, on camera, Gates walked through all of this slowly and deliberately. He knew about my grandfather's reluctance to talk about his childhood. In fact, I had explained in our pre-taping discussions how uncomfortable my grandfather had been whenever I'd pestered him for information about his father. I had explained that he had described himself as a bastard, using that word, almost wincing as he said it. Now Gates was stating on camera all that he knew—from his research, from my grandfather's journal, from my earlier interviews. He leafed through my deceased grandfather's journal, knowing that this mystery was something that my grandfather had **so** wanted to know—his father's identity, his father's story, his own roots.

Then came the big reveal. The DNA of Michael Hislop made clear that Dr. Stephen Henry Brown, born in 1873 in Catahoula Parish, Louisiana, was my great-grandfather. Gates showed me a picture of a man who looked like the white version of the grandfather I had known and loved so dearly. He showed me a picture of my great-grandfather, my flesh and blood.

As I looked at the photograph of this man, I felt a wellspring of emotions flowing up in me. I felt pain—**God,** I wished my grandfather could have known all this. I wished any remaining shame he'd felt could have turned to satisfaction. He'd deserved to know. I wished he'd had the peace of knowing his father and the solace of meeting his white siblings, nieces, and nephews in a time not so charged with bigotry. I wished that this branch of my family tree had known my grandfather—how great a man he was, that he had flourished despite the discrimination. I stared at my great-grandfather and wondered what he would have thought of his bloodline, his grandchildren, my mother. I wondered what he would have thought of me.

My parents and I would later meet Stephen Brown's grandson, Donald Brown—my mom's first cousin—and his great-grandson Michael Hislop, who had graciously agreed to have his DNA tested. They were informed that they had family in New Jersey, including a black man who was the mayor of Newark. They flew up to see my mom, my dad, and me. It was an incredible reunion. Here were people I would have walked past on the street, never imagining our connection. My conception of the word "family" forever expanded that day.

With all that had been revealed, I found myself focused on one of my ancestors that Gates had described only as "Slave Mother." She was along my grandfather's maternal line, and we knew that a man named James Stamper had owned her. Stamper had impregnated Slave Mother, and she had borne a child, Henrietta Stamper, who was both Stamper's daughter and property. I had heard stories about Henrietta from my grandfather and mother. And now I saw her transition: first as a slave in court documents; then in the 1870 census, where she was free; then in her death certificate, where James Stamper, at one time her owner, was cited as her father.

Knowing this history, I find myself angry that I didn't know Henrietta's mother's name, that I know her only as "Slave Mother." I find myself sad that her history, her parents, and her lineage were erased. I often think about what she might have endured and how she persevered. Who were her other children? Who are their descendants? There must be hundreds now. I think about her and her child, Henrietta; about their lives as slaves and as free people, after their release. I think about what dreams they must have had for their families, what hopes for the future.

Slave Mother and her descendants are now real to me; I can speak some of their names. They challenge me to see family where I once saw only people. I look in the mirror sometimes and search for them in the lines on my face. I find myself looking for Slave Mother in the faces of others. I am not looking for the many unknown branches of my tree, but Slave Mother certainly knew poverty, was devalued, had her dignity assaulted. She was seen as less than human, less than American—or not American at all. I look for my family, for my connection to people who today struggle with such challenges.

Gates also found out a lot about James Stamper, who impregnated Slave Mother. The man who **owned** my great-great-great-grandmother, the man who **is** my great-great-great-grandfather, had a remarkable American history that Gates laid out before my eyes, going all the way back to a John Stamper of Virginia who was either born in America in 1640 or came to America as a child around that time. Jamestown, founded in 1607, was the first permanent English colony in what would become the United States. The Pilgrims founded Plymouth Colony in Massachusetts in 1620. Not long after, John Stamper walked our nascent nation's soil.

I think about John Stamper, too. I wonder about his life as one of the earliest settlers of this country. I wonder why he came to what is now the East Coast of our country. I wonder what he endured, what challenges he faced, how he survived. I also wonder about his dreams for himself and for his descendants. I realize he never could have imagined me, but I live because he lived and dreamed and believed in this land.

I didn't know it when Henry Louis Gates Jr. invited me on his show, but my family and hun-

dreds of others in New Jersey owed a special debt
to John Lewis and the other civil rights organizers who marched from Selma and stood so bravely
on the Edmund Pettus Bridge. As they marched in
Alabama, they changed the destinies of families in
New Jersey.

A young lawyer in Hackensack, New Jersey,
named Arthur Lesemann watched the horrific
events of that march, which would soon become
known as Bloody Sunday. He went to work that
next morning and confronted his partner Leo with
a thought:

> **I said, "Leo, why aren't you in Selma, Ala-
> bama?" Well, get this. This wasn't really
> a joke; it was a poignant way of pointing
> out that we had to do something to get in
> to the most important fight that we would
> probably ever witness in our life.**

Arthur and Leo, two white men, one Protestant
and the other Jewish, were moved, angered, and
inspired by what they saw in Selma and on that
bridge. They believed that they could not just be
spectators to history. They **had** to do something.
Both were just beginning their legal careers and
were not making much money as they tried to
support their young families; it wasn't practical
to just close up shop and head south to help out.
So Arthur and Leo decided that they would look

around for people they could help—to be a part of the civil rights movement in New Jersey. As Arthur remembers:

> **I asked another lawyer up here who had a lot of civil rights contacts if he knew of any organization that looked like they needed some legal assistance. Lo and behold, he mentioned the Fair Housing Council, who he'd had some conversations with a few days earlier. He gave me the appropriate people to call, which I did. We met and we signed on as members. . . . That's when it all began, for us.**

A small group of Bergen County lawyers volunteered to join the efforts of the Fair Housing Council. At the time the council was a cadre of dedicated black and white leaders fighting against housing discrimination, which was rampant in northern New Jersey.

When Arthur and Leo joined in 1965, the president of the council was Lee Porter, a black woman who herself had been helped by the Fair Housing Council a few years before when she and her husband tried to move into Bergen County. Real estate agents refused to show her family homes in most of the seventy towns in the county save for the few that had black neighborhoods. Lee Porter and her husband were able to buy a house thanks to the Fair

Housing Council, yet they still faced challenges actually moving into Bergenfield:

> **Through the Fair Housing Council volunteer, I saw this house in Bergenfield, and I bought it. We're the only black family in that area. We were met with a mob who said, "We're not ready for integration. We don't want you to move here." They were pretty nasty but then some of the other people in the neighborhood said, "No, no, no. We welcome you." Leadership was important because the mayor . . . Charlie O'Dowd was the mayor. He heard about it. He said, "We're not having this in my town. These people are entitled to move here. If they want to move, we're going to protect them."**

After that experience, Lee Porter left her job and dedicated herself to the Fair Housing Council full time. In 1969 she was introduced to a couple looking for housing in Bergen County—Carolyn and Cary Booker.

My parents were living in Washington, D.C., at the time. In 1969 my brother was two years old and my mother was pregnant with me. With help from the Urban League, my father was able to get jobs as the first black salesman for two different companies; then he became IBM's first black salesman in their Arlington, Virginia, office. My father excelled there, eventually making it to the director level of the Golden Circle, which meant he was in the top 5 percent of IBM salesmen in the world. With his success in Virginia, my dad was offered a promotion. He'd be working in the IBM Office Products Division's headquarters in New York City at 590 Madison Avenue. My mom, who worked for IBM as well, got a transfer to work in White Plains. IBM also had an office in Franklin Lakes, New Jersey, so my parents wanted a home that was in the middle of that triangle, close to an airport because of how much they would have to travel for their jobs, and in a town that had good schools for their children. Bergen County was ideal.

My father began searching for homes and found that real estate agents kept directing him to the same few neighborhoods in Bergen County that had significant black populations. At the time you couldn't just find out about houses for sale in the paper and go see them; you had to go through real estate agents. The agents would usually insist on meeting you first, and they would assess you, ask you questions, and determine in their minds where you should or could live. For black couples this meant that agents would simply not show homes in certain neighborhoods—they would "steer" blacks away from some towns and toward others. This injustice angered both of my parents, and they sought legal help. They were referred to the Fair Housing Council.

With the council involved, they began to see homes in predominantly white towns around Bergen County, near Franklin Lakes. My father said when they pulled up to a home they instantly became a neighborhood attraction. Often by the time they walked out, they were greeted by onlookers. It seemed many found an excuse to be outside—watering lawns, walking dogs, pushing kids in strollers. My mother told me that at one point my father rolled down the window, smiled at one of the people on the side of the road, and said, "Don't worry, we didn't like the house."

For the houses that my parents did like, they would be told that the homes had already been sold or been pulled off the market. So Lee Porter and the Fair Housing Council decided to begin to send out white "test couples" to see if indeed the homes were sold or off the market. They weren't.

Porter reached out to Arthur Lesemann and gave him my parents' case file. Arthur, busy with a number of cases for the Fair Housing Council, referred the case to his colleague Marty Friedman. Friedman handled all the legal elements and helped to plan the sting operation that would follow.

My parents visited a home in Harrington Park on Norma Road. They loved it, but as usual, they were told the house had already been sold. The next day, a test couple was sent in by the council. When they looked at the house, they too expressed interest. And to their feigned delight, the house was indeed for sale! With Marty handling all the legal details, the white couple put a bid on the house that was identical to what my parents wanted to offer. The offer was accepted. The white couple went to the real estate agent's office and drew up the paperwork, but they did so without a lawyer. They claimed that they had to meet with their lawyer and would take the contract with them to get a legal review, and then they'd come back on Monday morning with their lawyer to finalize the contract. Marty and the test couple now had the evidence they needed to prove the house wasn't already sold and the agent was in violation of New Jersey law.

On Monday morning at the time of the appointment, as the real estate agent was waiting to close on the house, the white couple didn't show. Instead, Marty Friedman showed up with my father.

My father said he knew there would be trouble when he saw a large Doberman pinscher curled up in the corner of the office. Marty told my mom that what cut through the tension—and the ominous presence of the dog—was a sign hanging in the office that claimed they supported equal opportunity in housing.

The real estate agent looked up, more than a little surprised to see my father. Marty, having been part of sting operations like this before, didn't waste any time. He marched right up to the agent and walked him through the fact pattern. He informed the real estate agent that he was in violation of New Jersey state law and his real estate license was at risk. The Bookers, he explained, would be purchasing the home.

My father said that Marty didn't get much further into his speech. At this point, the real estate agent stood up and punched Marty in the face, then grabbed his paperwork, trying to yank it away and destroy the evidence. The agent called the dog's name, yelling at the dog to "Get 'em! Get 'em!" My father turned toward the dog as it ran at Marty and managed to corral it. He held the dog back as Marty and the real estate agent fought. Things slid off desks, a table and chairs were upended, and Marty was shoved against a window, breaking it. When things settled down, the real estate agent began pleading with my father, swearing that if we moved into Harrington Park, we would wreck the town. He kept insisting that we didn't want to move there, that we wouldn't like it, that we should want to be with our own people, that we didn't want to be responsible for destroying a community.

Lee Porter said the real estate agent was yelling about my parents being black. She recalled that the real estate agent went "ballistic." "There were fisticuffs and then he put the dogs on Marty," she said. My dad always insisted there was only one dog, but I often joked with him that every time he told the story, the dog got bigger—growing from Toto all the way to Cujo over the course of my lifetime. But I do imagine what this must have been like for my father: growing up in the segregated South, making it to college, then integrating company after company, facing biases and bigotry, only to distinguish himself, to excel, and then, at thirty-three, to literally fight his way into a town.

Still, my father never complained to me in telling this story. He even told it with humor: **We moved into Harrington Park and became four raisins in a tub of sweet vanilla ice cream**. My father and mother often talked of it to make a point about people—not the bigots or those who in the face of bigotry did nothing, but those in Harrington Park who embraced us when we moved in. My parents used the story as an example of the conspiracy of love: the lawyers inspired by Bloody Sunday; the volunteers, black and white, who gave up hours and hours to help families like mine; the leaders like Lee Porter, whose steadfast and tireless direction of a small organization has impacted the lives of thousands alive today and those of generations yet unborn. They told me the story to show me that good people doing the right thing can make a tremendous difference.

Marty Friedman is now dead. I never thanked him for what he did for my family, including taking a punch so that we could open a door to walk through.

My mom, modeling Lee Porter, went from a Fair Housing Council client to a volunteer. She went on to become the president of the Bergen County Fair Housing Council's board and helped to bring IBM on as one of the organization's biggest donors.

To this day Lee Porter, almost ninety years old, remains the executive director of the Fair Housing Council—a job she has held for nearly fifty years—and she is still fighting for equal housing rights in Bergen County and beyond.

My parents loved to remind me of what it had taken for us to move into Harrington Park. They reminded me that bigotry and hate can have very different consequences for well-connected IBM executives and their family in Harrington Park than for other, less fortunate people in our country. And this point would often be a launching pad for their discussion of the two American ethics and my place in the world. **Privileges and opportunities say nothing of character and honor,** they would tell me. **Only actions do.** We are ultimately responsible for our actions. We are defined by what we do. Actions, small and large, radiate out into eternity. What we do or fail to do—to one another, for one another, or with one another—leaves a lasting imprint beyond what we can imagine.

Yes, we do drink deeply from wells of liberty and opportunity that we did not dig. We do owe a debt that we can't pay back but must pay forward. We are the result of a grand conspiracy of love.

2

TALENTS

The most important thing to remember is this: to be ready at any moment to give up what you are for what you might become.

—W. E. B. Du Bois

I WAS TWENTY-FIVE YEARS OLD, AND YET I MAR-veled at how my mother could make me feel like a child. Here I was, I had made it to Yale Law School, and my mom still had the power to make me feel like a failure. Or maybe she was simply forcing me to confront my fears of failure. Either way, I was annoyed, and I wanted to be left alone.

"Son, what are your plans for after law school?"

An honest inquiry, a very practical one, but it made me squirm. In reality, she probably didn't ask the question all **that** often—but it felt unrelenting. (In fact, I started hearing the question before I even arrived for my first day of law school.) I hated the question because I had no answer. All I had was worry. For the first time in my life, I couldn't clearly articulate what lay in my future. It frightened me.

I was a focused, goal-oriented kid. Ask me what I wanted from life, where I was going, what the next years held for me, and I could tell you in exacting detail. Not that this was some rare feat. My suburban life was pretty clearly laid out in terms of school, and I loved sports, so my goals focused on excelling in both. I knew what was expected of me and what I wanted for myself—and those were usually the same thing. Until my twenty-fourth year, I lived life with clarity of ambition, a compelling vision of what I would do in the immediate years before me. It gave me comfort, certainty, and strength.

In grade school, my ambition was to get good grades, to be a kind person, and to excel in sports. In my freshman and sophomore years of high school, it remained the same, with the added goal of playing three varsity sports: football, basketball, and track. In my junior and senior years, it was to be a man of character, kindness, and service, and to win a football scholarship to the best academic university I could get into. At Stanford, my goals were similar to those I had in high school—play varsity, get A's, and be deeply involved in public service. College led to a master's degree, which led to a Rhodes Scholarship, which led to law school. Every step of the way, I had whiteboards up in my bedroom or dorm room with my goals written out. I woke up and went to bed determined and focused. There is a blessing, a **gift** in knowing where you are going and what your goals are, to have a feeling every morning that you are waking up with a definiteness of purpose.

Yet in my first year of law school, my bright vision for the future suddenly went dark. My experiences working with kids, engaging with nonprofits, and serving in cities had sparked a powerful drive to dedicate myself to working in these areas. My firsthand experience, my academic studies, and eighteen years of my parents making the point had convinced me that our nation wasn't living up to its promise, that we had work to do to address savage inequalities, persistent injustice, and unequal opportunities. I was good at declaring, detailing, and describing these points, but beyond possessing a knack for making grand statements, I couldn't articulate exactly what I intended to do about them. I was ambition without focus; I had a passion to make a difference but no plan for how to do so.

In law school I wasn't alone. I had a good number of friends who were trying to figure out what they would do next. For many, young adulthood is full of questions and insecurities: What are you going to do? What will your career be? With whom are you going to share the journey? Your twenties are a decade without clear paths, as if you have been walking for a good while on a well-lit road and now it ends at a dark forest; there are hundreds of directions you could take, none of them obviously right. Like many, I found myself standing and staring, hoping for a sign.

For a law school graduate, there are some standard options. There are clerkships, where some of the best and brightest work for judges on the state and federal levels. There are jobs with law and consulting firms. Just months after arriving in law school, many of my classmates were interviewing with firms for summer internships that could lead to first jobs and healthy six-figure salaries.

One of the reasons I picked Yale was because it had a generous loan repayment program for people who wanted to do public interest law. So I never put on a suit for a law firm or consulting group interview, and I had no interest in working toward a clerkship. Instead I threw myself into working at legal clinics that served the New Haven community, I took on a "little brother" through a local mentoring program, and I focused on direct service, hoping that engagement would lead to a clearer idea about what I wanted to do after law school.

During this time my dad didn't put too much pressure on me. His inquiries about my future would usually come amid playful teasing. His way of asking the big question without asking the big question was to invoke an old family joke: "Boy, you got more degrees than the month of July, but you're not hot. When are you going to get a job?"

My mom, however, was persistent and direct. On phone calls home, I was artful at dodging her questions or distracting her with stories of the ongoing work I was doing through the legal clinics. Now, though, I was home on break, my dad was off in a different part of the house, and I was sitting with my mom, relaxing and catching up. Then the question came, and I was cornered.

"Son, what are your plans for after law school?"

"Mom, I don't know," I said. "I haven't figured it out yet. I just want to help people, whatever form that takes. So stop worrying about me. I'm going to be okay."

My mom said nothing. I wondered if I had taken the wrong tone. But she didn't appear angry. She seemed to be studying me, sensing my distress. She was looking at me with compassion.

In the moment before she began to speak, I readied myself to engage in defensive listening—not intending to really hear her, just deliberating in my own mind about the best way to respond or, better yet, change the subject. I knew my mom's lectures well, and by this age I thought I had heard them all. Even when she wasn't around, I often could hear her in my head—my own maternal Jiminy Cricket, persistently propped on my shoulder as I navigated life.

But my mother surprised me. She told me something she'd never said before, and it was a life-altering moment for me. This is how I remember it, all these years later:

Son, you will be okay. I know you will, because God has plans for you. I've known that all your life. But that won't ever stop me from worrying about you. I'm your mother; that's what I do.

You want to serve, you want to make a difference; I'm proud of that. But "whatever form that takes" doesn't sound like a statement of confidence. I wonder if you are saying that out of weakness or strength, out of fear or faith. What is motivating you? How are you looking at the world and what it has in store for you— with fear or faith? You know, son, fear cuts off possibilities, faith expands them; fear locks doors, faith opens them; fear hides, but faith takes risks. God wants you to be courageous, to be faithful. He wants you to use your blessings, not diminish them.

What does it say about you, with all the blessings you have been given in life, that you can't be faithful? All that you have been given, all that you have accomplished, by the grace of God—it would be an affront to Him, an insult, if you weren't

willing to step out with courage and even enthusiasm, if you weren't willing to step out on faith.

Where is your sense of gratitude and the obligation that goes along with it—to show your gratitude by doing for others?

When God gives you blessings, why would you respond by diminishing them? Why would you act small when God created you, commanded you, to be large?

You know the parable Jesus told of the talents?

I looked at her, the woman who'd taken me to Sunday school at a small church in Closter, New Jersey; the woman who at times had taught that Sunday school; the woman who had had me memorize passages from the Bible; the woman who absolutely knew the answer to the question she was asking.

"Yes, Mom," I said, knowing that she was about to tell me the parable anyway.

A master gave three of his servants talents (an ancient unit of money) to take care of while he was away for a long journey. Two of his servants took the talents out into the marketplace, risked them, put them to work, and doubled what the master had given them. But the third was afraid that he would lose the master's money, and so he buried the talent, hiding it from the world. When the master returned, he gathered his servants. He praised the men who had taken risks, who had gone into the marketplace and increased their count. He said to each of the two, "Well done, my good and faithful servant." He rewarded them by bestowing on them more riches. And then he turned to the third, the one who had buried his talent out of fear. He admonished him, called him wicked for his conduct, and took the talent back.

Son, don't bury what God gave you. Don't be the wicked one. This world doesn't need your self-imposed limitations; it doesn't need your fear. You were born to magnify the glory of God, not shrink it. You want to serve this world? Well, the world needs the full measure of your faith, your courage, your boldest thoughts, your most inspiring dreams. This world needs you and the talents God gave you.

I want you to ask yourself something, Cory. Ask yourself what would you do if you could not fail. If you knew for sure you would be successful, what would you do? Who would you be, how would you behave, how would you feel, how would you serve? Answer that question. Feel that.

Act like that. And even if you do fail, I promise you that you will be better for it—wiser, stronger, and more capable. And, success or failure, if you press your talents forward with passion, courage, and faith, when all is said and done, I know God will look upon you and say, "Well done, my good and faithful servant."

My mom had brought the church! And in response, I sat quietly. She had laid waste to my defenses, and she'd planted in me a question that took root in my heart: **What would I do if I couldn't fail?**

It was a question that began to keep me up at night—not with anxiety but with energized thought. The question awakened my imagination again; it ignited dreams.

What would I do if I could not fail?

I took the question everywhere. And I began to love all the questions; the ones that used to haunt me, I was now grateful for them. Questions sparked my creativity. A reaffirmed sense of purpose had been awakened, and I was on a mission to make substantive, meaningful contributions.

I looked around for ideas. If I couldn't fail, what would the elements of my plan be, the steps toward this eventual success? If I were to do good for others, what would I need in order to excel? Whom would I need to meet? How would I need to invest my time?

The most powerful conversations we have in any day are the conversations we have with ourselves. And now my inner dialogue changed. I asked myself empowering questions that generated energy, not ones that sapped it.

I began resurrecting lessons that had served me in years past. Like when I arrived at Stanford as an eighteen-year-old wide receiver to play football and felt overawed by the size, strength, and speed of the older players on the team. After anguishing for a while as I fell on the depth chart and began to believe the coach's estimation of me, I decided to focus on the team's best wide receiver and make a study of him.

I focused on his behavior, how he distinguished himself, how he dared to be different. I listened to the questions he asked, watched what he ate, how he conducted himself on the field and in the gym. I saw that he had an unyielding attention to detail; he not only worked harder, but also worked smarter. He taught me that you cannot have extraordinary success if you don't put in extraordinary effort. I dramatically changed **my** conduct, absorbing and implementing what I observed, and I got results. Not only did my body transform—I lost weight, gained strength, and decreased my time in the forty-yard dash—but my confidence grew. I might have remained low in the coach's estimation, but my feelings of strength and possibility were higher than ever, and they overflowed into all areas of my life. It would take until my junior year for me to make meaningful contributions on game day, yet I still credit the lessons I learned at the bottom of the depth chart as some of the most valuable of my life.

This idea of modeling myself on others, of developing habits that reinforced my mission and my willingness to put in the work, served me well on the field. In law school I reasserted this strategy. I set a goal of having a career path that excited me. I couldn't define that path yet, but I could move ahead with confidence, trusting that the way would soon become clear. I also began looking in earnest for role models—people who were engaged in a bold mission of service; organizations that inspired me and fueled my sense of what was possible in the realm of public service.

At Yale, I immersed myself further in the community of public interest students, faculty, and lawyers. I peppered everyone I knew with questions about who in our nation was doing things that might resonate with my goals. Which were the nonprofits that were improving, even transforming, urban communities and neighborhoods? Which were the organizations working with city youth, nurturing them, empowering them, giving them the tools they needed to soar? Who were the grassroots organizers, activists, and lawyers getting results?

Through my questioning and research, I started discovering and visiting with inspiring organizations and leaders. I found the Vera Institute of Justice, which did hands-on policy work that had led to larger systemic change. I learned about The Door, a nonprofit that provided direct service to youth, including urgently needed legal work. I discovered more about Covenant House, which opened its doors to homeless kids, and helped put them on the path toward stability, strength, and promise. One of the most inspiring people I met during this time was Geoffrey Canada, who led the Rheedlen Centers for Children and Families—an organization that would eventually become the Harlem Children's Zone. He took time to meet with me, to introduce me to his organization, and to answer my many questions.

Not long before, the view at the end of my well-lit path had been of a dark forest. Suddenly, I saw a way forward. More than this, I realized I didn't desire a well-worn path; I wanted to forge my own. I was compelled by the idea that I could be a part of something larger than myself. I wanted to be part of a community that had within its heart and neighborhoods a profound purpose, an underestimated strength, an unappreciated nobility—a place that possessed a stirring civic courage.

That place was Newark, New Jersey.

• • •

I felt connected to Newark before I truly knew it. Newark was about eighteen miles from where I grew up in Harrington Park. As a young child I knew the city through my parents, their friends, and our periodic visits for church or cultural events. Further, when I would ride anywhere with my father or when I just spent time with him around our home, he would listen to the legendary Newark jazz station WBGO—a station that proudly reminded listeners in every station identification that it was "WBGO Newark."

Those Newark-generated sounds were the soundtrack to my childhood; WBGO Newark was, for me, deeply associated with my youth and my father. In a town that was mostly white, my friends' houses and their parents' cars would often resonate with Bruce Springsteen, the Doors, Billy Joel, and AC/DC, or the softer sounds of James Taylor, Frank Sinatra, and Barbra Streisand. My father, though, would play the blues or Motown albums or the radio station's jazz. From Thelonious Monk to Alberta Hunter, from Nina Simone to Charlie Parker, WBGO sent out a cultural beacon for my father, a soul-soothing signal that brought him bliss. He would make me wait in the car with him until a song ended, or gesture to me to hold off on interrupting him in his home office so he could listen just a little more, just a few more notes, and thus reabsorb into his DNA something that had been drained from him in a day of work at IBM. As I grew, I saw that the flavor of WBGO was everywhere in Newark.

My parents' closest friends, Colden and Frances Raines—or Uncle Colden and Aunt Frances, as I called them—had a dental office on Clinton Avenue in Newark's South Ward. I grew up listening to them sharing stories of their city, their love of the people, and the help and kindnesses they extended to folks in the neighborhood beyond dental care. They spoke of Newark with a spirit of defiance, cutting against the harsh criticisms of the city that I heard in other places. When I was growing up in the 1980s, Newark was a place often maligned or feared in the suburbs. Mentions of the city inspired concern or even pity expressed in a way that was often insulting. But Uncle Colden and Aunt Frances would have none of it. They wouldn't let stereotypes undermine the truth they knew of the city and would impart to me. Even in Newark's toughest years it had unassailable points of pride and was undeniably critical to the region. New Jersey was happy to place in Newark a state prison, a county jail, waste disposal sites, sewage treatment facilities, halfway houses, drug treatment centers, a grossly disproportionate share of public and low-income housing, and other necessary public goods that wouldn't be located in surrounding suburban towns. Despite this, Newark still boasted New Jersey's finest cultural institutions, including the state's largest public library and museum. It was the state's largest college town, and it was home to massive job generators such as Newark Liberty International Airport and the nation's third-biggest seaport.

As a young black man who at times felt misunderstood, prejudged, or assaulted by biased notions and reflexive assumptions, I felt a kinship with a city that had endured the same. Yes, I felt at home in New Jersey's predominantly white, more affluent suburbs. I grew up in Harrington Park, Old Tappan, and surrounding suburban townships; these towns, the people, and some of the closest friends of my life are a part of me that I could no more remove than my own heart. But there is something about Newark that is intrinsic to me. I was inspired by the city's resilience, its determination, its defiant attitude, its unshakeable belief in its unappreciated beauty. I felt at home in Newark. Newark was a kindred spirit, a soul-mate city. Newark was family.

In my second year of law school I began visiting Newark with increasing frequency and was more and more energized by the conviction of its people. Among the activists, leaders, philanthropists, and citizens, there was an ever-present and stubborn love for the city—a pride of place that I found infectious. Nobody denied the city's problems, but at the same time people pushed back against anyone who exaggerated them or focused on them and ignored the good, the great, the improving, or the potential. There was a tenacious resolve in Newark to show the world a truth that would upset shallow assertions that Newark was dead. There was a vast communal will to demonstrate that this once great city would rise again. It reminded me of Maya Angelou's poetic declaration: "You may write me down in history / With your bitter, twisted lies, / You may trod me in the very dirt / But still, like dust, I'll rise."

What others scorned, Newarkers defended. Where others saw fault, Newarkers described possibilities. Where others tore down, they sought to elevate. I was taken with this spirit. It spoke to ideas I had about America and our need to see one another for who we are, fellow citizens with interwoven destinies. Here were folks who challenged others: **I stand proudly here in Newark. You may be afraid to even drive through it, but this too is America.** Newark activists seemed to know, at their very core, something vital: if Newark fails, the very idea of America fails.

In my second year as a law student, putting countless miles on my beat-up Mitsubishi Montero, I found Americans rendering incredible service across the tristate region—in Connecticut, New York, New Jersey. Yet in Newark, New Jersey, I found all of that, and I also found the place I wanted to call home. With the determination to go to Newark, I began reaching out with greater focus and frequency to people in the city to learn as much as I could about how

I might contribute. I met with people involved in Newark nonprofits—people who worked at them, ran them, funded them, and advised them. Almost everyone I met impressed and encouraged me. And each new contact would generously introduce me to others, who would in turn suggest other people I should speak with.

By the end of my second year in law school, I had met with hundreds of people in Newark and around the region. In the meetings I consistently bumped into people who were just out of school. They were peers who worked in nonprofits, community development corporations, and advocacy organizations. A handful of us began meeting for breakfast, informally calling ourselves the "Breakfast Club," and we strategized about how the next generation of activists could help Newark. I savored this community of friends as well as many of the elders in the greater Newark community who took an interest in me and who would serve for years as mentors, advisors, and at times constructive and honest critics. One thing about Newark is that there is a refreshing candor and directness about the civic culture—friendship isn't about how nice you are, but rather about how helpful you are to each other.

I split the summer after that second year of law school between doing landlord/tenant legal work at Yale and an internship with a start-up in East Harlem, the Youth and Family Justice Center, that provided legal education for teenagers. This program was started at a time when kids in New York City were increasingly being stopped by the police. It was clear to those of us working there that our summer legal classes for kids had a practical urgency about them. We taught kids about how to interact with the police, what their rights were, and how to avoid unnecessary confrontations. I felt that working with this new nonprofit would not only offer meaningful work and be incredibly fulfilling, but that it would also be the ideal apprenticeship if I was going to start a nonprofit in Newark.

The weeks I was at the Youth and Family Justice Center, I lived in a spare bedroom in the apartment of Doug Lasdon. Doug ran an organization I admired called the Urban Justice Center. Doug and I put together the beginnings of my career plan: I would work for the Urban Justice Center when I got out of law school; then I would apply for a Skadden Fellowship—a public interest law fellowship funded by the law firm Skadden, Arps, Slate, Meagher & Flom LLP—which would fund my salary as a staff attorney for the nonprofit. Doug agreed that he would support my nonprofit in Newark and allow it to operate, in its early stages, under the umbrella of the Urban Justice Center.

That summer I wrote a comprehensive five-year life plan. My boldest dreams flowed out of me and into my journal. There was my business plan for the nonprofit in Newark, but I didn't stop there. I envisioned the life I would lead, all the way down to my hopes for getting married and starting a family. I wrote a personal financial plan for how to get by on my fellowship salary, and even tried to account for a little saving for the future. My plan included spiritual practice and development as well as health goals. When I was finished, I believed it was a masterpiece. I had the clarity I was looking for. As it says in the Bible, "Without vision, the people will perish." Well, I had a vision. I could feel my future; when I closed my eyes, I swear I could see it. With vision, I thought, the person will thrive.

There is an old saying: "If you want to make God laugh, just tell him your plans." And God probably got a hearty chuckle out of my five-year plan. But this was an essential step for me. I had gotten myself moving. Course corrections are a part of life, but they can't happen if you are standing still.

Sometimes in life friends extend to you small kindnesses that have a life-changing impact. In the fall of 1996, such a friend asked me to go with her to a black-tie fundraising event at the New Jersey governor's mansion, Drumthwacket. That night, as I was mining the crowd for Newark contacts, I met two people of special significance.

One was a woman I fell in love with at first sight. I had never before felt such immediate chemistry, and I was so certain she was **the** one that, later that night, I called a friend and told him that I had met my wife.

The other person I met was a man named Ray Chambers.

Ray was born in Newark in 1942 and later graduated from Newark's West Side High School. He came from a humble background and went on to become one of Newark's many great success stories. He amassed extraordinary wealth with his private equity company through buyouts of companies such as Avis and Gibson Greeting Cards. Ray would become a global humanitarian. And though he was involved in causes around the world, he remained one of Newark's most determined and generous philanthropists. For Ray, Newark was a personal mission, and he was directly involved in the city in countless ways. When my friend introduced me to Ray, I talked to him about my vision to contribute to Newark. He seemed keenly interested in my plans. I was struck by how modest and self-deprecating he was. As we wrapped up our conversation, he invited me to his office to talk some more.

It was a few weeks before I would meet with Ray—and it remains to this day one of the strangest meetings I've attended. I felt immediately comfortable with this man—too comfortable, given the short time we had known each other. Ray had a Zen-like aura about him; he seemed sincerely excited about my determination to serve Newark, and his gentle tone and spirit made me feel that he had opened a space in which I could bare heart and soul.

I must have rambled on for a half hour about two things—the woman I loved and the city I wanted to serve; the person I wanted to marry and the nonprofit I would start. Ray listened . . . and listened . . . and listened. He didn't interrupt or seem the least bit impatient. He gave me all the space I needed; I took it, and more. When I finally finished, he said two things. I remember it like this: **Cory, what you are feeling right now is not love. It is infatuation, but it isn't love. You just met her; you don't know each other yet, and more likely than not you will break up with her. And I like that you want to serve Newark, which is so good. But if I may . . .** He paused for a moment, studied me. **Newark doesn't need another nonprofit. If you want to make a difference in the city, you will run for mayor.**

As much as I tried to pretend otherwise, I was undone by Ray's comments. Who **was** this guy? With a few short sentences, he had dashed my dreams. For the first time during that meeting, I contained myself. I was suddenly polite, all the while thinking that he didn't know me, that I was going to prove him wrong with my success in nonprofit work and with my glorious marriage. At the end of the meeting, he generously gave me the names of more people he felt I should talk to, and I left.

The woman I had met that night at the governor's mansion and whom I had begun dating was accomplished in the financial industry and was also involved in philanthropy. She was self-made; while I came from the suburbs, the product of two IBM executive parents, she came from a tough urban neighborhood, raised by a single mom who through work and sacrifice helped her daughter get a set of Ivy League degrees and achieve professional success. She lived at a nice Manhattan address and made a considerable salary; I was actively seeking to find a tough neighborhood I could move into, and while I was thrilled I had won the Skadden Fellowship, it paid about $32,000 a year for each of its two years. She wanted badly to have children as soon as possible and to be a full-time mother; I, on the other hand, was itching to start my professional life. I could see that my five-year plan didn't fit hers. It was a gut check: Should I hold fast to my dreams? Should I alter my path? Should I seek a better-paying job to better support a family?

We broke up after a couple of months of dating. Ray Chambers's prediction came to pass—and quickly. It wasn't love, and it wasn't meant to be. And while I had been angry with Ray that day in his office, sure that he was wrong, he had earned my respect for telling me the truth.

In the autumn of 1996, after asking advice from numerous people about the right neighborhood to move into in Newark, one that faced challenges and would be a good place to start my work, I rented a room on Dr. Martin Luther King Jr. Boulevard across the street from two tall buildings called Brick Towers. One of the members of the Breakfast Club called to give me a key piece of advice: if I was going to live and do nonprofit work in that neighborhood, I had to meet Ms. Virginia Jones.

3

MS. VIRGINIA JONES

That only which we have within, can we see without. If we meet no gods, it is because we harbor none. If there is grandeur in you, you will find grandeur in porters and sweeps.

—Ralph Waldo Emerson

Ms. Virginia Jones insisted that I follow her, so I did as I was told. She was the 68-year-old president of the tenants association at Brick Towers, a pair of sixteen-story low-income buildings that stood at numbers 685 and 715 Dr. Martin Luther King Jr. Boulevard. She slammed and locked her apartment door, and I followed her down the hallway, to the stairwell, down five flights of stairs, through the lobby, across the courtyard, and past the wall that separated the courtyard from the street. Young men stood near the wall; I suspected some of them were drug dealers. On the street she stopped, turned, looked at me, and asked me a question that I will think about for the rest of my life.

My Breakfast Club friend had told me that I had to get to know Ms. Jones before I started working in the neighborhood; in fact, it was critical that I get her **permission.** So I called her and made an appointment to see her.

We met in her apartment and I told her of my good intentions, of my determination to make a difference. I told her about my past experiences helping to run legal clinics, working for nonprofits in four different cities on a host of issues. I told her that I was now living on Dr. Martin Luther King Jr. Boulevard, across from Brick Towers, and that I wanted to help her. She seemed barely interested—gruff, a bit dismissive, very skeptical. I could tell she was assessing me; it was almost like an interview with an employer who seemed to have no time or need for another employee but was nonetheless mildly curious. As I spoke she hardly looked at me, focusing instead on a stack of papers; when the phone rang during our conversation, she answered it and started barking out commands to whoever was on the line. But I persisted, filling silences with my earnest testimony and my thoughts about what I might be able to do to help around the neighborhood.

Then she started asking me questions: Would I be there today only to be gone tomorrow? Would I be committed to the Brick Towers community?

I had assumed I'd be greeted with excitement as a new recruit, that my own commitment would be obvious. These buildings appeared to be in crisis. The conditions inside and out screamed for help, and the street looked to me like a war zone, one battle in the larger and failing drug war. I'd thought she would draft me and put me to work. But now all I could think was that I was failing my interview. And I didn't fail interviews.

This early conversation with Ms. Jones mirrored my first weeks on the street, which weren't going all that smoothly, either. I had worked in cities since I was nineteen, but now, at twenty-seven, I was no longer living on a campus I could return to at day's end. I was renting a room in a boardinghouse in the community. It was a redbrick house built in 1871, and I was in a room in the back of the house that was about ten feet by ten feet with windows that looked out on the backyard. My room was old and run-down. The whole place felt frail, as though if I jumped up and down too much on my floor I would fall through. Setting up my electronics, I realized I couldn't plug too many things in at once because I would blow the house fuse and annoy the other renters.

I encountered the challenges of Dr. Martin Luther King Jr. Boulevard the day I moved in. My best friend from fourth grade, Chris Magarro, helped me move. Chris is a six-foot-seven-inch Italian, a former Rutgers tight end, one part man, one part mountain. We made several trips, carting boxes from his car to my room. After one trip up, we came back down to the street to find that his car had been broken into. And a lot of my belongings were gone. Chris and I looked across the street at Brick Towers and at the guys standing there; they looked back at us. I could tell that this huge friend of mine was intimidated and so was I. We did nothing about what was stolen. We let it go and just kept moving.

There was constant drug dealing on the street. This section of Dr. Martin Luther King Jr. Boulevard, from before Spruce Street to just past West Kinney, was one of the most notorious in the city, and perhaps in the state. It had been the subject of local, state, and federal law enforcement actions, but the dealing remained constant, more brazen than anything I had ever seen. There was boldness, a brashness, a fearlessness to the way the men conducted their trade. Drivers slowed their vehicles and rolled down their windows as they approached, the dealers came to meet them, money and product were exchanged, and then the cars drove off. White friends of mine who came to visit were often mistaken for buyers; guys would knock on their car windows or push drugs at them if their windows were open. My home was next to a vacant building that was nicknamed "Happy House," a place where people of all different backgrounds would come to use drugs. The dealing didn't only disturb me, it fascinated me. I had seen open-air drug dealing before, but this was like nothing I had ever encountered, and far beyond any Hollywood depiction. In those early days, I sometimes knelt in the bathroom at the front of the house and peered out the cracked-open window at the street below. I listened to the men yelling signals back and forth at each other as cars drove up. I watched the efficiency with which they moved their product, all in the open, as if they had no fear of police—as if they had no fear of anything.

But I had fear. I occasionally heard gunfire at night. There were periodic shootings in the area, and people whom I met in the neighborhood often detailed past shootings and murders that occurred in connection with the drug trade. When I walked my street I felt like the guys were watching me. Years later, I tracked down a number of the guys who had dealt drugs in front of Brick Towers and interviewed them, including the man who in the 1980s and early 1990s ran the Brick Towers drug trade, Jace Bradley. They told me that they'd suspected at first that I was in law enforcement; realizing I wasn't, they still found me suspicious. Who was I and how had I gotten there? They told me that they'd wanted to test me, to challenge me to see how I would respond. They'd resented me: Who was I to think I would show up in their neighborhood and change things? As one of the men put it to me: "My thing, yo, is that this motherfucker is cocky, right? He just don't care. I wanted to know everything about [him]. Why is he so cocky like this? Where is he from? Who is he? Who the fuck is he, really?"

My worst confrontation happened early on, before people in the community knew me well. I was walking into the buildings one afternoon to see Ms. Jones, crossing through them, and for the first time I looked at them and did more than just nod; I said something along the lines of "Hello" or "Hey man, what's up?" And that triggered it—they were on me. One of the young men lit into me: "I don't know who the fuck you are! You don't know who I am! Don't you fucking say hello to me, you don't fucking know me! You don't fucking know me!"

Other guys crowded around. I didn't show much emotion in response. I knew instinctively I had to find a balance between not showing fear and not showing aggression—too much of either would have invited more of a confrontation. I stopped momentarily, paused, looked at the guy yelling at me, looked around at the others staring at me, and then just started walking past them, through the courtyard and into the buildings. Only then did the rush of adrenaline hit me, and my heart began to race. I shot up the stairs to see Ms. Jones. I didn't speak of the incident, but I was shaken, and though Ms. Jones didn't say anything, I worried that she could tell something was wrong. And then I began to wonder if something could happen, if I could get shot or killed. Was I willing to die for this?

One of the men I interviewed later told me they had done some homework on me, that they'd found out I wasn't law enforcement and knew I wasn't from Newark but from Bergen County. He said that in this confrontation, they'd been trying to send me a message: "Take that shit back to Bergen County somewhere. Take that shit back there. You ain't from Newark, man."

In time, the guys on the street decided to give me a pass. As one dealer explained, "We didn't think it was a threat because you was a pacifier. We knew that you were making your mark in the hood but didn't know to what extent. But we still continued to conduct our business. We see you do your jogging. You'd come out [of Brick Towers]. We just continued to do what we needed to do. It didn't faze us because you didn't have that badge or that gun on your hip. You had a phone, but that ain't going to do but so much."

When I became a council member, though, my presence was bad for business, and the dealers considered taking action. In interviews, Jace alleged that he intervened on my behalf and convinced the younger ones not to shoot me. "They were just going to shoot you in the leg, scare you," he told me, as if to give me some comfort.

Ms. Virginia Jones and I were standing on Dr. Martin Luther King Jr. Boulevard. She had walked me down her building's steps, through her courtyard, and past the men in front of the building, finally stopping in the street. She was almost a foot and a half shorter than me, but I felt safe with her, like I had a bodyguard. I liked that people were seeing me with her. She was standing in front of me, staring intently into my eyes. I had told her upstairs how much I wanted to help her, and now she had something to tell me.

"You say you want to help, but first you need to tell me something. You need to describe to me what you see around you. . . . Describe the neighborhood."

What? I thought.

I hesitated, and she repeated, "Tell me what you see."

So I began. Tentatively. "I see Brick Towers. Two buildings in rough shape. I see the street. I see the house I live in, the bodega." I probably pointed at Happy House and described the abandoned building, and I may have mentioned the guys in front of Brick Towers.

As I continued to speak, she looked more and more disappointed. At some point, she raised her hand and spoke curtly: "You can't help me." She turned back onto the sidewalk, walking away from me.

"Wait," I said. "What do you mean?"

She whirled around, looked at me hard, and launched in.

"You need to **understand** something," she said. "The world you see outside of you is a reflection of what you have inside of you. If all you see are problems, darkness, and despair, then that is all there is ever going to be. But if you are one of those stubborn people who every time you open your eyes you see hope, you see opportunity, possibility, you see love or the face of God, **then** you can be someone who helps me." And she walked away.

I looked down at my feet, struck by what she had said, rolling it through my thoughts again and again. **Okay, grasshopper, thus endeth the lesson.**

Perhaps it was something I'd said in her apartment that had set her off. Perhaps I'd said something judgmental about the buildings or the community that ran counter to what she knew in her heart and saw with her eyes. Perhaps she sensed that I was struggling in those days, a bit rattled, and that, everywhere I looked, I was seeing things that I perceived as staggering challenges. Perhaps she thought I'd give up, retreat from Brick Towers, get a nice apartment in a better neighborhood, and never become part of her community. Perhaps she knew I wasn't seeing the community with loving eyes, that my connections with people were being obscured by my inability to see beyond my fear and my own implicit biases.

And now she was speaking to me of vision. With people who were addicted to drugs or dealing them, what did I see? Was I reducing them, drawing conclusions, summing up the totality of their being by the least of their actions? What of their histories— what of their past, present, and possible future? Did I see the complexity, the potential for redemption, the depth of their humanity? Did I lead with love, extending it from inside to out, recognizing an essential connection to a shared humanity and destiny?

In his "Letter from a Birmingham Jail," Dr. Martin Luther King Jr. wrote:

> To use the words of Martin Buber, the great Jewish philosopher, segregation substitutes an "I–it" relationship for the "I–thou" relationship, and ends up relegating persons to the status of things. So segregation is not only politically, economically and sociologically unsound, but it is morally wrong and sinful. Paul Tillich has said that sin is separation. Isn't segregation an existential expression of man's tragic separation, an expression of his awful estrangement, his terrible sinfulness?

Here I was in a neighborhood that was segregated along lines of race and economic status, a result of decades of profoundly biased public policy—the result of redlining by banks and mortgage companies and the federal government, the result of bigoted Federal Housing Administration practices, the result of prejudiced decisions to cram low-income and public housing into urban centers and refuse it in suburban towns, and more.

Standing out there on the street, I realized that every person nearby—children, seniors, hardworking parents, and, yes, buyers, sellers, and users—was my neighbor. In major world religions, there is no commandment more fundamental than to love your neighbor as you love yourself. Now I was being challenged to manifest that love: this was a test of my love, of my vision. **The world you see outside of you is a reflection of what you have inside of you.**

I would come to know that Ms. Jones embodied a critical ideal of leadership: you can't lead the people unless you love the people. She was a leader in that community because people knew she loved them, no matter what. She had an infinite reservoir of love.

At the dawn of my professional career, a senior citizen who led the tenants association was telling me that the most important and immediate work I needed to do in that neighborhood was to tend to myself: to cultivate a love within and let the world partake of the harvest. It was clear to me: if I was going to come to her neighborhood, I needed to come correct.

I went back to Ms. Jones. I went back more ready to listen than talk, more ready to learn than assume, more willing to love than judge. I became her student, her protégé, her assistant. Before I even realized it, I became her son.

Years later, Jean Wright, one of the other tenant leaders I worked closely with, teased me. "Cory, Virginia knew as soon as you moved across the street that you were hers," she said. "Virginia said that she would get you to move into Brick Towers. She took to you right away. You didn't know it, but you were her son from the start. She was calling you her son to all of us."

The men in front of the buildings involved in the drug trade told me that Ms. Jones talked to them about me, too. I didn't know until I sat down to write this book that she had done so. One guy told me that after he came at me hard, intent on intimidating me, Ms. Jones came at **him** hard and said, "Look, don't you be doing this. Cory is okay. Cory is all right. He's family."

When I moved onto Dr. Martin Luther King Jr. Boulevard and met Ms. Jones, I saw a tough woman who could hardly be bothered with me. And when she met me, she saw family.

In 1998 I moved from across the street into Brick Towers, and I lived there until the buildings were closed in 2006. Ms. Jones and I were among the last residents to leave.

In 2006 the life of Brick Towers was over. The twin buildings were empty shells awaiting the final blows of a wrecking ball that would return them to the earth. They had risen to life in the late 1960s, with the first building completed in 1969—the year Armstrong and Aldrin walked on the moon, Nixon took office, **Sesame Street** began, and Woodstock happened, the year of Vietnam War protests and the Stonewall riot, Marvin Gaye's "Abraham, Martin and John," and the Beatles' "Come Together."

Each building was sixteen stories tall with spacious one-, two-, and three-bedroom apartments. The towers were erected on a hill aside a long boulevard that cut through the Central Ward of Newark and was appropriately named High Street. The buildings offered dramatic views of Newark's downtown, seaport, and airport, and a glorious vista of Manhattan's skyscrapers, just twelve miles away. Their main entrances faced inward, toward each other, and between them was a courtyard, a large central space elevated above the two streets on either side of Brick Towers: High Street on the east and Quitman Street on the west. From those streets, there were only two ways into the courtyard: through the two openings in the walls that surrounded the buildings.

Those walls were formidable barriers, and the bounded courtyard created a safe space where kids could play, seniors could sit and relax, and adults could unwind after work or on the weekends. The courtyard was where Brick Towers residents became a community, where they looked out for each other, and where tenant leaders heard complaints.

The first residents felt fortunate to be there, especially because they had earned their way in. There was a lengthy application process, one that included interviews and inspections of their current residences. Admittance was not easy.

Ms. Jones easily made the cut. At age forty-one, she was a correctional officer who worked at the local youth facility, and moved in with her three children, two girls and a boy. In 1970 her family became one of the first to rent an apartment in the southern tower. Hundreds of families would move into the buildings in the months after Ms. Jones and her family settled there. And they would learn, upon arrival, that Ms. Jones was the true towering presence at that address. She set the tone in Brick Towers. She was a stern woman; she could intimidate and instill fear. She would bark orders to kids, letting everyone know what was unacceptable behavior in and around the buildings. Yet underneath that gruff exterior, people learned, was a woman of rare warmth and honor, a woman who possessed a deep compassion for the people of her community.

Working in the youth lockup facility for the Department of Corrections, Ms. Jones saw that too many children were being lost because of sexual, physical, and emotional trauma, because of a lack of structure, engagement, discipline, and love. She was determined to see that the children of Brick Towers wouldn't fall prey to forces devouring too many of our country's youth, chewing them up and then falling into the hands of a system ill equipped to resurrect their promise. The community she sought and achieved in the 1970s was one where every child was hers and every adult was expected to exercise parental responsibility toward all kids, not just their own. As a community, they would raise the children.

Kids who grew up under Ms. Jones's tutelage remember that she minded every child who crossed her path as if that child was her own. "She was stern," one young man remembered. "She was no-nonsense. She'd talk to you like you were her own damn kid." If you stepped out of line at Brick Towers, you could count on Ms. Jones to call you on it. "Boy, I'll beat your ass myself" was an often-heard refrain. But the ferocity with which she scolded kids did nothing to dampen her affection for them. As the same young man recalled, "We had nothing but love for Ms. Jones."

In the 1950s and '60s, hundreds of public housing buildings sprang up in Newark—some tall, some sprawling and low—and the city was transformed. The skyline of the city's Central Ward was suddenly full of brick complexes, acres and acres of them punching into the sky, giving Newark a nickname that would last: "Brick City."

At the same time, the Northeast also saw dramatic losses of urban manufacturing jobs. As work vanished, poverty rose; with poverty came crime, which accelerated the exodus of people, businesses, and investment, shrinking Newark's tax base and creating a downward spiral. With fewer resources to address increasing problems, schools suffered, as did the kids who attended them. The responsibility of principals, teachers, and staff expanded well beyond academic instruction into having to grapple with the collateral social consequences of extreme poverty.

Further driving tensions was the overt racism that pervaded the city in the 1960s. Though blacks and Latinos accounted for the majority of the population, they had almost no meaningful political representation. What's more, mostly white officers policed predominantly black sections of the city, like the Central Ward. There were widespread reports of police brutality, and tensions built up around the all-too-common experiences of black youth who were stopped and harassed by the police.

Newark was certainly not the only major American city experiencing such tensions. In many of the country's metropolises, rage and frustration fueled violent behavior in the form of riots. In April 1967, Dr. Martin Luther King Jr. addressed that turmoil in a speech at Stanford University entitled "The Other America." He pointed out that many activists, motivated by the extreme behavior of domestic terrorists such as Bull Connor and Jim Clark, were quick to march with him in Selma and Birmingham to address the injustices there, but they weren't active in the cities near their homes, cities where the deteriorating economic and housing conditions had a different kind of impact on people. "It's much easier to integrate a lunch counter than it is to guarantee a livable income and a good solid job," he said. "It's much easier to guarantee the right to vote than it is to guarantee the right to live in sanitary, decent housing conditions." He condemned riots and violence as "socially destructive and self-defeating," creating more social problems than they solve. But he also called riots "the language of the unheard."

"I think America must see riots do not develop out of thin air," he said. "Certain conditions continue to exist in our society, which must be condemned as vigorously as we condemn riots. . . . Social justice and progress are the absolute guarantors of riot prevention."

For Newark, Dr. King's speech proved prophetic. Three months later, riots would consume the city's Central Ward. About a year after the riots, construction on the buildings began. And in 1969 Brick Towers was born.

In the first Brick Towers tenants association meeting, Ms. Virginia Jones was elected president. Around her gathered a core of strong members, mostly women, an impressive group of activist leaders. They took every child, every family, every aspect of the building as their responsibility: their arms embraced the community, and their love was large.

Beyond creating a working relationship with building management and organizing the tenants to handle the basics—such as setting up schedules by which each resident took a shift mopping their own hallway floor—they focused on the children. Ms. Jones and her colleagues rallied the buildings to build meaningful traditions that would last for years. They held cookouts and parties for every holiday from Halloween to the Fourth of July and an annual fashion show where families would model clothes, handmade or store bought, everything from eveningwear to back-to-school gear. They took the kids on trips around the region: to movies at the Loew's State Theatre downtown, to Island Beach on the Jersey Shore, to Coney Island, to museums in New York City. They went to Six Flags Great Adventure, Action Park, the Bronx Zoo. In

1978 they took a special trip to see **Timbuktu!** on Broadway and dine at Tavern on the Green. In the summers they shut down Montgomery Street behind the towers and created a "play street" where they placed Ping-Pong and foosball tables. Brick Towers also started a city summer job program for the kids, where teens did work cleaning up the community and earned their first paychecks.

Ms. Jones and the residents were innovative and industrious in how they found ways to provide opportunities for the kids. To pay for parties and events, they pooled their own money and wrangled donations from local businesses, the buildings' management, and anyone else they could find. They participated in the political upheavals that brought into office Ken Gibson, Newark's first black mayor, and used their connections to city hall to benefit the buildings. They threw support behind three different Central Ward councilpeople who held that office during the 1970s, leveraging their political influence for help.

In the early 1970s leaders in Newark renamed High Street in honor of Dr. Martin Luther King Jr. Dr. King spoke eloquently about how we have made our whole world into a neighborhood but have failed to use our spiritual and moral prowess to make it into a brotherhood and sisterhood. Living on Dr. Martin Luther King Jr. Boulevard, though, Ms. Jones and her fellow tenant leaders in Brick Towers accomplished just that in the 1970s.

They turned Brick Towers into a community of love.

By the mid-1980s, however, Brick Towers was grappling with two threats: the building management and the drug trade. Over the course of a decade, building management's relationship with tenants had gone from symbiotic to parasitic. The buildings were being drained of their resources for the enrichment of the owners, imperiling the structures and the people. Capital maintenance was constricted, and dilapidation set in.

When things broke around the buildings, from lighting to common room furniture, they stayed broken for weeks, months, or forever. Elevators stopped working with regularity, stranding seniors and those with groceries in the lobby or, worse, between floors. Basic building functions such as garbage removal were not properly attended to and led to roach and rat infestations. Once-pristine common areas grew dirty and full of unpleasant odors. The management collected rent and federal subsidies such as Section 8 payments and benefited from federal programs that brought in additional resources to help the buildings and their inhabitants, but little of the money seemed to be used for the purposes intended.

At some point, the management also stopped the strict screening of tenants. Gone were the lengthy application process, the interviews, and the home visits. Some new residents brought with them their involvement in drugs, introducing fissures in the community that would be exploited and expanded. Soon the walls that enclosed the Brick Towers courtyard could no longer keep out the menace of narcotics. Cocaine, heroin, and marijuana gradually seeped in, destroying what once had been a refuge.

In this overwhelmingly black neighborhood, residents witnessed more and more white people driving up to the buildings—not deliverymen, elevator repair crews, or management, but white people of all different ages and backgrounds who parked, walked into the courtyard, and then emerged again and hurried away. Before long, in the early morning there were actual lines outside the walls, folks of all races and socioeconomic status waiting to be served. As one former dealer described it, "Big moves were being made. We had lookouts on all the higher floors, lookouts on the roof with walkie-talkies. We had a gunman standing right there with a gun for the knuckleheads, you know, anybody who wanted to come up and try to rob us. It was like **New Jack City.**" Residents tried to confront the drug dealing—Ms. Jones, unwilling to surrender her buildings, was among them—but they had limited success. They called the police, and occasionally the police came to scatter the drug dealers and make arrests, but the menace would not retreat.

In the early 1980s a young Jace Bradley completed his military service and came back to Newark to live. At first he tried to follow the straight and narrow. He got a job working at a Kmart for about $6.00 an hour. But newly married and with an infant daughter at home, he longed for greater financial stability. "Working at Kmart wasn't making it," he said, "so I looked for other ways."

"Other ways" turned out to be a role in a vibrant and surging American business: illegal narcotics. He quickly gained a reputation as a brilliant strategist, and for his ferocious use of calculated violence. Jace recognized that Brick Towers was an ideal place in which to run a drug operation, and he decided to take over the buildings. Within a year he had designed and implemented an operation that, according to his estimation, was grossing more than $50,000 a day. The properties were ideal for drug dealing for the same reasons they had offered residents sanctuary. They were like watchtowers rising above sturdy castle walls, with only two entrances and excellent visibility. Anyone approaching the buildings or the entrances could be seen long before they drew close.

For those who had intentions of robbing Jace's workers, the walls offered a formidable deterrence. Approaching stickup men had to ask themselves if it was worth it to confront one of the dealers when there was an armed gunman behind a wall or high up in the building while they stood in the open below, vulnerable.

Police were also at a severe disadvantage. Officers who approached the buildings had no ability to surprise. The young men dealing for Jace could scatter long before police got close, sprinting into the buildings, slamming the front doors, which locked behind them, and vanishing into a maze of floors and apartments.

But Jace layered on even more protection and sophistication. He alleges that he bribed management, that several of the security guards who worked at Brick Towers collected a salary from the buildings' management and then took double that income from his team to look the other way. Jace gained complete access to the buildings and created an information flow that allowed him to know about threats to his business and opportunities. His access to higher apartments and to the buildings' rooftops allowed him unobstructed views for miles. He equipped his team with top-of-the-line walkie-talkies and used them in a sophisticated strategy to integrate the lookouts at street level with the eyes in the sky and his central base of operations.

Jace's operation employed dozens of young boys and men in specified roles. He lived a life of flash and abundance that enticed too many young men who thought there was no way to achieve that for themselves except by joining him. Jace pulled them into this world, offering membership in an exclusive organization that watched over its men. He paid his crew on a daily basis, and paid them well; when there was trouble, he provided bail money and lawyers. For many kids, the attraction of affirmative mentors or role models, church or after-school programs, nurturing and empowering schools, and pathways to college was too weak to win them away from the inducements of the criminal world. It was a tug-of-war for their destinies, and it wasn't a competition.

Decades later, when I interviewed them, many of these young men were in their late thirties, forties, and fifties. Having served jail time and found little opportunity for gainful employment, they often described the dealing as the only game in town. Though most seemed to regret their choices, they had perceived few other options at the time. They came of age after a rapid shift in American cities: the steep decline of industrial jobs coincided directly with the rise of housing projects such as Brick Towers and the drug dealing that consumed them. Michelle Alexander, author of **The New Jim Crow,** writes about this in her introduction to a report on public education and black males:

We could have taken a different path. . . . For example, as late as the 1970s, more than 70% of African Americans in Chicago worked in blue-collar jobs. By 1987, due to de-industrialization and jobs moving overseas, hundreds of thousands of African Americans nationwide (a majority of them men) found themselves suddenly jobless. By 1987, the industrial employment of Black males in Chicago had fallen to 28%. Staggering numbers of Black men across the country found themselves suddenly trapped in racially segregated, jobless communities struggling for survival. The economic collapse of inner cities happened almost overnight.

In this complex, Jace had one of Newark's most thriving businesses—an illegal, dangerous, and destructive one that consumed long-term promise in exchange for short-term payments. I listened to Jace boast of his business acumen. He'd identified the best suppliers in the region and ensured that he got high quality at low cost. He was able to offer product at lower prices than his competitors around the city, which gave Brick Towers a reputation as a hot place to buy.

Jace is in his fifties now and lives in rural Pennsylvania, where he takes care of his elderly mother. It seems like a lifetime ago that he drove the latest-model cars, flew in private planes, and had stacks of cash so plentiful that it seemed like Monopoly money. "The more I think about it, though—I'm much older—it wasn't life, what I was doing," he told me. "I put up basketball courts. I put swings in for the kids. I always thought if I could give back to the kids that the ends would justify the means. But in reality, it wasn't worth it."

To hear Jace tell it, respect for the elderly was a cornerstone rule for the soldiers in Jace's crew. After all, his mother lived in Brick Towers throughout the nearly two decades of his reign. As a result, residents of the buildings were well aware of the drug trade but did not know the intricacies of the operation or the extent to which it had infiltrated the buildings. Ms. Jones and other residents battled with management about the drug problem but had little understanding that they were engaging with people who had no incentive to change.

It wasn't in Jace's interest to affect the residents' life more than was necessary. In fact, he worked to keep the narcotics operation from interfering with building events, and he paused sales during the hours children were going to and from school. He also instructed his team on what they already instinctively knew: keep the sales away from building leadership, especially Ms. Jones. He said to me, "Ms. Jones, God bless her, she knew what we were doing, but we showed her respect by staying away from her and the elders."

But as another dealer from that era described it, the sheer level of open-air drug dealing in the courtyard made it hell for the hardworking residents of Brick Towers. "The whole courtyard would be filled," he remembered. "Ms. Jones and other tenants would have to U-turn and go out the back to go to work. Everybody started going out the back door."

Amid these challenges, Ms. Jones and other residents continued to step up for the children in the 1980s. They continued to hold events, serve meals, and plan trips. The tenants association leadership watched out for families as best they could, connecting people with work opportunities, drug treatment, or legal assistance.

Perhaps the best illustration of her tenacity is the often discussed story of how Ms. Jones was once sued for punching one of the buildings' owners. As the story goes, in the middle of an argument about building conditions she got so frustrated that she leapt up and punched the landlord square in the face and had to be held back from pummeling him further as she shouted a torrent of colorful words. The landlord didn't retaliate with his own fists but saw an opportunity to evict her, so he dragged her into court. Before the judge, Ms. Jones played the diminutive elderly woman. The judge looked at the much larger and younger landlord and then at the small, fragile senior citizen and dismissed the case.

Still, the tenant leadership of Brick Towers could not solve all of the problems that inundated their buildings in these years. And sometimes the problems visited unimaginable tragedies upon them.

It was in 1980 that Ms. Jones got a knock on her

door. The woman who stood there was in tears—which wasn't uncommon, as folks came often for help, sometimes in crisis. But this woman looked like she was in shock. Unable to speak, she pulled at Ms. Jones, leading her out of her apartment, down the five flights of stairs to the lobby of 715, then out into the courtyard, where a crowd had gathered in the lobby of 685. Ms. Jones ran over and the crowd let her through.

There on the lobby floor was Ms. Jones's son, Charles. He had been shot multiple times.

Over the years there would be many stories about why Charles was murdered. His sisters, Ruby and Bessie, say that the day before his murder Charles had stopped a robbery in the lobby, and the criminal had vowed to pay Charles back for interfering. In the late 1970s, residents say, before Brick Towers became an open-air drug market, there were a lot of stickups in the building. It was a terrible kind of irony that when the drug trade offered young men a chance to make a lot of cash dealing in the courtyard, now watched by Jace's armed men, crime within the building dropped.

Ms. Jones had the means to move, to leave the buildings and even the city, but she didn't. And even when, over time, she went head-to-head with the drug dealers, the deadbeat landlords, and other criminal types who destroyed the quality of life in the towers that she loved, she never feared for her safety. Her daughters say that it was her experience as a corrections officer that offered her a kind of protection. "Her inmates loved her because of who she was to them," Ruby recalled. "She didn't mistreat them, she didn't step over or on them, she helped them. People protected her, they loved her; they really did. With that type of power, you have your enemies, but you have the people that protect you and look after you."

Ms. Jones could have blamed Brick Towers for taking her only son, but she didn't. She took even greater responsibility upon herself, and instead of hating, she loved more. Her love was defiant, stubborn, resolute. Her fierce tenderness let people know she was more than their neighbor; she was watching out for their well-being.

My dad loved Newark. During most of my years there he lived in Atlanta, but he delighted in coming to the city and visited me there as often as he could. While I was busy working, he would make his rounds: he'd wake in Brick Towers, take early-morning walks in Weequahic Park, have brunch in one of Newark's soul food restaurants, visit one of the city's many senior citizen high-rise buildings, meet with friends around town, and perhaps end the evening with a quick stop in a neighborhood bar like Carl's Club Vanity, where he would enter as if he were Norm from the TV show **Cheers**. It was always something to see, the way people called out his name and welcomed him, as if they'd known him all their lives, as if he lived right down the street. My dad developed so many relationships with folks independent of me—people who were happy to see him, folks who thanked him for help and advice. I don't know how many problems he fixed without my help, because it was only when the situation required assistance he couldn't provide that he'd come to me and say something like, "Now, son, you need to help Ms. Brown here, she's good people."

This was my father, a man who never met a stranger. He recognized the dignity of everyone he met no matter their circumstance. Every walk or outing with my dad came with an unspoken agreement that we'd take it slow, because his great joy was the time he spent talking with people along the way.

Even in brief interactions, my father had a way of leaving folks feeling elevated. In the checkout line in a grocery store, the clerk—who at first glance seemed bored by the monotony of his day—would be laughing, smiling, or opening up to my dad as they shared personal stories about challenges and frustrations or about the simple joys of children and family. Car valet, coat check attendant, the guy handing you a towel in the men's room—he saw them all, delighted in them, and connected. He affirmed humanity with dignity.

He often rolled around Newark without me. I

think, at times, he felt I was a wet blanket—I don't drink, and have never have been one to hang out in bars or clubs—and I think he found it a drag to have a politician in tow. In that sense we were an odd couple, with me the Felix to his Oscar. So his nights out would often be with partners of his like Phil Grate, his peer in age and one of the most active volunteers in my many Newark campaigns.

In April 2004 my father came to visit for my birthday. He would sometimes show up like that, unannounced, with the intention of surprising me: one of those things parents do that make you feel loved. The first time my father ever made such a visit was when I turned twenty-one and he traveled all the way from New Jersey to Stanford to surprise me. Refusing to have my first drink, I ended up being the designated driver as my father and some of my Stanford classmates threw a few back at a Palo Alto restaurant.

But this day in 2004 was my thirty-fifth birthday, and my dad and I went for a walk around Newark. This walk took us from Brick Towers through the Central Ward. He and I were lost in conversation as we headed toward one of our stops on 18th Avenue near Bergen Street. We were walking to visit a family that had been supporting me since I first knocked on their door while campaigning in 1998. The family matriarch, Ms. Rosalie Powell, is like an adoptive parent to me, and she delighted in reminding my biological parents of this every time she saw them.

As we were approaching her door, we heard what sounded like explosions echoing between the buildings behind us; yells and screams followed. I knew it was gunfire. I turned and sprinted toward the sound, leaving my dad on the street. I didn't realize it at the time, but an off-duty police officer, Kendrick Isaac, was right behind me, running full speed up the hill as well, his gun drawn. All around, there was panic. Young kids raced past us, running in the opposite direction. When I got up a small grassy hill between the buildings, I saw a young man on some stairs, holding on to the banister, and people yelling and screaming around him. As I approached him from behind, he fell back against me; I looked over his shoulder and saw his shirt filling up with blood. With the help of others, I laid him on the grass and put my hands on his chest trying to stop the blood that seemed to be coming from everywhere. I asked his name and the people around me shouted, "Wazn." He wasn't speaking.

I began talking to him and asked someone to bring me towels. A woman sat at his head, holding him as well. I called his name, begged him to stay with me, and felt for a pulse, which was faint. Foamy blood started coming from his mouth, and I desperately tried to clear it away with the towel, hoping it might help him to breathe. But he wasn't breathing. Again I begged him to stay with me, yelled at him. I felt once more for his pulse; this time there was none.

After what seemed like an eternity, the ambulance arrived. Officer Isaac would tell me later that he scanned faces as he paced around the immediate area, working to make sure that the shooter wasn't still nearby. When the EMTs charged up the hill, they pushed me out of the way and cut open the young man's shirt, revealing the bullet holes. I just sat on the grass, watching them work. They hoisted him onto a stretcher, loaded him into the ambulance, and took him off to the hospital. But I knew he was dead, that he had died right there on the grass.

More police were arriving as I walked down the hill toward my father. He stood there and said nothing. I looked at him and asked him to leave, to go home and wait for me. And then I turned and talked to the police on the scene. The director of the Newark police department, Anthony Ambrose, arrived. Years later, Anthony would become a trusted and valued friend and advisor. He would go on to become chief of detectives of the Essex County Prosecutor's Office, helping my mayoral administration with law enforcement strategy and criminal investigations. But in 2004 I saw him as an adversary; he was the police director for Mayor Sharpe James, whom I had lost to in the mayoral race two years earlier. My campaign and I believed the police had engaged in biased and rough campaign activities and that many in the department, including Anthony, helped secure Sharpe James his relatively narrow victory. But standing there in front of Anthony at that moment, I felt no animosity. I was lost, in distress. I had never watched someone die before, and it was gruesome, a godawful end to a young life. Anthony would tell me years later that I seemed to be in shock, that I was shaking as I stood there in jogging shorts and a T-shirt with blood all over me. I vaguely remember him asking me more questions, but what I remember vividly is how this guy, whom I had come to dislike and imagined to be mean and hateful toward me, was so kind at a time when I needed it. I felt compassion from him; he seemed to be genuinely worried about me, and I was grateful.

I left the scene and walked the mile or so back to Brick Towers in a daze. I can barely remember that walk, whether I took the elevator up to the sixteenth floor or if, as was often the case, the elevator was broken and I walked up all those flights of stairs. I remember my father being at the door when I opened it. I remember the look on his face when he saw his son covered in a boy's blood. It seemed as if something broke in my dad just then, as if his usually incandescent light had been shot out. I know he wanted to hug me, but I just wanted to go to the bathroom. That was what I muttered as I pushed past him, heading into the bathroom and shutting the door.

I turned on the water in the sink and began to wash my hands. I kept rubbing them and rubbing them; they were shaking, I couldn't get them to stop shaking. I kept the water on, as hot as I could stand it, and kept rubbing my hands together, feeling as if I couldn't get the traces of blood off my hands. I stripped off my clothes, full of my sweat and his blood. Leaving them in a heap in the corner, I turned on the shower until the water was as hot as I could bear. I climbed in, put my hands against the wall, bowed my head, and let the water cover me.

Later, friends reminded me that in the days and weeks after the shooting, I was different. One said it seemed as if I was in a fog of depression, a dim version of myself. I couldn't get Wazn out of my mind. I'd once had some distance from murders, but no more.

Two conversations from that time stay with me, and I reflect on them often. The first was with my dad. I had always been close with my father, but this was a time where he probably felt that he couldn't reach me. I was too distant for him to get his arms around me. I could tell he was struggling with this, with not being able to find the words to comfort me. I think this was because he was struggling, too.

As we sat together in the aftermath of the shooting, my father looked at me, and in what felt like an indictment of my generation he said, "Son, I worry that a boy growing up like I did—poor, black, to a single mother in a segregated town—would have a better chance of making it in America if he was born in 1936 rather than being born today." My father—born in 1936, a man who participated in the civil rights movement, who through his and others' foot-soldier activism helped to integrate our world and advance American ideals—seemed to be wrestling with a thought like this: **All this work, advancement, and progress, yet a kid like I was faces more challenges today than ever before. How could it come to this?**

Facts support my father's haunting assertion. African American boys are two and a half times more likely than their white counterparts to be suspended in grades K–12. If a black boy doesn't graduate from high school, he is more likely to go to prison than have a full-time job. A black boy born today has a one in two chance of being arrested—more if he is poor and from a single-parent family. The leading cause of death for young boys who shared my father's circumstances is murder.

My father didn't intend to do it, but with his comments he kicked me when I was down. In the years I had lived in the neighborhood, violence had affected me—but now I could see with a terrifying clarity what was happening. I had no distance anymore, no comfortable gap that allowed me to keep moving the way I had in the past. And my father's angst only aggravated my despair.

In the aftermath of Wazn's shooting, my dad, who as a boy was taken in by a loving family and grew up in the funeral home they ran, learned just how much funeral homes had changed. Funeral homes were no longer places that marked the sad but graceful passage of a life fully lived, but sites of unnatural and abhorrent pain. Weekly deaths by gunfire in Newark, hundreds in cities across our country, our children being put into boxes, elders burying the young.

And beyond the murders, hundreds more were being wounded and crippled on Newark's streets. I once asked an emergency room doctor what the cost of one gunshot wound in Newark was to taxpayers—specifically, the medical costs associated with the uninsured men who are rushed to hospitals, clinging to life, and are often saved by talented women and men with the skills of front-line military medics. He said it could easily be up to $100,000—even $200,000 or more—for the medical costs alone, depending on the severity of the wound. Of course there are other costs, too, and financial metrics alone don't measure it all. What is the cost of the emotional and spiritual damage to children, to a family, a neighborhood, a nation?

For the eight years that I lived in Brick Towers, and during my almost twenty years as a Newark resident, my neighbors struggled with the emotional wounds of violence. This is not America; it is not who we are. It is a cancer on the soul of our nation. Like many cancers, the true peril comes from not detecting it, not recognizing the threat and thus not taking the appropriate action.

We are one body, one nation under God, indivisible. As has been said, injustice anywhere is a threat to justice everywhere. But what happens when we are unaware of the trials and tribulations of our countrymen and women? Do we become complicit in that injustice? Do we contribute to its spread?

And there I was, facing my father's judgment of my generation and me. I was angry. I was questioning myself. I wanted a revolution of consciousness, of activism, and of love—but I couldn't even muster that spirit in myself.

But there was another conversation in those days after Wazn's death. While my dad's was a painful challenge, this one was instructive. I received nurturing wisdom that I've often repeated to myself since, that I've held on to when I've sat with children traumatized by violence, or when I've tried to console people in the midst of tragedy, or when I've made mistakes, let people down, failed to be the man I want to be.

I was young, brash, and at times overly eager when I moved into Brick Towers, and perhaps I still am two of those three things. But Ms. Virginia Jones, the president of the Brick Towers tenants association, taught me about humility and love through her example. She taught me that yes, love sometimes yells, but most often it is a whisper or doesn't make a sound at all. Not speaking, just doing.

All those years that Ms. Jones lived in Brick Towers, the things that she did may have seemed small to some: helping someone cover their rent when they came up short, planning a beach excursion for the kids during the summer, fighting for the heat to be turned on in a cold winter month when the slumlords left the buildings to freeze. But living in Brick Towers, I came to see, in really no time at all, that Ms. Jones and the women like her were the ones that bound us together and kept us whole.

The morning after the shooting, I felt like I was twenty feet underwater. I got up early and left my apartment. My dad was still asleep; he knew I had work and would understand my absence when he woke. As I walked out of my building, through the lobby where her son had been murdered, I saw Ms. Jones standing at the front entrance to Brick Towers. Her back was toward me. I stopped about fifty feet from where she was and stared at her.

For Ms. Jones, hope was relational. It didn't exist in the abstract. Hope confronts. It does not ignore pain, agony, or injustice. It is not a saccharine optimism that refuses to see, face, or grapple with the wretchedness of reality. You can't have hope without despair, because hope is a response. Hope is the active conviction that despair will never have the last word.

As I stood there, staring at her, Ms. Jones turned

around. She saw me, waved me over, and opened her arms as I approached. She hugged me. I'm six foot three and she was barely five feet tall, but I felt as if I disappeared into her arms. As I broke down, she said two words to me over and over again: "Stay faithful. Stay faithful. Stay faithful. . . ."

4

DO SOMETHING

It is not enough to be compassionate. You must act.

—His Holiness the Dalai Lama

In July 1999 I almost quit politics.

I slammed down the phone in my City Council office, pounded my fist on the desk, and collapsed back into my chair. I was disappointed in myself because I had just raised my voice with Elaine Sewell, the president of the Garden Spires tenants association. I had disrespected an elder, an ally, a friend—something in utter opposition to who I am and how my parents raised me.

My tone with Elaine, I knew, was about much

more than the subject of our conversation; it was the result of a year of being fed up with my role as an elected official. I had believed that if I got elected to the Central Ward seat, I could change things. But now, one year into the job, I felt like I couldn't; I felt like I had volunteered to go to the front lines and ended up sitting in a trench with no weapon. And now I was exchanging anger and frustration with Elaine, insisting that I did not know what to do about the problems she was bringing to my attention.

Why did I run for office in the first place? In 1997 I graduated from law school with a legal fellowship that allowed me to help tenants in Newark full-time, to be there for them, to keep them in housing, to help improve conditions, to battle slumlords, and to lay the groundwork for a nonprofit that I believed would eventually do significant work to empower kids, families, and neighborhoods. And I gave it all up to be something I had once considered a suspect profession: a politician.

Now I was beginning to regret that decision. In my first year in office, I was achieving little of the transformative change I sought. I poured my heart into the job and had a tireless staff who did the same; we'd helped many people, I felt certain of that. And yet I was failing to make anything approaching a systemic difference. I found out immediately upon entering office that being a legislator is a numbers game—and one is indeed the loneliest number when you need a majority to get things done. I felt like I was blocked everywhere; I must have been breaking records in Newark history for being outvoted eight to one.

For a guy who talked a lot about change, I went about it in a boneheaded way. I didn't seek common ground with my colleagues; instead I walked in and sought to distinguish myself from them. I wanted to be the reformer, but by separating myself from them I undermined my ability to advance change.

Even though being a council member is a part-time job, the Newark City Council is the highest-paid city council in the state, and the job promises a host of privileges that I felt were wrong. I did not accept many of the lavish perks. I gave up a city car and refused to use expense accounts for things like personal meals and travel. But doing the right thing in the wrong way is often wrong. I regret the holier-than-thou, sanctimonious posture I sometimes took—the way I didn't just refuse those things but wielded the decision like a sword of condemnation against some fellow council members. Some of my colleagues had been in office almost as long as I had been alive and had made sacrifices and rendered admirable service to their community. I was taught to respect my elders, to acknowledge the experience of those senior to me, and to show deference to those who faced challenges and hardships that my generation will never know. I didn't live up to those lessons in my early days on the City Council. This failing undermined my mission of service.

I'd been elected to get things done, and the biggest issue for my constituents wasn't City Council compensation or expense accounts—which I didn't have a shot at changing anyway. People hadn't elected me to point out what was wrong with my colleagues. They'd elected me to find ways to work with them and to get something accomplished. My tactics were brash, and they left my colleagues feeling disrespected; I think many of the veteran council members viewed me as an obnoxious upstart looking to score points at their expense.

Legislating demands that you have a working relationship with your colleagues. No matter how much you disagree with them, there must be common ground or you render yourself ineffective. I didn't earn my colleagues' trust, but instead ignited their suspicion. As one of the more senior men on the City Council, Donald Tucker, used to say about our nine-member body, "You need to learn to count to five."

My challenges with my fellow council members were the least of my problems. The mayor of the city, Sharpe James, was making my life miserable. My suggestions about anything related to how the city operated were ignored or dismissed. I was told I couldn't communicate directly with department directors and had to take my issues up with the mayor's office; in fact, I had few opportunities for substantive conversations with the mayor. I had believed I would be able to engage him on policies, city programs, and practices—so far, I had experienced none of that.

I was thrilled when I got my first invitation to the mayor's office to speak with him. The office was grand. The walls were covered with tributes to himself, from shovels from many groundbreakings to more plaques than I could count. There were pictures of him with all the right people, from famous athletes to Bill Clinton. I entered the mayor's personal office and sat down in a chair at a conference table. I was eager and jumped into my thoughts on how the city was using its Urban Development Action Grants (UDAGs)—a federal program I had studied and believed could be put to better use. In fact, I believed we weren't in compliance with the federal requirements of the grant. The mayor looked at me and then proceeded to dismiss my points. His remarks made me doubtful that he even knew what a UDAG was. He launched into a lecture about what my job was, about separation of powers and what I needed to learn: **You can't tell city inspectors what to do, you can't tell the police what to do. You are a legislator, not an administrator. You need to know your role.**

It was clear that the mayor had no use for me. He already had his votes on the City Council. I was a problem and possibly a threat, commanding attention from the community and local press disproportionate to any of my actual accomplishments in government. Here I was, a twenty-nine-year-old first-year first-term city council member sitting before a veteran mayor in his sixties. I was hopeful and eager to discuss issues, but he just wanted to set me straight. He began coaching me on my career path. He advised me to follow his: a term or two as a ward council member, a couple of terms as an at-large city council member, and maybe in twenty years—2018, perhaps—I should think about running for mayor.

Then he said something that frightened me.

You spend a lot of time in Montclair, don't you? Up on South Fullerton Avenue? He then stated the exact address of a law school classmate of mine, a home at which I did indeed spend a considerable amount of time. All I could do was stare at the mayor, shocked at what he had said and wondering how he knew this. It felt like a threat.

Ever since I began my work in city hall, many things had started to happen that were unsettling, even frightening. City workers told me they were afraid to talk to me because they might lose their job. My car began to get ticket after ticket when legally parked, even in front of city hall. One afternoon I saw the ticket writer doing it. I confronted her, not out of anger but to plead, "Come on, are you serious? You know this is my car. Why are you ticketing it?" Looking afraid, she said, "I was told to do this—I have to do this." I instantly understood. This wasn't her doing. I ended up having an aide take the tickets to court and demonstrating that I had been legally parked, and many were dismissed. But things got worse when I realized there were other tickets, ones I hadn't seen on my car, as if they had been written and then kept by the traffic cop. My driver's license was put in jeopardy because of all those tickets, and I had to work hard to prevent it from being suspended.

So the fact that the mayor had mentioned a place where I spent much of my time, and that he brought it up in a smug fashion, suggesting he had power over me, confirmed what some police officer friends of mine had warned me about: I was being followed.

From the day I started driving a car, my parents gave me detailed instructions on how to interact with police if I ever got stopped. Their concern for my safety, their worry that a minor infraction could turn into a life-altering altercation—these things made me afraid. Indeed, in my teenage years and in my early twenties I was followed and stopped by police with greater frequency than my white peers. But in that moment in the mayor's office, he injected into me a fear I had never had before: what could the police do to me under the direction of a mayor who was fast becoming a political adversary?

My father was particularly worried about this

new world I had entered. He had raised me to embrace the world, to live passionately, to give my heart to others, to trust the universe. But he feared that I would be taken advantage of, that I would underestimate how sinister the world could be, that I would overestimate my margin for error. He began to worry my professional accomplishments, which he had so enthusiastically encouraged, put me at risk of experiencing the kind of incident that could bring my life crashing down.

This was an example of something I admired about my dad: his ability to hold two opposing ideas in his head and somehow, more often than not, find balance. On one hand, he raised me to believe in the goodness of the world, to trust that the bargain so celebrated in America was fair, that hard work will be rewarded, that the decency you put into the world will be reflected, that you reap what you sow. But he also came of age at a time when this bargain wasn't always honored; he knew that, to some degree, my experience of the world—kinder than his—was a lie. My father, a man who worked his way up from poverty, who lived his own Horatio Alger story, **still knew about the lie**. Despite the fact that he could be pointed to as living testimony to the fairness of the bargain, he was haunted by the lie. In his time, he witnessed unprovoked cruelty, unjustified hate, unmerited punishment, and unrelenting evil. He knew too many victims of hate, both explicit and subtle. This was his American experience: he was deeply in love with his country, and yet he was anguished over its inability to extend the bargain to all of its people.

He raised two black boys in Harrington Park, a safe and nurturing suburban community. My brother and I flourished there. We became believers, seeing firsthand that if you worked hard, played by the rules, and gave more than expected, you would be rewarded. And my father and mother were prodigious examples of this ideal. Their hard work, unyielding discipline, respect for others, and unusual kindness empowered my brother and me, instructed us, informed us, inspired us to excel. In this context, my brother and I are not exceptional. Under these conditions, what would have been exceptional would be for us not to succeed by society's measure.

But I saw the warring contradictions in my father's admonitions and I understood. Harrington Park and my parents' privilege afforded my brother and me room for error. And yet we were to make no mistakes, there were limits, and we shouldn't test them. In my youth, my dad's fears for me manifested themselves in his insistence that I always be cautious; he was at times explicit, as were other family members and friends. As one uncle would say to me once when he saw me cutting up in an upscale suburban mall, "Boy, don't forget you are black." He meant, of course, that he believed I wouldn't encounter the kind of tolerance or lack of judgment that white children would be afforded.

When I was young, my dad and I had long talks about the importance of knowing when to walk away from a situation, about why it was essential to stay alert in crowds, about how to defuse a tense encounter. My dad seemed to be indicating that even if I was wronged, called a racial epithet, or harassed by an authority, I should turn the other cheek—not purely out of some Christian ideal, but as a survival skill.

So when I told my dad about my challenges in city hall and with the police, it triggered his worst fears. I remember a strange conversation I had with him around that time, so strange I suspected he'd been drinking.

"Son, you need to be careful, you need to take extra precautions."

"What do you mean, Dad?"

"Before you get in your car, check the backseat."

"What?"

"Before you get in, check the backseat. See if anything you didn't put in there is in your car."

"Really, Dad? You want me to walk around my car and study it every time before I jump in?"

"Son, someone could put something in there, they could plant something. You have no idea how folks can play."

I soon stopped talking to my parents about my

uncertainties. I didn't tell them about incidents that alarmed or concerned me. They had once been an outlet for me; now they were two people from whom I hid my heart. I was unsettled and feeling new anxieties, but I kept them to myself.

Later in my council term I was alerted that the police were tapping my office phones. A chill settled over my team when we were notified. We reached out to the state and other authorities as well as the press. There was a formal investigation, which concluded that the incident was a mistake, that someone had hit the wrong button or something along those lines—an excuse I found to be unacceptable.

It was barely a year into my term, and I was weary and stressed. I was gaining weight; I began to get severe headaches and had trouble sleeping. I had frustrations about an inability to move legislation, about not being able to affect the broken budget process; even when I could put money in the budget for programs or initiatives, I couldn't get the administration to follow through on them. This all was going on amid a constant concern for the safety of my team and my own well-being. I hated feeling like I had to assume a level of suspicion that belied my nature to trust people. I couldn't find the balance my father did, and I was too embarrassed to confide in anyone.

The words the mayor had spoken to me in private had been chilling, but they would soon be matched by his periodic slams in public—

comments that rose in a crescendo when I finally decided to challenge him for his office. At first his comments shocked me; I couldn't believe a high-ranking public official could speak about anyone in such a negative way. But being publicly dressed down by the mayor soon became routine, even predictable; it became so commonplace that our local newspaper largely ignored it. But when national media started focusing in on it, the mayor's rhetoric and tactics drew fascination. As **New York** magazine wrote at the end of my four years as a city council member:

[Sharpe James] . . . toss[ed] off every hot-button insult in the book: In a March breakfast for a City Council candidate, James called Booker "a Republican who took money from the KKK." To a group of his own supporters, he claimed Booker took money from the Taliban. In an encounter on the street with a group of Booker supporters, he said their candidate was "collaborating with the Jews to take over Newark." And in a recent public confrontation between the two men and their supporters, James referred to Booker as "the faggot white boy." ("That was an emotional reaction" was James spokesman Richard Mc-Grath's rather understated explanation.)

Sharpe James's war on his upstart opponent isn't only being fought with words. Booker

supporters have been trailed by the cops, del-
uged with blizzards of parking tickets. Booker's
phone has been tapped. He has been escorted
out of public housing and city parks. Tenants
in public housing have been told by Housing
Authority employees they could be evicted if
they keep Booker signs in their windows.

The truth is, I think the mayor's rhetoric was hardest on my dad. The two men were of the same generation. Both had ridden a tough road out of difficult
circumstances; both knew the ravages of America's
race realities. For my dad to listen to his son being
baited with racial epithets by another black man
was deeply insulting to him. But in a sense, the
mayor was teaching me lessons as valuable as some
my dad had taught me. This was Politics 101. I
wasn't running for president of my Harrington
Park seventh-grade class. This was Newark; this was
Brick City. If I was going to come, I had better bring
it. As I had done after the first bone-rattling hit I
took playing Division I college football, where the
linebacker was seeking not just to tackle me but to
end my career, I needed to get up, tighten my chin
strap, and decide: take the hits or get off the field.
Sad to say, in the first year of my job I wasn't
sure if I wanted in or out. I hadn't passed a single meaningful piece of legislation, I hadn't reset
Newark's budget priorities, I hadn't authored some
lasting initiative. I had to go through a lengthy

bureaucratic process just to suggest to the administration that a pothole needed to be fixed. As a nonprofit legal activist, I wouldn't have to look over my shoulder, wouldn't have to worry about getting into my car, wouldn't have police officers warning me **not to do anything you wouldn't want filmed and used against you.**

It was at this moment that I had my heated conversation with Elaine Sewell. And it was at this moment that I had to ask myself: Is this what I want to be doing with my life?

Elaine had called me because of some challenges she was facing at Garden Spires. She had demanded that I do something about them at the very moment when I felt most incapable of helping.

Garden Spires and Brick Towers had a lot of similarities. Both were deteriorating twin buildings, both were notorious centers of drug activity, and both housed strong, determined communities surviving amid crime and violence, trying with noble determination to find their American bargain.

Garden Spires was often called Academy Spires, as it stood on the site of a former school called Newark Academy. But when the school relocated, in 1965, two twenty-one-story towers were built. They sit adjacent to a major roadway that cuts from the New Jersey Turnpike through Newark and toward some of the more affluent suburbs in New Jersey. At its busiest, it functioned like a drive-through: people didn't even have to get out of their cars to buy drugs. The dealers catered to them with a speed and efficiency that would have made McDonald's jealous.

I came to know these buildings through one of Newark's legendary tenant organizers, Frank Hutchins. And in my early months out of law school, I worked to help him address some of the buildings' many issues. This is how I met Elaine Sewell, president of the Garden Spires tenants association. When I made the decision to run for City Council, Elaine became one of my most ardent campaigners. She was relentless on my behalf. She was in her sixties, but she outworked nearly everyone on my campaign. I remember personally knocking on every one of the doors in those buildings and talking with just about every resident; Elaine did the same.

Every time I walked those buildings, I was struck by the dignity of so many in the Garden Spires community. Single parents who worked eighty- or ninety-hour weeks and still were unable to make ends meet for their families, parents who had to make awful choices between being home for a sick child and bringing home a paycheck to feed that kid. People who filled out hundreds of job applications but could find no one willing to hire them because of a drug-possession charge from years before. People who felt they couldn't let their kids outside and fretted at the lack of structured recreation for their children. And then there were the elders, people who had worked their entire lives and were now trying to live off their meager Social Security checks, who felt disrespected because of the conditions inside the buildings and the drug problem outside.

In a city council election I won by just a handful of votes, these buildings had made a difference for me. The residents believed in me. Elaine Sewell believed in me.

And on that July day, before I raised my voice, Elaine had called to ask me for help. A violent incident had occurred at Garden Spires. As she explained it to me, guys involved in the drug trade had attacked the security guards. "Cory," she said, "it is the Wild Wild West out here! The Wild Wild West."

My response wasn't "I'm on it." Or "I will get the authorities out there." Or "I will bring in the cavalry." No, I figured that if I couldn't get the mayor to stop making the police ticket my damn car, then how could I get him to protect the people at Garden Spires? The mayor's words kept ringing in my head: **You're a legislator, not an administrator.** So I got defensive. I began to explain to her over and over again that I didn't know what to do. This only made her frustrated. She demanded action, and I told her I would call the police or the mayor's office. She said she had already done both of those things.

"We elected you, Cory. If you can't help, then why did we elect you?"

Hearing that, a part of me crumbled. A year's worth of stress and frustration rose up in my throat. I felt the need to defend myself. I tried to hold it together, but I couldn't. My voice raised, I told her that I was pouring my heart into the job, that I was sorry she wasn't satisfied with my work. I rattled off small assistances I had provided for her Garden Spires community—food for her meetings, money for community events, resource books for her residents, job opportunities for this person, drug treatment for that person. I labored to make my list long, but by then neither of us was listening; we were just talking over each other. And then I slammed down the phone.

I walked out of city hall, took the steps down to my car, and drove back to Brick Towers. All I wanted to do was go to my apartment, close the door, and douse my anger with ice cream.

But there was an obstacle.

There, standing in front of Brick Towers, was Ms. Virginia Jones. The project's own sentinel. I had never wanted so much **not** to see her. Should I go around back? Scale the walls? But it was too late. She saw me; we made eye contact. Her mouth creased up ever so slightly. Her brows furrowed.

I walked up the steps and tried to move past her, using all of my energy to send out a message: **Don't mess with me today, I'm not in the mood**.

"Boy, don't you just walk past me."

I stopped. She could tell I was distressed, because she opened her arms. It wasn't a request; this was a command. "Come here and give me a hug." I stomped over to her, gave her the least sincere hug I'd ever given, and then tried to escape. She grabbed my arm.

"What is **wrong** with you?"

That was it—she had asked for it. So I unloaded on her. I let loose a torrent of complaints: **Why did I run for office? What is the point? I'm not getting enough done! The city government is dysfunctional! I was doing more for the Central Ward before I got elected!** Like an angry kid, I probably whined something like, **Sharpe James is mean! The other City Council people don't play nice!** My list went on and on, and then I came to Elaine Sewell. I told her all about the incident at Garden Spires, and about my call with Elaine and how we argued. "I don't know what to do to help her," I said. "I just don't know what to do. I don't know what to **do**."

"I know what you should do," Ms. Jones declared.

She said it with such certainty that the music playing at my pity party came to a screeching halt.

"What?"

She folded her arms and took a deep breath.

"Yup, I know exactly what you should do," she said again.

"Look, Ms. Jones, I don't have time for games. What should I do?" I barked—that is, I barked in the most respectful way I could.

"Cory, you should do . . . something."

"Something?" I said. "That's it?"

"Yes. You should do something," she said, as if she had given me some precious gift. Then she smiled.

I wasn't about to give her any more gratification. I swung around, not caring how rude I was being, and scampered away into the lobby of my building. The elevators weren't working. God may reign supreme on the earth, but he had abandoned the elevators of this damned building to the devil! So I hiked up sixteen flights of stairs, banged out of the stairwell, opened my apartment door, walked through, and slammed it shut.

There on the table in the living room was my Bible. I took a breath and picked it up, and turned to a page that I had read often. It was in chapter 17 of Matthew: "For truly I say to you, if you have faith the size of a mustard seed, you will say to this mountain, 'Move from here to there,' and it will move; and nothing will be impossible to you." I paused and read it again.

And then Ms. Jones's words came back me: **Do something**.

I took another breath, and then another, trying to jump-start a meditation practice I had given up on months before. I was so focused on what I **couldn't** do, so focused on the obstacles, that I had lost an appreciation of what I **could** do. I was allowing my inability to solve a problem undermine my will to contribute something to the solution. I was allowing my inability to do **everything** to undermine my determination to do **something**. To myself I said, **Ms. Jones, you are the most infuriating, pain-in-the-posterior teacher in my life. Next time, I will hug you right!**

An idea formed, sharpened, and then crystallized in my mind. At a time when I felt vulnerable, at a time when I felt powerless, this felt right.

The reactions from my staff members when I told them my plan were pretty much 100 percent against. Jermaine James and Darrin Sharif both counseled that it would diminish any political capital I had left, that it would most likely fail to garner support, that I would look silly, that it was dangerous.

Jermaine was twenty-two at the time. He remembers saying to me, "Cory, we're not trying to be martyrs. We're not trying to get killed out there. Those of us who were born and raised in Newark know that there are certain projects you just don't go to. I was never allowed to go to Garden Spires as a kid, and I had no reason to go there until I joined your staff."

Jermaine seemed to have the most passionate concerns, so I decided to put him in charge of executing the plan. It turned out to be a wise choice: he did an incredible job.

My plan was to call Elaine Sewell back. I would admit to her that I didn't have the answer to the problems at Garden Spires, but I would no longer surrender to the idea that I couldn't help. I would move to Garden Spires—not into an apartment but into a tent that I would place on the pavement between the two buildings. I believed that I could disrupt the rampant drug trade, and unlike members of my team, I didn't think there was going to be violence. I believed that if we set up a tent, if we submitted ourselves to prayer, and if I fasted as long as it took until we found some kind of satisfactory conclusion, people would pay attention. That in fact that bit of pavement could be transformed into one of the safest places in the city.

My staff went to work. I was insistent that we not wait, that we get what we needed and get out there. My friend Jay Zises donated money that allowed us to rent a tent. Jermaine, exercising wisdom and forethought, got a huge one; it looked like a wedding tent. My staff secured cots and blankets. And then I went to see Elaine. I wanted to talk to her face-to-face.

I found her in front of the buildings. She looked at me sternly, but I could tell that hers was the kind of anger that could be defused. Love hadn't left us;

our bond hadn't been broken. I went up to her and came right out with it: "Elaine, I am sorry I disrespected you." My voice broke as emotion welled up in me. "I am just so sorry, I shouldn't have yelled at you, I was . . ." I couldn't speak anymore because she was hugging me. And now she was speaking, saying what I wanted to hear, what I needed to hear: **I love you, Cory, I love you.** She was crying, too.

In Newark, the capacity to forgive is profound. I have had to rely on that spirit many times over the years, and from a good number of people. In Brick City, I found tenderness, compassion, and an understanding of our common fragility that has been instructive and redemptive. Yes, there is brokenness in the city, but there is also gentleness. This obviously is not universal or absolute, but often an allowance is made for our mortal reality: people break, we make mistakes, we do wrong, we sin, we sometimes sin horribly, but we are human.

The challenges I faced in Newark forced me to confront my own weakness. This in turn helped me become more tolerant and less judgmental; it helped me fall more deeply in love with people, with the fullness of humanity. There is wisdom in recognizing one's own fragility, in acknowledging the fact that we humans are by our nature capable of mistakes and even depravity. That understanding ignites an appreciation of grace: "But there for the grace of God go I."

Grace, by definition, is not assigned by merit. It is extended freely—we are worthy of it despite ourselves. One reason I love Newark is because I witnessed a prodigious grace in the city, not in a religious sense but in a human one. I encountered folks all over the city who exemplified the highest ideals of grace. In tough circumstances and harsh conditions where you might expect an every-man-for-himself attitude, I found people exhibiting empathy, compassion, and generosity. I saw the awesomeness of grace. In that moment, out in front of Garden Spires, Elaine extended grace to me. She hugged me despite myself. She fully embraced not just my peaks but also my valleys. Elaine was an agent of grace: doing for others, advocating for opportunity, fighting to improve conditions for all, opening doors for others to walk through, accepting people where they were—all while never asking anyone to supplicate before her, to beg for forgiveness, to submit to her assessment of their worth.

After our embrace, I told Elaine that I still didn't know what to do about the problems at Garden Spires. Just saying it as I looked into her eyes felt liberating; admitting I was incapable somehow made me feel stronger. I realized in that moment that she wasn't looking for me to wave some magic wand and fix everything. My inflated ego and overblown sense of self had convinced me that that was what she wanted. Elaine knew I was human, and she just wanted me to be present—to connect to her and the residents, to bear witness to their frustrations, to show I cared and that I would do something.

I told Elaine that I wouldn't leave Garden Spires until we could figure something out. I told her that I would live in a tent between the buildings, that we could hold meetings with the residents, management, and others, and that maybe we would find a way to make a difference. I told her about Matthew 17. She, like many Christians, knew the "Faith the size of a mustard seed" verse, but I told her I was taken by the next verse, which is less known: "But this kind does not go out except by prayer and fasting." I told her that this was what I wanted to do: while I was living in the tent, working with the residents, I would also fast, and I would pray with anyone who wanted to join me.

As the tent was erected, I did something most politicians learn to do early in their careers: I called a press conference. The Essex County executive, Jim Treffinger, agreed to join me, and he rolled in with a trailer hitched to a truck that opens on one side to reveal a stage.

On the hot afternoon of August 15, 1999, I sat in a pair of khakis and a short-sleeved polo shirt next to Elaine, who was in a line of officials that included state assemblyman Craig Stanley, an official from the Drug Enforcement Administration, a local minister, state senator Ron Rice, and the county sheriff, Armando Fontoura. Not a single city official came to the event.

I spoke about how we, as a community, could no longer tolerate places where people live in fear, where people are afraid to walk outside or let their children play. I stated that this was the United States of America and that people in a nation this great shouldn't live under conditions so poor. People from the buildings were out and about; the area around the tent was crowded. There was no sign of the drug dealers. The atmosphere suddenly felt light; it was August, but it felt as if summer had just begun. People asked constructive questions and held impromptu strategy discussions. People were listening, talking, and connecting with one another.

Both the owner and the manager of the buildings had come to the press conference, as we had alerted them to what we were doing. I was worried that the pavement was private property and that they could take action against us, but we discovered that the lot right in front of the two buildings was city-owned. Still, we showed respect to them anyway—and starting from that posture turned out to be the correct approach. They were amenable to discussions and made it clear that they were willing to meet with tenant leadership to discuss changes.

As the sun went down, the officials began to leave, but the block party atmosphere continued. I was surprised by how many kids were there—more than I had seen on any previous visit to the Spires. It was clear that we had brought with us a sense of security, and folks were taking advantage of that.

Twenty or so people agreed to sleep out in the tent, from my staff to elders such as Phil Grate and Elaine Sewell. No one got much sleep. Many of the young folks stayed out there, talking with us past midnight, and it wasn't until one or two in the morning that we began falling asleep.

As we drifted off, we began to hear things hitting the pavement and slamming against the top of our tent. We jumped to our feet to investigate. I opened the tent and looked up to see something in flight from a high floor hit the ground: It was a used diaper. There was food and filth strewn all around the tent. Clearly not everyone was happy about our presence. I went to bed worrying if the warnings of my staff were correct, worrying that the initiative would fail—and worse, that someone would get hurt.

On the second day of our vigil, Monday, August 16, I was awakened early by a handful of men. They came to the tent, poked their heads in, and asked if I was available to speak with them. We stepped outside, and they introduced themselves as correctional officers at a local facility. They had seen what I was doing on the news and had come to let me know that they wanted to help. They wondered if I needed security for the residents and the folks camping out, and offered to take shifts throughout the week, keeping an eye on things. I wanted to hug them, but, sensing that they were not the hugging type, I settled for a handshake.

When the sun came up, some people who'd slept out left for work; others walked over toward one of the buildings to pray. As we prayed under the buildings, I found myself praying that nothing would be dropped on us. We went around the circle and each person testified, fervent and determined, lifting up his or her hopes, faith, and passion. The words of some of the seniors struck me. They beseeched the Lord for help, detailing their experiences of living in fear and tough conditions, asking for deliverance. Several of them extended their prayers to others: "God, please help these young men. They are misguided, they are lost, they know not what they do."

The rest of the day brought nothing but good news. All the media coverage and word of mouth triggered more and more people to come out to the tent and support us. Community leaders from across the city visited. Frank Hutchins and members of his low-income housing advocacy group, the Greater Newark HUD Tenants Coalition, came out again, and provided invaluable guidance on how to engage the management and how to organize around the key issues of concern. Frank saw how many people were present and suggested that the coalition hold a tenants rights seminar for all the residents the following evening, as people came home from work. After that we could get food and hold a larger tenants meeting under the tent.

Still more people came and I found myself playing the role of greeter. People who led or represented organizations and nonprofits—law firms, the YMCA, members of the NAACP, members of the Newark environmental group the Greater Newark Conservancy, local businesses, and more state and county officials—showed up and offered further support. No city administrative officials came, though.

The day was racing by, and I was so busy that I didn't have time to think much about my hunger. Throughout the day, Jermaine spoke further with management. In the late afternoon my staff, Elaine, and I huddled to discuss strategy. Jermaine informed me that he was getting a lot of calls from people who were offering to help. Jermaine believed we could begin to coordinate donations of food, clothing, and other essentials.

That night we again went to bed very late, but this time nothing was thrown at us.

On Tuesday, August 17, we again prayed in the morning. Our group was growing larger. It was now a true mix of people, from young volunteers to seniors, Christians, Jews, Muslims, and more. As people left for work, they joined in the tent to pray. Others hovered just outside to listen. I noticed that some people who joined us looked like they were struggling deeply. One woman, skinny and weak, looked as if she was a survivor from a prison camp; I knew that what she was actually surviving was addiction.

Jermaine, Darrin, Richard, and other staff members were extraordinarily busy organizing for the evening's tenants meeting. We would huddle often, and with Elaine and other tenant leaders we discussed creating a larger schedule of events.

That evening I saw two police cars enter the grounds. It wasn't the sheriff's office or the state police, both of which passed through with some regularity. The two police cars that came up were from West Orange, a suburban town to the west of Newark. With the police cars came the mayor of West Orange, John McKeon, and other city officials. This was something I hadn't expected—a suburban mayor and his police coming to offer help. The mayor said he had read about security concerns and wanted to provide a measure of safety. (He joked that I shouldn't let people in West Orange know about it, so I hope the statute of limitations has expired by now.) He also wanted to know what we needed. With offers of help coming from everywhere, I didn't have a long list, but he had his own ideas. The owner of a Panera Bread, he said, had offered to donate to our cause, and I agreed. Every morning, delivered by West Orange's finest, for the rest of the campout, we were blessed with an abundance of muffins, bagels, and breads—as much as I wanted to, I continued my fast and did not partake.

The Greater Newark HUD Tenants Coalition's tenant rights seminar was an enormous success in giving residents a greater sense of empowerment. This led into a tenant meeting, where we separated the issues into four categories around which we could strategize: building security, building conditions, senior issues, and youth opportunities. We quickly uncovered some ways to help—from connecting people with the services of nonprofits to connecting resident leadership with building management. We discussed other goals as well, from having recreation on-site to having better access to affordable daycare for the youngest children.

On Wednesday a street sweeping company came by with one of its trucks. The pavement on which we had set up camp was strewn with broken glass and debris. We had swept up a good amount, but this truck did a thorough job; when it left, our little patch of pavement was pristine.

We now had so many volunteers that we decided to more formally engage the kids hanging around our tent. With college students coming from around New Jersey and even New York University students coming from across the Hudson, we began to do activities with the kids: arts and crafts, face painting, sports, and tutoring.

Religious leaders from around the city continued to visit Garden Spires. We got deep into the planning for a gospel concert on Sunday as well as a church service under our tent. I was particularly grateful during this time for a handful of pastors who offered to fast with me. The first three days of the fast had been difficult, but by Thursday, the hunger pains began to dissipate. And it helped that pastors took time to teach me about fasting in various traditions.

By the weekend, Garden Spires was full of activity. The pavement was thick with residents and volunteers—in fact, every one of us was a volunteer, pitching in to help one another: a community fixed on inspiring Garden Spires. Amid it all, there was a constant cookout happening, with hundreds of hamburgers, hot dogs, sodas, and juices—all donated. The live music and DJ contributed to a block-party feeling.

Virginia Morton, a tenant leader from another area in the Central Ward, asked me to end my fast after the weekend. I had not eaten solid food for seven days and had lost considerable weight. No, I said, I wanted to press on into the next week, insisting I wasn't going to eat or end the campout until we had some assurances that the problems surrounding the buildings would be addressed. I wanted someone from the city to come out and hear us.

Journalists came in and out, interviewing me and others. But the most significant press that weekend came from the **Star-Ledger,** which took the mayor to task in an editorial about his failure to send city police to Garden Spires.

> It is not unusual for politicians to grandstand. But once in a while, an elected official has legitimate reason to dramatize a point . . . Newark Councilman Cory Booker camped out at the Garden Spires housing complex to draw needed attention to complaints over safety, drugs and deteriorating local services. He built a mini tent city to highlight these issues, invited supporters to join him overnight and held job and health fairs during the day. . . . [W]hile state and county officials showed up to cheer Booker on, city officials stayed away.
>
> Worse, the Newark police refused to provide extra security for the church members and other supporters who spent time at the tent with Booker. Police Director Joseph Santiago said Booker violated protocol by contacting the North District precinct captain instead of contacting him or the city's business administrator.

This is political pettiness brought to a new low. . . .

On Monday, an official from city hall finally showed up: the mayor's communications director. I think she came out to assess my posture toward the mayor. I wasn't hostile or angry; instead I welcomed her with kindness. Perhaps that's something that happens after a week of fasting and prayer: I felt no animosity toward the mayor at all.

On Tuesday afternoon, in the lull before people started getting home from work and the evening bustle around the tent began to build, the mayor arrived without fanfare. He came to sit with me and to see for himself what was going on. We discussed the key issues, and I told him this could be a win for him and for the community. I pointed out that the vacant land we were on was city property and suggested he build a park there.

The mayor left, and soon word got out that he was going to come again the next day to lay out a plan.

On Wednesday, August 25, the tent was packed as Mayor Sharpe James and I both stepped inside. It felt, I remember thinking, like a boxing match. There was applause and chanting, with some people yelling his name and others yelling mine. I stepped forward to speak first.

Some people probably expected me to take a jab

at the mayor or to slight him in some way. But on my tenth day of fasting and praying, I felt light; I felt no negative emotions whatsoever. In fact, I felt love for him. In the months and years ahead he and I would battle and I would not feel so enlightened. But in that moment I felt unthreatened by him. I had a feeling that all was okay, all was as it should be.

Instead of condemning Sharpe James, I praised and thanked him. I made the point that he had a city to run, one beset by challenges; we were fortunate to have a mayor who wasn't stuck in city hall but was out in the community, a man who knew the streets as well as anyone in the tent did. Sharpe James was our mayor and he was here that day for us, I said. I was grateful to him because he wanted to help.

I think my words surprised the mayor. He had been holding some papers in his hands, which I figured were prepared remarks, but now he folded them, and we did something we had never done before: we hugged. The **Star-Ledger,** our state's largest newspaper, captured the hug and put it on the front page of the local section. It may sound strange, but I remember in that embrace smelling him. It was the closest he and I had ever been and I breathed the moment in deeply. He smelled familiar, like the older men in my family. I don't know if it was his cologne or aftershave or what, but his smell was like family.

Here's how the **Star-Ledger** reported my remarks, our embrace, and Sharpe James's promises:

Ten days ago, Central Ward Councilman Cory Booker showed up to camp out at Garden Spires with water, juice and hope that he could bring attention to drugs and poor living conditions that have plagued the housing complex.

What he got yesterday was a promise from Mayor Sharpe James that the city will build a park adjacent to the complex, will provide an on-site police command post and will ask the federal government for money to hire more security guards.

James, however, went even further. For one of the only times publicly, James, who at 63 has had a foothold in Newark politics for 29 years, talked about passing political power to younger people, like Booker.

The mayor's comments followed a passionate and unexpectedly modest speech from Booker, 30, who called James "the father of Newark."

"I consider myself his son under a larger political family," he said to a crowd of more than 200 people who spilled out from under the big, white catering tent, where he fasted and slept for 10 days.

James, who also is a state senator from

the 29th District, was thrown off by the remarks and didn't follow a prepared speech. "I'm somewhat scared to come up as an old man who understands that I have to pass the baton," James said after he hugged Booker.

When Sharpe James made his promises to build a park, establish a police command post on the site, and spend more money on security, the crowd erupted in cheers. He and I hugged again, and then we went out. We climbed into a bucket lifter and were raised high into the air. To the applause of the crowd, we cut down sneakers hanging from an overhead wire—a perceived symbol that drugs were being sold in the area.

My fast was over, and we took down the tent. The mayor did indeed bring police out to Garden Spires, and for months the residents enjoyed increased police protection; the ten-day reprieve from open-air drug dealing that had started during the campout lasted for months. Eventually, though, the police left and the drug problem returned, as did many other issues and challenges that afflicted the buildings. The mayor never built the park. I swore to do better. And years later, when I became mayor, my administration worked to get a park and a preschool built.

●　●　●

Before I went back to Brick Towers to have my first meal in ten days, we gathered for a final prayer. There were more than a hundred people there to pray, the biggest group we had had with the exception of the church service under the tent the previous Sunday. My body felt weak, but when we joined hands I felt the strongest I had ever felt in my thirty years of life. I felt connected to those in that circle; there was an energy that flowed through us all, that united us. I felt as if I was having a revelation. We were young and old; we were believers and nonbelievers; we were black, white, Latino, and Asian; we were Christian, Muslim, and Jewish.

When it was my turn to pray, I spoke the words I heard in my head. They flowed to me unbidden; I didn't have to search for them or pull them forth. I had a clarity of thought and a spirit that rose up and into my words. I didn't speak as loudly as I would have normally. I knew people would hear me.

I spoke of our great nation. I spoke of how much I loved our country and her ideals and how grateful I was to our ancestors. I spoke of our need for each other, how we are each other's hope, how when we come together we are strong. How we know that if there is no enemy within, the enemy without can do us no harm. And the enemy within is indifference. It is apathy. It is convictions without courage and ideals without action. It is division. For we know that where there is unity, there is strength.

We know, as the African proverb says, that sticks in a bundle can't be broken.

I talked about how we belong to each other, how differences of race can't change that, how living in different places can't change that, how practicing different religions can't change that, how even having differences of opinions can't change the fact that we belong to each other, we owe each other, we need each other to be successful.

I said we had work to do, that there are great injustices in our midst, that we couldn't fail now, we couldn't give in, give up, or surrender in the face of all that is wrong—that we couldn't let love lose.

Lord, I prayed, we need strength now. Give us strength, God, because the times are tough, the hour is late, and the price being paid by too many of our children is too great.

Help us, Lord, help us to remember who we are. Help us to remember that we are the United States of America, that we have pledged to be one nation, under You, indivisible.

Lord, I prayed, help this group invoke strength, grace, love, the limitless potential that comes from unity. And though we will leave this place and go our separate ways, help us to remember this connection, help us to remember this strength, help us to remember the love we witnessed here and the power that flowed forth. Lord, help us, though we will soon be separated by distance, to remain always united in purpose.

5

MY FATHER'S SON

A human being is a part of the whole, called by us "Universe," a part limited in time and space. He experiences himself, his thoughts and feelings, as something separated from the rest—a kind of optical delusion of his consciousness. This striving to free oneself from this delusion is the one issue of true religion. Not to nourish the delusion but to try to overcome it is the way to reach the attainable measure of peace of mind.

—ALBERT EINSTEIN

HASSAN WASHINGTON'S WAKE WAS HELD IN the basement of the Perry Funeral Home. All other viewing rooms were on the first floor, but Hassan's service was in the basement. I walked down the narrow, steep stairs; I always felt when I went to this part of the funeral home like I was descending into the hull of a boat, with its low ceilings and tight spaces. This compartment was packed with people, so many of us crowded in on top of each other. Pain and grief lay everywhere; there was moaning amid murmurs and hushed tones. None of us wanted to be there. I wanted to leave, but there was no escape. All of us in the bowels of that building were chained together by our proximity to a too-common American reality: another child was dead, in a box.

Surely there was a time in our history when a dead teenager held the heart of our nation in a powerful grip—wasn't there? When Emmett Till was murdered, his death moved millions of citizens to call out the brutal, internecine reality of Jim Crow and to further advance the revolution that was the modern civil rights movement. William Faulkner was outraged that such a heinous crime had taken place in his beloved home state, Mississippi. From Rome, where he was living at the time, he wrote:

> If we Americans are to survive it will have to be because we choose and elect and defend to be first of all Americans; to present to the world one homogeneous and unbroken front, whether of white Americans or black ones or purple or blue or green.
>
> Perhaps we will find out now whether we are to survive or not. Perhaps the purpose of this sorry and tragic error committed in my native Mississippi by two white adults on an afflicted Negro child is to prove to us whether or not we deserve to survive. Because if we in

America have reached that point in our desperate culture when we must murder children, no matter for what reason or what color, we don't deserve to survive, and probably won't.

Are we so moved today by the deaths of thousands of young people? Mamie Till chose to keep her son Emmett's casket open, so the world would be forced to see the truth of the brutality, the violence, the injustice; today, are we open to the enormity of our truth? Do we see?

Faulkner spoke of "we," of an interwoven destiny. Of collective responsibility. The murder of children "no matter for what reason or what color" should be an assault on the conscience of our country, a unifying national tragedy. But does this carnage now pass as if it is routine? Not worthy of our notice?

I stood in the cramped basement, familiar faces full of grief streaming past. Brick Towers was well represented; Central High School was there; friends, family, neighbors, community leaders, clergy, and activists, all in a basement now swollen with sadness. We knew Hassan, we watched him grow up, we knew his laugh, his natural charisma—and yes, we knew of his troubles.

There was no press camped outside the Perry Funeral Home looking for comment, trying to capture the outrage and agony. No one even had to make a decision as to whether to send a reporter or a camera crew. The larger world kept moving on as we kept descending into that basement.

I was the mayor of Newark, but in that basement, my inauguration weeks before seemed totally inconsequential. I knew a mayor had a responsibility at a wake or a funeral, but I didn't rise to it. I didn't do my part in comforting or encouraging others. I just stood in the back, pressed up against the wall, with Hassan's body in front of me. Friends and neighbors came over, hugged me, shook my hand as they shook their heads; beautiful people, sparks of light and glory now dimmed by this loss. I was grateful for every touch, every handshake and hug. I was leaning on their light as I struggled with the darkness of my own guilt.

I had to leave that basement. I couldn't breathe. I turned to Kevin Batts, a detective on my new mayoral detail, and told him we had to go. Back up the narrow staircase, now working against the stream of people coming down, I tried not to make any eye contact with friends, neighbors, and others. I couldn't confront or share in the grieving any longer; I just wanted out.

We headed through the lobby and out the door, then climbed into my SUV. I told the detective driving to take me to city hall even though all I wanted to do was go back to Brick Towers and climb into my bed. Once we arrived, I shot up the two flights of stairs and rushed past our receptionist, past my assistant, and into my office. I slammed the door and locked it, trying to make myself clear: **Do not bother me.** I sat on the couch before my new desk in my grand new office. I didn't fight it any longer: I surrendered and let the grief fall upon me, along with that other emotion, shame. I cried.

I was taught of a courageous love—of people who could love those who hated them, despised them, and cursed them. A heroic love that leapt lines of segregation, compassion that tore down walls, a determined empathy that saw value in every child regardless of race, geography, or circumstance. An activist love that ignited a nation's moral imagination and galvanized a collective will. Heroes of every faith, color, and sexual orientation, who left behind the comfort of anonymity and marched knowing they would be beaten, boarded buses knowing they would be burned—we are a product of their love. A love that asserted the fundamental idea that we are in this together, bound by destiny, that what happens to my American brother or sister affects me, that our connection mandates an obligation. I was taught of a courageous love.

But I wasn't feeling it.

As I sat on that couch in my office, heavy with self-doubt, I knew I was also taught that love doesn't simply leap canyons of injustice. More often the greatest love, the most needed, advances in small steps and is seen in consistent acts of kindness. We descended into that basement because we loved Hassan. So many of us showed up, but it cut at me: we were there, assembled for his death, but where had we been during his life?

His choices led him to that box, but so did ours.

When I moved into Brick Towers, apartment 16C, Hassan Washington lived four floors below me with his grandmother in 12C. On warm evenings I'd hang out in the courtyard of our building, talking to elders such as Ms. Jones, Ms. Jacobs, and Ms. Wright. We would strategize about addressing the buildings' issues and share the news of the town. The courtyard was full of kids, and Hassan—outgoing, enthusiastic, and funny—was one of my favorites. In his grade school years Hassan distinguished himself as exceptionally bright and curious.

As I took on the role of Newark's Central Ward council member, engaged in the hard fights of city politics, Hassan and many other kids from Brick Towers were a constant in my life. I watched Hassan grow up. He'd help his grandmother, Mrs. Holliday, carry groceries up the stairs when the elevators in the buildings were broken; he'd stand, still and respectful, as Ms. Jones lectured him to use the sense that God had given him and stay out of trouble.

As Hassan grew into a teenager, I saw him more on his own, away from his grandmother's watchful eyes. He started hanging out in the lobby of my building with a crew of other teens. I had countless conversations with him and the other boys, but I saw troubles; I saw danger descending. It seemed to set upon them quickly, almost as if I'd looked away for only a second and then looked back to find that they were no longer kids but young men walking a perilous line. On many nights I came home and noticed the smell of marijuana in the lobby. Their graffiti spread like mold through the lobby and into the mailroom, into the elevator and the stairwells. In that graffiti were Bloods signs and their tag: "Brick Tower Red."

Right before my eyes, at my building's front door, Hassan was riding the wheel downward. I tried to take action. I began to have more serious conversations with him and his friends. I'd bring home food at the end of my days and hang out in the lobby with them as we ate and talked. I'd push them about their futures and try to advise them, inspire them, and warn them. As a further intervention, I took Hassan and his friends to the movies. We went out to eat at my favorite diner, Andros, and I brought a crew of my own, friends who knew about dealing drugs from direct experience. One friend captured their attention with his story of dealing drugs and getting out right before his world collapsed. I was happy that they seemed to listen to these guys, who had stories more relatable than the ones I could bring from my straitlaced suburban high school experience. We made more plans and tried to set up mentoring opportunities, but just as our connections deepened and grew, just as I began indulging in thoughts that we might be breaking through, I got busy with my career pursuits, and my focus on these kids dwindled.

I was running for mayor and, having lost once, I was determined not to lose again. I was all in, and had around me a campaign team whose passion and work ethic matched mine. It was an intense time, and I told myself I would pick up with Hassan and his friends after the election was over. And so I went back to seeing them only late at night when I came home exhausted from the grueling days of campaigning.

Hassan and his crew were great to me. Night after night they encouraged me, sending me off into the elevator with cheers, gentle teasing, and words of support. Hassan told me they'd make sure everyone in Brick Towers voted; he told me **he** had **my** back. One night they had gotten hold of some "Booker for Mayor" lawn signs, and when I showed up they raised them high and shouted the title I so ardently sought: **"Mayor Booker! Mayor Booker!"** I went to bed that night thinking of all the things I would do for Hassan and his crew when I was mayor, what I could do for so many other kids, and I felt so good about myself, my mission, my dreams. . . .

I was taken by Hassan: his spirit, his inner light, the goodness he showed toward me. I think my appreciation of him was heightened because I saw some of my dad in him. Both were charismatic, both were born leaders, both lived in segregated black neighborhoods—one segregated **de jure,** the other **de facto**. Both were born poor to single moms, both had absent dads, and both were raised, for a time, by their grandmothers. My dad used to say he was a hardheaded young man who survived and thrived because of a community that wouldn't let him fail; he admitted to getting into his share of trouble, but he claimed he had benefited from hundreds of people who stepped up, and that it was their small acts of kindness, love, and decency that saved him.

Despite all my father and Hassan had in common, plenty of differences separated them. But as I sat slumped on that couch in my regal new office, I could focus on only one: a community had been there for my dad and would not let him fail, and still we let Hassan fail.

In the weeks between the evening Hassan cheered me as I got into the elevator and the day of my inauguration, I lost track of him. Immediately after the election, the FBI learned of death threats against me, and the county sheriff, Armando Fontoura, quickly surrounded me with a security detail. Consequently, from the moment I was elected, Brick Towers—our buildings, with a long reputation for crime—had the best security in the city. What this meant for Hassan and his crew, however, was that our lobby was no longer suitable for hanging out and smoking weed. And in my new world of unrelenting crises and 24/7 work, I barely noticed that Hassan wasn't there to greet me anymore when I came home to steal a few hours of rest.

I was inaugurated as Newark's thirty-sixth mayor on July 1, 2006. I pushed the bounds of my endurance racing around the city at all hours. I spent many nights in police cars, riding along with patrols. If a shooting occurred, I'd often be one of the earliest on the scene. Once on the scene, I'd huddle briefly with police and investigators, engage with any crowd that had gathered, answer questions, listen to concerns. Sometimes I'd take the brunt of their anger, fear, or frustration. I'd share with residents our strategies to meet these challenges and my belief that we could take our city back from the rising violence.

On August 14, 2006, just blocks from Brick Towers, two young men were shot. I arrived as the ambulance was taking one away. The other was covered with a sheet. I got the report from the officers on the scene, and talked with residents. I spoke with passion and determination about what we could do together to make a change. I was at the scene for over an hour. Over an hour, and yet I never asked the name of the dead teenager. I didn't ask anything about him. Was his humanity not important enough for me to ask? Instead, with seniors and others gathering, I walked right over to talk minister to the living—to be mayoral.

That night I returned home exhausted. I pounded out messages to my staff on my BlackBerry. I then went to my email inbox and opened the police reports and alerts that had come in during the day. I scrolled through until I saw a subject line that said "Homicide." I opened it. It contained the details of the Court Street shooting. Two black males shot. One dead. The victim was eighteen years old. His name: Hassan Washington.

And now, in the Newark mayor's office, behind a locked door, six weeks after my inauguration, I was trying to make sense of his death.

God had put Hassan on my doorstep, right in front of me, day after day. But, unlike all those who had helped my dad in the 1940s and '50s, I had not stepped up. I hadn't paid it forward. I felt a profound sense of failure. I had become mayor, but I didn't feel like I was the man I wanted to be. I was so caught up in my big mission that I failed in the small acts of love that mattered most. I had won an election, but felt as if I had failed my history.

My father was raised in the funeral home business. He had been born in 1936 to a single mother with health problems so severe, she couldn't care for him. In the earliest years of his life, he was cared for primarily by his elderly grandmother, but when it became clear that even she could no longer provide for him, they gave him up to live with James and Eva Pilgrim. Eva was an elementary school teacher, and James owned a local funeral home. Pilgrim's Funeral Home was known back then as the colored funeral home, because white funeral homes didn't tend to black bodies.

My father taught me early in my life that attitude is a conscious choice; it is a currency available even to those with no access to money. No matter what the circumstances, you exercise your power, you demonstrate your worth, when you decide how to act and react in the face of it all. If the world punches you in the gut, that doesn't define you; it's what you do **next** that speaks your truth. My father's truth was relentless positivity; he radiated it and seemed to believe that he could affect the world around him with the force of his spirit. He would tell me, "Son, there are two ways to go through life, as a thermometer or a thermostat. Don't be a thermometer, just reflecting what's around you, going up or down with your surroundings. Be a thermostat and set the temperature."

My mom and dad were constant mentors, my first and greatest teachers. But as I grew, I also learned that behind my father's courageous positivity and humor was unreconciled pain. The Pilgrims loved my father well; in the funeral home he not only gained a nurturing family but learned the connection between hard work, discipline, and reward. But he did carry pain with him, a pain I also saw in my mother's father, who was born to a single mother and never knew his dad. Both men, in moments of honest conversation, used the word "bastard" in reference to themselves. It always made me feel uncomfortable; it struck me as an unnecessarily aggressive anachronism, a self-indictment for a crime committed by no one. For my father, I know now that he was part of a pattern going all the way back to slavery. He was born poor to a single mother, Jesse Lucille Booker, who was born poor to a single mother, Mary Willie Booker, who was born poor to Nannie Bailey, who was born to Talithia Givens, who was most likely a slave.

My father often talked about how fortunate he was. He had a profound work ethic; I've never encountered anyone who could outwork my dad, and he took great pride in this. Yet he was cognizant of the fact that hard work had been necessary but not sufficient to break him out of the circumstances of his birth. It was also the small and consistent acts of kindness from folks in that segregated town that freed him to live his American dream. And even though he carried with him hurt and shame about the circumstances of his birth, the love of a town, a strong church community, and the nurturing Pilgrim family made him feel an unending sense of gratitude. This gratitude emanated from my father. He would never be able to pay back this country or his Hendersonville, North Carolina, community for all they had given him, but he would do his best to reflect their goodness, by being a tireless agent of gratitude.

And so, from my earliest years, funeral homes weren't places of dread but places of joy. Some of my fondest memories, in fact, were of running in and out of the rooms with my older brother and our beloved cousins, the Pilgrims' other grandkids. We would play games around the house and sometimes peek in on bodies that were being prepped for a funeral. The constant shushing from my dad and my mother's admonitions to "be respectful" barely slowed us. Perhaps I delighted so much in Pilgrim's Funeral Home because my soul knew that this place had helped save my father's life.

Charlton Holliday, Hassan Washington's father, had pulled the trigger. The shotgun went off, and pellets exploded forth, lodging in the man's head. The man fell, collapsing hard on the ground. He clung to life for about a week in the hospital. Then he was pronounced dead. Charlton had murdered a man.

It was spring 1989, and Charlton had gone to the man to collect a debt—not his own debt but a friend's. The friend was afraid to confront the man, so he enlisted Charlton's help. Charlton decided to bring the weapon.

"My friend was acting all scared," Charlton said

years later when I spoke with him. "He acted like he didn't even want to ask him. When I ran up on him, I'm like, 'Run and cry, bitch,' and he just brushed off on me like whatever and then when I grabbed him he turned around and tried to swing at me. That's when I pulled the shotgun and he tried to run and I just pulled the trigger."

Days after the murder, Charlton was back at Brick Towers, his home. It was early one April morning and he was hanging in front of the buildings. Police stormed up on the high-rises, coming from the back and the front. They were looking for Charlton, but they didn't recognize him as they flew up the steps, through the courtyard, and into one of the two buildings. They passed him without notice. Charlton knew why they were there and where they were going. He told a friend, who seemed surprised by Charlton's certainty.

After the police flooded the building, Charlton darted into an apartment on the third floor. He grabbed the phone and called upstairs to 12C, where he lived with his mother. His mother answered the phone. The police had stormed their apartment. They had warrants, they told her, and they wanted Charlton. She was afraid. She asked him to come to the apartment, to turn himself in, but Charlton refused. He waited the police out nine floors below. When all was clear, Charlton left the buildings. But it didn't take long until the police were on him again. This time it was away from

Brick Towers up on Astor Street, and now Charlton did not run or hide. He surrendered without resistance.

Charlton was twenty-one years old at the time. In the preceding year, he had had three children by three different women: Hassan, a boy named Hakeem, and a girl named Charleen. Charlton was convicted and sentenced to twenty-one years, and so Hassan would never remember a time when his father was not behind bars.

Hassan would also scarcely know his mother, who was eighteen when he was born. When Charlton was locked up, she spiraled downward and became consumed by the fire of narcotics that was blazing throughout Newark at the time. "It was like as soon as I got locked up," Charlton recalled. "Hassan was at my mom's house all the time so my mom was like, 'I don't know what's going on.' Then everybody started telling me, 'Your baby's mom, she's out doing this stuff . . . getting high and selling drugs.' . . . So my mom was like, 'I'll take him.' My mom, she tried to make an example to help Hassan's mother get herself together. But you know, the streets was calling any and everybody back then."

Looking back, Charlton realized that he owned her descent into drugs and addiction. That his crime started a ripple of devastation that would resound for decades. Others would bear the wounds of his actions, those he didn't know and those he most loved.

• • •

It wasn't supposed to be this way. In 1974, v
the Hollidays moved into Brick Towers, the hig.
rises offered some of the finest housing available
in Newark. But the 1980s brought different management, landlords who no longer enforced high
standards for entry and who cut maintenance to
the bone, and the larger problems of the city in-
fected Brick Towers. Residents still talk about the
first murder in their tight-knit neighborhood. It
was in the late 1970s, and in the aftermath, things
changed quickly. Crime rose and conditions in
the buildings steadily worsened. Across Newark's
Central Ward, schools struggled, job opportunities
vanished, and the drug trade exploded. Amid these
savage storms, more and more loved ones got swept
away. Brick Towers had a solid nucleus of women
who protected the children, and the tenants association was strong. They fought the series of slumlords, organizing, assiduously working to preserve
the strength of their buildings physically and spiri-
tually. But eventually the dam broke, and drugs and
violence swallowed up the buildings. Even then the
tenants association didn't give up. When I arrived
at the buildings in the late 1990s, I witnessed their
indomitable determination firsthand.

Yet in the late 1970s, Charlton Holliday wasn't
saved. His early minor crimes were a warning sign,
but no one heeded it. In **my** early life, I saw kids do

wrong, veering off course, only to have their courses dutifully corrected by vigilant adults. I grew up at the same time—I'm eighteen months younger than Charlton—and lived only about eighteen miles north. I witnessed my peers engage in similar mischief, from shoplifting to experimenting with drugs and alcohol. But in Harrington Park there was a wide margin for error, with second, third, and fourth chances. At their worst, our run-ins with police would mark not an end to our opportunity but the beginning of an intervention. Charlton's path was different.

Before the Newark riots and civil disturbances of 1967, most people in northern New Jersey thought of Newark as a shopping mecca. Before suburban New Jersey became known for its malls, there was Newark with its boutiques and glittering department stores like S. Kleins, Hahne & Co., and Bamberger's. The flagship store of the Bamberger's chain was founded in 1893 in Newark. The store took up a whole city block and had its own phone exchange. The store was among the first in the country to offer a delivery service to shoppers in the suburbs; all you had to do was dial a 565 number and a Bamberger's delivery man would carry whatever you needed to your doorstep.

Around the time he was in sixth grade, Charlton Holliday and a group of his friends began shoplifting at Bamberger's. His shoplifting crew were not his friends from Brick Towers. Brick Towers boys were good kids, as he told me. These were kids from other neighborhoods, and their first offense as sixth-graders was shoplifting ladies' gloves. It was the height of the disco era, and these gloves were coveted items. They lifted them, then went back up into the neighborhood and made good sales that gave them extra money for food, movies, and other things that eleven-year-olds covet.

This is where Charlton Holliday's story should have shifted. Petty shoplifting should have resulted in constructive discipline that would have put him back on course. But these kids didn't receive help from positive role models; instead they were approached by people who accelerated their descent. One of these men was Jace Bradley, who ran the Brick Towers drug trade. A young Charlton looked up to Jace, who drove around in a fancy car, wearing expensive clothes and jewelry. Jace exuded wealth, power, and style, and that was seductive to Charlton.

When some of the dealers saw how good Charlton was at selling stolen gloves from Bamberger's, they recruited him to sell pills. By the time he was thirteen, he was dealing drugs and bringing home good money, anywhere from $50 to $100 a day. His natural skills and God-given talents were focused now, but perversely so—not on school or sports, but on selling drugs.

Charlton had numerous run-ins with the police as a teenager, including being picked up for truancy, fighting, and car theft. At seventeen he was arrested for drug dealing as a juvenile and was sent into the system for a short time. Three years later he killed a man and was on the way to prison for a long time.

His mother came to visit him every month with Hassan, sometimes two or three times a month if she could manage it. In their brief conversations, Charlton tried to encourage Hassan to keep his head down and stick to his books, but more and more Charlton met folks in prison, fresh from the streets, who would tell him, "Yo, man, he's just like you."

Hassan was becoming his father's son. Charlton warned against this, but his admonitions rang hollow and hypocritical—in prison, Charlton had become a bigger drug dealer than he ever was on the streets. "I was running hard," he recalled. "I was running harder in prison than I was in the streets because in prison you ain't got to worry about somebody getting shot, you've got to worry about somebody getting stabbed. But at the same time I had my mind on my kids by supporting them financially as best as I can."

Charlton convinced himself that the money he made helped his kids; he convinced himself that he could look out for Hassan through his connections. That was, of course, a bad assumption.

I moved into Brick Towers in 1998 and met Hassan when he was ten years old. When Charlton heard about this in jail, he said, he had felt hope for his son. Once I became a city council member, my presence affected the drug trade at Brick Towers, scattering the dealers who sold in the open-air market in front of the building. "I watched the news every night in jail, every night," Charlon told me. "When you moved in that building I was so happy because I figured maybe it is just going to change now. It did change to a certain extent . . . you tried to show the community like, 'Man, I'm here.'"

But my presence brought no revolutionary change. And when I lost the mayor's race in 2002 and was no longer on the City Council, the quality of life declined. Brick Towers was eventually taken over by the Newark Housing Authority, which did an even worse job managing the buildings. There was less security and shoddier maintenance; troubles for all of us in those buildings grew. Some families moved out. Squatters started moving in—and to prevent this, the Housing Authority started welding doors shut. By the time I was gearing up for my second run for mayor in 2006, there were vacancies on just about every floor of the two buildings. Graffiti was everywhere, marking the buildings as Bloods territory. And Hassan was one of the people running the drugs.

After my victory in the July 1, 2006, mayoral election, I was elated because I now could influence the Housing Authority to step up and do right by the residents. This was the moment for Brick Towers; we were now in control of our destiny. But a month later our community gathered together not for a mayoral victory celebration, but in the basement of Perry's Funeral Home.

Charlton was granted a special dispensation to go to the funeral home and say goodbye to his son. Two prison guards escorted him into the basement. It was early morning when he arrived, as the Department of Corrections would not allow him to be there with the other mourners. Charlton said he sat for a while with his son: "I talked with him," he said. "I cried with him."

This was the end point for Hassan, but it was also an end point for Charlton. He shaved his head, giving his dreadlocks to his niece so she could put them in Hassan's casket to be buried with him. Perhaps he wanted a part of him to descend into the earth with his son, to be close to him forever in death the way he hadn't been able to be while his son was alive. But perhaps it was a modern take on the Samson story. He had been so hard for so long. He was a man who believed toughness was necessary in the world in which he chose to live. Now with his shaved head, that brand of toughness left him:

"I think about the boy that I killed, and then I think about Hassan, and I can't help but think that's on me, what goes around comes around. . . . Once my son got killed, I asked the Lord, I said, 'God, get these demons out of me.' I don't smoke weed no more, I don't drink no more. I rarely curse. They say that God takes away from you so you can straighten up, and that's what happened with me."

When Charlton was released from prison, he set out to start his life anew. He worked hard to escape his environment. He tried to get a job in Newark but wasn't able to. Jobs for ex-offenders are difficult to come by not just in Newark but across our nation. In frustration, and determined not to fall back into the life of destruction, he moved to West Virginia. There, he was able to convince a warehouse manager to take a chance on him. He landed a job driving a forklift at a warehouse.

"It was hard for me to sell myself to them, to the idea that I'm not going back. I was honest with them about my past because I knew if you lie, they're going to find out. So me and the manager, I told him, I said, 'Look, man, I really need a job because I'm not going back to jail, but it's getting to the point where I might have to do something for some money and I don't want to do it. All I'm asking for is this opportunity.'"

Charlton still returns to Newark, still visits with old friends and, when he can, attends our annual Brick Towers reunion. He mourns when he hears about people he knew getting shot and killed. And he tries to do everything he can to talk guys out of the game. He talks to the young men and tries to tell them what he needed to hear back then but didn't. He tries to stop the cycle.

Charlton knows he is only one person, but he tries. Unfortunately, the men he confronts seldom believe they can escape; they don't believe they can get work, get a break, get free. Their chains—real or perceived—are our chains. One to another, we are chained to this collective fate that defines our nation more than we want to admit.

Here, my father's words come back to me: **No matter what the circumstances, you exercise your power, you demonstrate your worth when you decide how to react, how to act in the face of it all. If the world punches you in the gut that doesn't define you; what you do next, that speaks your truth.**

My father's circumstances were dire. He was born poor, in the Jim Crow South, fatherless, to a mother who couldn't take care of him. But in the face of those circumstances, hundreds of hands, through modest actions, reached out. In the face of terrible circumstances, they responded and collectively freed my father. They broke chains, freed a child from his circumstances, set in motion a cycle that affected generations yet unborn.

Charlton knows what has been unleashed by what he did earlier in his life. "What goes around comes around" is how he put it to me. Charlton served his time, twenty-one years, and he paid his debt—but he is still working to atone.

But what about us? Do we need to atone? Hassan failed. We failed Hassan.

Hassan's death, like all deaths of our children, cannot be in vain. I am my father's son. I am the son of a man who was born from poverty to a mother born from poverty to a mother born from poverty going back to slavery. I can't imagine the failures they confronted. I can't imagine how they survived the journey along this grievous path worn into the American soil. I can't imagine how they kept going, facing unthinkable tragedies, forging forward, stumbling, falling, getting up, falling again. Despite it all, they never gave up. They never gave up on each other. We can't, either.

6

I SEE YOU

This is the true joy in life, the being used for a purpose recognized by yourself as a mighty one; the being thoroughly worn out before you are thrown on the scrap heap; the being a force of Nature instead of a feverish selfish little clod of ailments and grievances complaining that the world will not devote itself to making you happy.

—George Bernard Shaw

I SAT IN THE ROOM OF A HOSPICE CENTER IN East Orange, New Jersey, in November 2009, beside the bed of Frank Hutchins, seventy-five, a longtime housing advocate and tenant organizer. Cancer was ravaging his body, but not his stature. Frank was a father to me, one of my most cherished teachers, a man who changed the course of my life. He was dying, but no disease could obscure his truth.

Before my electoral interests were ignited—before

Frank Hutchins—when I lived across the street from Brick Towers, renting a room in a house with a handful of other boarders, I dreamed of starting a nonprofit. All I knew of Brick Towers, the two large sixteen-floor buildings, was that they had an incredible group of tenants who had created and nurtured a strong community despite the outrageous conditions of their buildings.

As a wannabe community warrior, I soon met Ms. Virginia Jones. She didn't simply hand me a black belt in community-revolution karate. Instead she put me through an intense initiation process, where, it seemed, I had to convince her both that I was committed to her community and that I was worthy of working there. She had me performing tasks around the building. I carried everything from tables and chairs to cases of sodas and hot dogs for cookouts. She put me to work posting or handing out flyers for tenant meetings, other building events, or important announcements. I was her sidekick as she confronted management about elevator repairs. In my last months of law school and first months of being a graduate, I didn't get started building a nonprofit; I just did the unglamorous tasks Ms. Jones assigned to me. And I loved it.

One summer day in 1997 Ms. Jones asked me to her apartment for a meeting. When I knocked, she opened the door and greeted me impatiently. I was on time, but she acted like I was an hour late: "Cory, come on now, get in here and sit down."

There was another person in the apartment, and Ms. Jones introduced me. His name was Frank Hutchins. It was clear that he was important to Ms. Jones. In her introduction, her voice took on a tone I hadn't heard from her all that frequently—it was just a hint, but I swear there was a sweetness in her voice. I was suddenly excited for the meeting.

Frank had gray hair, a mustache, and a day or two of scruff around his face. He was dressed in slacks, a shirt, a jacket, and very worn shoes. He looked a bit disheveled, as if his appearance was of minimal concern to his larger mission. In short, he looked the part of the tenant activist.

Frank was the head of an organization called The Greater Newark HUD Tenants Coalition. He worked in low-income buildings all over Newark that were subsidized in one way or another by federal money through the Department of Housing and Urban Development. It seemed that Ms. Jones had called in Frank to help fix the larger problems in Brick Towers.

Frank seemed happy to meet me and treated me as if I were an old friend he had known for years but had lost touch with. As we spoke, Frank's eyes struck me: behind wide, large-framed glasses, they were gentle, kind, and patient. They put me at ease, made me feel comfortable sharing. When he looked at me it was as if his whole being was present and attuned to mine—it wasn't just a moment, it was an experience.

Ms. Jones began to put forth a damning theory about the landlord. She insisted that the landlord was exploiting the residents and scamming the federal government, pocketing money and grants intended for residents' benefit. She pulled out a bunch of papers and handed them to Frank; they were documents describing different HUD programs and funding streams. There was nothing conclusive, but they seemed to pique Frank's interest; they piqued mine as well.

We discussed strategy and tactics. We would collect more specific information from residents about the conditions in the buildings, we would let HUD officials know as many specifics as possible, and we would press them to come to future meetings and help address the building conditions. By using the Freedom of Information Act, we could demand more information about the funding streams that the building was receiving. And as we got information, we would inform the HUD inspector general for our region about what we discovered—which we suspected would be the failure of the landlord to abide by the requirements of grants and other payments. In short, we set out to shine a brighter spotlight on the buildings, letting federal authorities see how taxpayer dollars were being invested—and, perhaps, to expose the potentially illegal activities of the landlord.

This tenant meeting had a more powerful impact on me than I could have expected. I would go on to attend hundreds more with and without Frank, but this one—hours long, which allowed me to observe Frank in action—was particularly enlightening.

Our tenant meetings in Brick Towers occurred in the basement of the southern tower. From the lobby you would walk down one flight of stairs, go down a hallway, and turn left into a damp room the width of three or four bowling lanes and about the same length. A table sat at the front of the room, and rows of chairs were lined up in front of it. Ms. Jones, Frank, and other officers of the tenants association sat at the head table; I sat in a chair off to the side, holding a sign-in clipboard and a notebook.

The buildings had more than a thousand residents; about a hundred attended this meeting. To open the meeting, Ms. Jones announced in her commanding tone that she was fed up with what was going on and was determined to keep fighting—we just had to fight smarter.

She explained that she had met with Frank and that we would all have to collaborate if we were going to win more attention for the buildings. She closed with a strong sentiment: **that people needed to see what was really going on here**. Folks in attendance nodded in agreement.

She then talked about some of our tactics, saying that she, Frank, and I were going to reach out to HUD officials to get information about the buildings. "HUD needs to get out here and see how we are living," she said. "They need to come out here and listen to us." There was support from people in the room—nods, hand claps, and exclamations like "That's right!"

And then she invited Frank to speak.

He stood and, rather than starting to speak right away, looked out at the room, taking it in. Folks were quiet. And a moment or two before the silence would have become awkward, he smiled gently and began. His style, voice, and energy were different from Ms. Jones's. In fact, Frank was different than most speakers I had seen. He was not fiery or flashy; there was no booming voice, no roaring oratory, no jokes or attempts at humor. He didn't try to show the audience how smart or knowledgeable he was. In a community of gifted pastors, both licensed and self-appointed, Frank made no attempt at preaching, having little use for the rhetorical tools of that profession. He made no attempts to try to play to the crowd. Instead, he was soft-spoken and his comments were brief—basically, he stood up there and said he was there to help, would do what he could, and hoped to hear more from them about what was going on. In all, he said probably three or four sentences, and then sat down.

At first, I was disappointed. I had thought this man, a tenant organizing legend in Newark, would ignite the crowd, lift the room, or fill us with hope. But then I realized: in this basement, in a room full of people enduring conditions that made their home a hostile place, he deferred to them. His focus was on **them.**

When he was done, Ms. Jones opened the floor and people rose to speak. They asked questions, mostly of Ms. Jones, and she answered. Some expressed gratitude; some shared their grievances about what they were bearing and how it affected them, their jobs, their kids, their grandkids. There were complaints about the elevators that broke down with regularity, leaving the elderly and disabled stranded in the lobby and forcing so many to use the stairwells. And about how management didn't clean the common areas—most notably those stairwells. They were filthy, full of garbage, urine, feces, used drug paraphernalia. People spoke of how often the presence of a homeless or drug-addicted person sleeping in the stairwell made it more complicated to climb or descend the stairs. People talked about calling for help for those folks, and how nothing came of the call. It was clear that for many, merely venturing into the stairwells— many of which were dark because the lights had long since burned out—was an act of courage.

People spoke of mice, rats, and roaches that plagued the buildings and the toll such infestations took on their physical and mental health.

People spoke of the life disruptions that took place when heat and water failed. There were stories about heating apartments with open ovens and pots of hot water. I thought then how dangerous this was—but years later, living in Brick Towers, I would do the same thing. I also heard how it would get so hot in some apartments during the winter that you had to open the windows in order to tame the radiators' inferno.

People spoke of the lack of security in the buildings, how vulnerable they were to vandalism, theft, and occasional physical confrontations. Anything of value might be taken—often by the drug-addicted looking to sell something for quick cash. The constant lack of security, having to look over your shoulder, wondering if the sounds you heard when locked in your apartment were from gunfire, or a fight, or someone in trouble—there are limits to human endurance, both physical and emotional. And in this safe space of community, people opened up about their experiences. If someone showed emotion, they received nurturing responses from the crowd: "That's okay, take your time!" or "Tell it!" or "You know that's right!"

I took notes and tried to record specific information that we could use later, complaints that I could document in detail to HUD. I was clinical about it. We had a mission, and though I hadn't yet gotten my bar exam results back, I was trying to be lawyerly in collecting material for a compelling fact pattern.

I was moved by the testimony, joined in the supportive responses, and felt increasingly motivated to be a part of this fight—but I must confess that as the meeting moved into the second hour, I began to lose patience if folks digressed or repeated themselves. I had what I needed to confront HUD, and there seemed to be nothing new coming up. But people wanted to talk, so the meeting kept going. At times Ms. Jones and I would try to move people along if they got carried away. I tried to do it without being rude, but Ms. Jones was more direct. We were good cop, bad cop, trying to keep the meeting moving.

Frank, on the other hand, possessed a bottomless reservoir of patience. I shot him an occasional glance, hoping for affirmation of my feelings, thinking I might get a look of sympathetic solidarity: **Yeah, I'm with you, this is going on too dang long.** Instead, what I got was a gentle smile: **Hey, breathe, it's all right.** And then he would look at the next speaker, inviting him to take his time.

I realized that as he looked at each speaker, Frank **saw** that person. He connected to each of them with an expression of soulful kindness and an interest that seemed to emanate from the core of his being. When someone got personal or emotional, he would lean forward, growing even more attuned, letting the person know he or she was in a safe and supportive space. Though each person spoke in a monologue, Frank listened in such a way that there seemed to be a dialogue between them, a conversation. They spoke and he listened, and yet they were both communicating.

I suddenly noticed a detail I had missed earlier in the meeting, a detail that I would reflect on long after and still draw from today. In that meeting, Ms. Jones was the tenants association president, the person of authority, and there were other association officers at the table, too—people beloved and trusted in that community. Yet most of the speakers, after briefly addressing Ms. Jones, looked squarely at Frank when they spoke. They hadn't been instructed to do so, and there was nothing in his initial words to command the attention people were giving him. But they did. I marveled at how this frumpy older man drew each speaker's eyes. What made it particularly impressive to me is that Frank's presence was humble; somehow, he made each speaker feel like he or she was the center of attention. Frank changed the temperature for the people in that room. In this dank basement, people turned toward him to feel his warmth, and they were made better by his energy.

My attention wandered over the course of that meeting, but the love Frank offered every speaker never abated. In reflection, I realized that one of the most valuable things you can give someone is your time and attention.

• • •

After the meeting, Frank invited me to swing by his office the next day. He wanted to work with me on the HUD part of our strategy. His offices were not impressive. They were located on Broad Street in Newark, half a block south of city hall above T.M. Ward Coffee Co., a Newark landmark established in 1869 that sells teas, nuts, other treats, and many different types of coffee. The stairs to Frank's office were dusty, creaky, and worn, but as you ascended you were embraced by the delicious aroma of coffee.

Inside, Frank's office looked like a war room. Filing cabinets and boxes abounded; there was a handful of desks, a conference table covered with so many stacks of paper, it was hard to pull out the chairs. None of the furniture matched, and everything was worn from use. To a guy who was fresh out of Yale Law School and spoiled by Ivy League facilities, the computers looked like they belonged in a museum. Everything seemed to serve a purpose, however, to be in some kind of order—if only I could figure it out. As I would see during the course of our meeting, if Frank needed something—to illustrate a point, to refer to a template for our letter, or to cite a federal regulation—**boom,** he had it in his hand in a quick minute.

Frank and I sat down and discussed the previous night's tenant meeting. I shared my notes, which I had arranged into a fact pattern of building issues, and he helped me craft letters that we were going to use to press HUD about the problems in Brick Towers. I pumped him for information about his own history, for stories about his past tenant battles—and I couldn't help but make some allusion to the length of the meeting the night before. Frank obliged me by patiently answering all of my questions, and he seized the opportunity to make some points to me.

It is critical, Frank said, to bring things to light in meetings like the one we'd had. Yes, the mission was to address the conditions of buildings, but people themselves deserved attention, too. Frank believed that the physical condition of the buildings was causing spiritual harm, with good people facing unrelenting stressors that were damaging to their emotional well-being.

All this I agreed with, and I felt that it was the source of the urgency in what we were doing. But Frank went further. He insisted that the meetings served a vital function. They were more than just a forum to communicate information, to plan or strategize. There was mutual support there. Meetings and community gatherings were places to share and to be validated, places where you knew you weren't alone. Folks were there to help each other, to collaborate and to commiserate.

Frank explained that there is value in standing before your peers and figures of authority and having your struggle acknowledged; there is value in being seen, heard, and felt, value to being understood.

Frank was determined in his mision to address the condition of the buildings, but he also insisted that we shouldn't neglect what residents have endured. "This deserves attention," he told me. "It can't just be covered over, ignored or forgotten. There is a need for healing."

Again, I said I understood this.

Frank continued.

He stepped back with me and suggested we take a broader look at our nation. He questioned how we could have such intolerable conditions—not just around Newark, but all over the country. He linked this to what he believed was an empathy deficit. America is materially rich yet simultaneously has too much material poverty. What made this and other negative conditions persist, he believed, was an insidious poverty of understanding, a poverty of empathy. People's inability to see what is going on in the lives of their fellow citizens, to understand what so many Americans endure, creates an atmosphere that allows injustice to fester and proliferate. Frank had a faith in the goodness of humankind and believed that few people would allow such conditions if they truly saw them up close, if they saw how individuals suffered. He believed such awareness could be achieved—and that doing so would trigger outrage and motivate people to act.

Decades before, through creative acts of protest, courageous civil rights activists had revealed to the public at large the injustices that were rampant throughout our society. The resulting outrage fomented action that created change. But in Newark, in places all over our country, we are failing to see the fullness of the injustice. We are failing to see each other. Our distance from one another allows us to avoid seeing the conditions of our fellow citizens, and so no empathy is extended.

Frank insisted that the way we designed our housing policy in this country, from the local level to the federal level, was exactly what the civil rights movement was fighting against: segregation, discrimination, the erecting of walls between people. We designed housing policy so as to obscure our ability to see each other, to prevent ourselves from having to connect with others and confront the truth about what they were enduring. We allowed injustice to grow strong and persist in a way that is utterly contrary to our country's core values, that insults our best conceptions of humanity.

It was in this context, in that cluttered office above the coffee store, that Frank first said something to me that I hadn't heard before and that still has me thinking, all these years later. Frank asserted that civil rights—indeed, human rights—were not just about equal access to public accommodations and equal employment opportunity. Human dignity, security, freedom from fear, environmental toxins, and physical deprivation were also rights that should be defended and fought for. It was then that he said to me, looking at me with his kind eyes, "Cory, housing is a human right."

Frank came to Newark in his early thirties during the city's most turbulent period, in the aftermath of the riots and civil disturbances of 1967. By 1970 he was one of the city's best-known activists. His gentle nature could have been mistaken for weakness, but he quickly proved himself to be a formidable fighter: He was relentless, creative, a master of details who knew how to bring attention to injustice. He never turned vicious in his war against the forces that were condemning too many Americans to live in slums; he was, in the truest sense, always a **gentleman**. He was Newark's peaceful warrior.

In April 1970, Frank was a leader in an epic rent strike at the Stella Wright Homes, a series of now demolished brick public housing high-rises a few blocks west of Brick Towers. Run by the Newark Housing Authority, they were in horrific condition. The strike went on for three years and still stands as the longest in the city's history. Frank and the residents won in the end: the courts acknowledged the horrible conditions the residents were enduring, and even referred to the public housing agency as "Newark's largest absentee slum landlord." The court ordered improvements, granted the tenants an 80 percent cut in their back rent, and gave them nearly two years to pay it.

In 1972, Frank had a major role in writing Newark's rent control laws, saving thousands of Newark's low-income residents from sharp spikes in rent and affording them other basic protections.

Frank was relentless, but he was also innovative. As we worked together to get HUD officials to Brick Towers meetings, I learned how in the early days of his work he would highlight building conditions and ask high-level officials to attend community or tenant meetings—or embarrass them into it if they refused. They called these meetings "eyes and ears" meetings. The practice was replicated by tenant activists around the country and even adopted by HUD officials themselves as they went out into the field and met with residents in their homes and community spaces. Thanks to Frank, HUD officials from Washington had a steady presence in Newark during the 1970s and '80s, listening to folks at the bottom of America's economic ladder, witnessing their housing conditions, hearing their voices, acknowledging their struggles, and taking the time to see people who were all too often unseen.

But what frustrated Frank the most was how so many people fail to see that our housing problems—our inability to see each other, our dense low-quality housing, and the consequent ghettoization of people—are the result of deliberate policies, some of which persist today.

America's pockets of minority poverty were in many cases created or perpetuated by government policy, and Frank knew this. New Jersey is a state that is in the top three in median income, and yet it is home to some of the nation's poorest cities. Further, New Jersey is now the fifth most segregated state in America for blacks and the fourth most segregated state for Hispanics. Frank knew this was the result of conscious local, state, and national policy. He also knew that such segregation has a profound effect on education and job opportunities and on people's ability to escape poverty, violence, and despair.

After World War II, racially focused housing policies were set in place at every level of government—and many of them are still on the books. These policies included local restrictive covenants that banned the transfer of property to blacks, real-estate agents steering minorities away from white towns, zoning rules that allowed towns to avoid having low-income housing built within their borders, overtly discriminatory mortgage lending that undercut minority wealth creation through home ownership, redlining that effectively walled minority communities off from opportunity and investment, the secession of sections of cities into new towns so as not to have to share schools and other public resources, and Federal Housing Administration policies that rewarded financial institutions and builders who invested in white communities and created disincentives for investments in minority communities, starving neighborhoods of jobs and tax money. HUD policies were put in place that directed the building of densely clustered low-income and public housing into urban spaces. Newark's nickname, "Brick City," is derived from the federal policy to pack low-income housing into Newark and not diffusely throughout the state of New Jersey, where the impact of poverty on families would have been mitigated. As Kenneth Jackson writes in **Crabgrass Frontier: The Suburbanization of the United States**, "The result, if not the intent, of the public housing program of the United States was to segregate the races, to concentrate the disadvantaged in inner cities, and to reinforce the image of suburbia as a place of refuge [from] the problems of race, crime, and poverty."

The problems caused by housing policy have, over generations, compounded the impact of denial of opportunity in certain communities. Specifically, this denial of opportunity includes the denial of job opportunity, the denial of the opportunity to build wealth in one's home, the denial of the opportunity to live in a community free from violence, and the denial of equal educational opportunity—a denial that affects **all** children. As the educational resource organization Realizing the Dream wrote, "A growing body of research documents the educational benefits for all students of racially and ethnically diverse schools. Segregated minority schools are much more likely to be in poor neighborhoods, have lower graduation rates and offer New Jersey's minority students far fewer opportunities to take the kinds of academic enrichment courses that prepare them for college." This all hits home for me, because of what my family had to do to overcome these policies and practices. My family had to fight, engaging the Fair Housing Council and lawyers in order to move into a community with some of the highest-ranked public schools in the state. My parents were able to succeed only because they had courageous housing activists in their corner.

No matter what issue he was confronting, Frank's love of people never wavered. This was a core part of Frank's belief: that we are good people individually, but we are better together. For him, housing was a human right, and fair housing policies were as important for people in affluent communities as they were for people in poor communities. He believed that the battle to keep a person in a safe and habitable home was urgent, as was the larger cause of non-discriminatory housing policy in the United States. He worked tirelessly, locally and nationally, to create policy that undid the sins of the past.

I came to see Frank as someone who was fighting against the common notion of tolerance. For most of us, tolerance demands only that we acknowledge another's right to exist. Tolerance says that if **they** cease to be, if **they** succumb to injustice or disappear from the face of the earth, then **we** are no worse off. Frank devoted his life to working against this shallow notion. In his mind, our nation needed to move beyond tolerance to love. Because love recognizes that every person has value, that we need each other, that we are interdependent—that what happens to you matters to me. Love necessitates extending yourself, often out of your comfort zone, making the conscious choice to **see** that person, despite his or her circumstances, as worthy and as vital to you. Love recognizes that if another falls, fails, or succumbs, then we are all worse off and our lives are diminished.

Tolerance is becoming accustomed to injustice; love is becoming disturbed and activated by another's adverse condition. Tolerance crosses the street; love confronts. Tolerance builds fences; love opens doors. Tolerance breeds indifference; love demands engagement. Tolerance couldn't care less; love always cares more.

After my meeting with Frank, I sent a number of letters, some of which went to HUD and some of which went to the regional inspector general. I was surprised to see that using formal-looking letterhead, citing appropriate codes or regulations, and using a handful of five-dollar words got people's attention. Soon we were having conversations with

HUD officials, and eventually they were coming to the Brick Towers tenant meetings.

It was so affirming for residents to be able to speak to HUD officials about their problems. I could see how proud people were—heck, I was proud, too. We were being **listened** to; people in positions of authority were **seeing** us. For me, HUD became real. They weren't apathetic bureaucrats, as I had suspected. They were good people with hard jobs who were trying to do their best to help.

Ms. Jones's theories about the corruption of the landlord proved to be valid. Though it would take years for the investigation and legal proceedings to run their course, the landlord pled guilty to tax evasion in 2000: failing to pay taxes on profits he made in part from Brick Towers. The ill-gotten profits were related to the very things Ms. Jones pointed out in that summer meeting in 1997: instead of investing in the safety of the building, he was taking unjust profits—which he ultimately didn't report on his taxes.

Frank knew HUD rules and regulations well enough to realize that Ms. Jones was right in pointing out that the landlord couldn't keep getting federal money for the buildings when the buildings were in such horrific condition. He knew that the buildings didn't meet HUD's habitability standards. In order to receive federal funds, the companies formed by the landlord had to represent to the federal government what Frank knew couldn't be true: that the buildings were livable. Indeed, one of the landlord's companies that was designated as the managing agent for Brick Towers—BTA Properties Inc.—falsely certified that Brick Towers met the HUD habitability standards.

This corporation entered into a plea agreement to pay $1 million; while the court eventually waived the $1 million penalty, $362,987 was paid to HUD in restitution. And perhaps most significant, Brick Towers was turned over to HUD.

This ushered in two of the best years the buildings had seen in a long time. HUD invested a tremendous amount of money into the buildings to try to bring them up to code. They significantly increased security, and even kept the elevators operating relatively smoothly.

But the victory over the landlord didn't end Brick Towers' struggles. After I ran for mayor in 2002 and lost, the city of Newark pressed HUD to sell the buildings to the Newark Housing Authority. This would mean that Sharpe James, the man I had challenged for mayor, would effectively be our landlord—and the Newark Housing Authority was already recognized by HUD as one of the most troubled housing authorities in the nation.

We organized, protested, and marched against the Newark Housing Authority, but couldn't stop the sale. For one dollar, the housing authority bought the buildings and took over. Before long, security diminished, and the elevators started breaking down again as investments in maintenance dropped and overall conditions deteriorated.

From the moment I met Frank, I could tell that we would grow close. When I got word that I had passed the New Jersey bar exam, the first person I reached out to wasn't my parents, my brother, or my friends; it was Frank. He and I met with Bill Goode, another tenant activist, in a Newark diner tucked into a building on Hill Street and celebrated by consuming disturbing amounts of carbs—this teetotaler's favorite vice.

As a newly minted lawyer, I agreed to work with Frank on his efforts in other buildings around the city—and it was around this time that I started to seriously think about running for the Newark City Council. The idea had first come up in a meeting at Ms. Jones's apartment, in the winter of 1997, when she abruptly announced to the room, "It is decided then: you are going to run for the Central Ward council seat!" I was flattered by her suggestion, but I told her I thought I could be more valuable to the tenants as their lawyer. To which Ms. Jones said something along the lines of: **If you want to help us, then you will do what is best for us and run.**

Frank would be invaluable in my deliberations. What's more, when I finally decided to run, he became a key voice in my campaign. He organized his network of tenant leaders behind me and was essential to my victory. I had many young people involved in my first race for elected office, but I benefited from a distinguished group of elders who helped run my campaign, men like Carl Sharif, Phil Grate, Saidi Nguvu, and of course Frank. They—along with a group of tenants association presidents who included Virginia Morton, Elaine Sewell, and Ms. Jones—were essential to my victory. People like Frank not only propelled me into elected office but kept me connected to the reasons I ran in the first place.

In 2009, as mayor of New Jersey's largest city, I sat in Frank's room at the hospice and studied his face. I kissed his forehead. I prayed.

I thought back on how, over the decades of Frank's life in Newark, he had aided tens of thousands of residents in securing their homes, staying in those homes, keeping the heat on in the winter, keeping the water running, and shielding them from illegal eviction. Frank had been there for them, had served them, had seen them.

And I thought about how Frank inspired me in my work, as well. As mayor, I attacked housing issues. In the middle of a national housing collapse, we set an ambitious goal to double the rate of production of affordable housing in the city, and we accomplished it. More than this, as market rate housing arrived in Newark's downtown, we insisted that we create integrated housing—we would not tolerate ghettos of affluence. Instead, when we built new lofts and luxury apartments near the new arena or our train station with an easy shot into New York, we made sure to create significant percentages of low-income units as part of those projects. Further, we worked to turn around the troubled Newark Housing Authority. We moved it from one of the nation's worst to one of the nation's most improved; housing authority officials from all over the country came to study our turnaround and take lessons back to their cities.

Yet, as I sat there in his hospital room, I was unsettled.

I loved Frank; I knew what he had done for our city. I wanted the room to be full of flowers, balloons, cards, and tributes. I wanted his bedside to be crowded with people, I wanted folks waiting outside to get in to thank him and heap praise upon him for a life well lived. He was going to die, and I wanted him to have a hero's end. But there was no army of admirers there, only a modest group of us visiting.

Perhaps I also felt as though I wasn't being a good enough friend. As mayor, I was always running around, always pressed for time. I visited him fewer than a half dozen times in that hospice—and it might have been less if it hadn't been for my assistant, Sharon Macklin, who carved out time on my schedule so I could sit with Frank.

But then, all this was about my ego's needs and not Frank's. Frank never had need for adulation or the applause of crowds. There was a profound humility about him and his mission. He was about purpose, not popularity; he was about service, not celebrity. Like that first speech I saw him give in front of the Brick Towers tenants association, his life wasn't about what he could get for himself but about what he could give to others.

On my path of service, I have been overly concerned about what people think. It is a challenge of politics—knowing that the process of getting elected can demand a departure from the soul-feeding work of serving others directly. These realities were some of the reasons I initially resisted running for city council when Ms. Jones asked me.

I remember remarking to Frank how I identified with something I had heard an elected leader say about her political career: "Before I was in politics, if I helped an elderly person cross the street, I was a good guy doing a good deed. After I got into politics, if I helped an elderly person cross the street, I was just another politician trying to get a vote."

Frank's response: "Who cares? Just keep helping."

In my first three years as mayor, Frank's health began to fail. I would visit him occasionally in his apartment on Elizabeth Avenue. I would bring food or take him out to eat. During this time, Frank slowly began to lose his eyesight. At first it weakened; then it was severely limited; and then, at last, he was legally blind. As a result, I would greet Frank by announcing myself, "Frank, it's Cory."

He would laugh. "I see you, Cory."

This became our regular greeting.

"Frank, it's Cory."

"I see you, Cory."

I came to love hearing him say it, and Frank knew I loved it. It had layers to it.

As Frank's health got worse, we stepped up the attention we gave him. Frank had a small group of friends and family who helped care for him. When it was clear he was having trouble staying in his house and paying the rent, I worked with others to get him into an apartment—one run by the Newark Housing Authority. An agency he had fought for decades was now, thanks in part to his own actions, worthy of his presence as a tenant.

In his final months, Frank and I did things together. We went grocery shopping, and once he asked me to take him to the movies the way we had done in the past. I knew he couldn't see the screen, but we went anyway, and I marveled at how he smiled through the experience.

In those final months, Frank was Frank. Every time I saw him, he was glowing. He exuded peace . . . and he saw me.

"Frank, it's Cory."

"I see you, Cory."

A friend once told me the stars we see in the night sky are light-years away—literally, trillions of miles. In fact, some of those stars are dead and gone. Yet we still see the light of a star long after it's gone, as that light continues to travel through space, flowing outward forever. While those stars have burned out, their light has traveled for years to reach our eyes. To us, they still shine. The star may be dead and gone, but the energy, light, and warmth it gave off while living are eternal. Stars die, but their light goes on forever.

That last time I saw Frank alive, I knew it was the end, even before the nurses told me it wouldn't be long. His breathing was rapid and shallow. I placed my hands on his hand. I laid my head next to his. I fought back tears.

"Frank, it's Cory."

"I . . . see . . . you."

"Frank, I love you."

"I . . . love . . . you . . . too."

7

TO WASHINGTON

So let us not be petty when our cause is great. Let us not quarrel amongst ourselves when our Nation's future is at stake.

—John F. Kennedy

In the early 1990s, my father was diagnosed with Parkinson's disease, a ruthless thief that slowly robs you of your faculties, mobility, and basic physical gifts. He received this news with his usual mix of humor and determination. In the years that followed, I would get a master class in courage from my dad. With his symptoms worsening and his mortality hovering over him, he made the difficult choice not to surrender to fear. He chose to steal hope from despair, joy from sadness, and laughter—bad dad jokes and all—from the seriousness of the disease.

My father campaigned beside me for every one of my elections, from City Council to all three runs for mayor. No one was better at engaging with voters than this retired salesman now pitching one of his favorite products: his son. Through my campaigns, he became a sort of celebrity in Newark, especially with senior citizens. He told corny jokes, entered and won dance contests, walked in senior fashion shows, delivered food and shared meals, and even delivered condoms to senior citizens after hearing about the growing problem of STDs in some of our city's senior buildings.

But by the time New Jersey senator Frank Lautenberg passed away in 2013 and I entered a rushed campaign for a special election to the United States Senate, my father's Parkinson's had grown too severe for him to be with me on the campaign trail. He and my mom would remain in Las Vegas, Nevada, where they had moved. I felt their absence—and the reason for it pulled at my heart.

By the summer of 2013, Parkinson's was savaging my father's cognitive abilities. Our once vibrant, funny, and nurturing father-son talks were over. In our short conversations I would tell my dad how much I loved him, repeating it many times and hoping that at least one of my declarations would settle upon his soul. I would listen patiently to him, even when what he was saying didn't make sense.

I tried not to let the sound of my voice reflect my own pain. **Stay positive,** I thought. **Sound positive. Choose courage.** I would tell my dad stories from the campaign and let him know the truth: even though he wasn't there, he was empowering me at every step, motivating me, giving my work more reason. I just hoped that my Dad, a poor kid born to a single mother in the Jim Crow South, would live to see his son elected to the U.S. Senate.

Then, during the primary, my father had a stroke. I got the news right before a debate. From that point on, there were no longer any conversations with my dad, just my mom putting the phone to his ear and allowing me to talk. My father, a superhero to me throughout my life, was now terrifyingly mortal. I wanted to go to him.

My campaign manager, Addisu Demissie, supported my leaving the campaign and missing one of the debates, but my mom insisted that I keep campaigning; it would be what my dad wanted. My mom stayed by his bedside in Las Vegas and cared for him, and I continued campaigning, calling often to get updates on his recovery.

I didn't know Senate majority leader Harry Reid at that time. I had fielded phone calls from him before I made my decision to run and appreciated his encouragement and enthusiasm about my candidacy. But when he found out that my father had had a stroke and that I was sticking to the campaign trail, he and his staff immediately engaged. Senator

Reid himself went to my dad's bedside in Las Vegas, embraced my mother, comforted her, and showed my family a compassion that I will never forget.

I went on to win the primary and then flew out to see my father. His body was swollen, he was unable to speak, and his breathing was labored and erratic. I spoke to him, and as he vacantly looked up I prayed that he recognized me. I sat by his bedside and meditated on love, trusting that our connection hadn't been severed by this disease.

Because this was a special election, the time frame was compressed, which meant I had to rush back to New Jersey. The August primary led right into an October 16 election, and I struggled to balance my duties as mayor with the demands of the campaign trail. Each day moved slowly without my parents around and with my dad in a hospital room. The final week of the election could not have come quickly enough.

Six days before the election, I was driving to a press conference on my mayoral schedule that was both a public triumph for Newark and the culmination of a seven-year quest for me: we were announcing that a Whole Foods would be coming to Newark. This was about more than a supermarket. It was a sign that Newark was rising, that a city, long overlooked and underestimated, was now experiencing development at a rate not seen since the 1960s. Whole Foods, usually a more suburban supermarket, was important in symbol and substance.

But on the way there, I got a text from my brother: "Call Mom." I knew before I made the call; I felt it. I jumped out of the car and walked away, trying to find a place to be alone. I called my mother. Six days before I would be elected to the United States Senate, my father was gone.

On October 31, 2013, the day I was to be sworn in, I was uplifted to see how many people had made the trip to Washington, D.C.: family and friends from all over New Jersey and as far away as California and England; countless people who gave up so much of their time and energy to work on my campaign, to support it, and to earn this day. But my dad was not there, and I felt it.

My staff planned the day so very well. They managed meals, transportation, and events for the hundreds of people who attended, assigned the handful of Senate gallery tickets with diplomacy, made the overflow viewing room comfortable, and flawlessly organized the receptions, all while abiding by the strict Senate rules and protocols. But I was most grateful that right before I took the oath of office, I was gifted the opportunity to have breakfast with my mother and Congressman John Lewis.

John Lewis helped to fill the absence I felt that day. What my dad could often achieve by lifting me up and teasing me, the congressman achieved with the gravity of his presence.

To have John Lewis sit with my mother and me in his office, the walls of which could easily serve as exhibits in a civil rights museum; to have him pray with us; to have him, despite my protestations, actually serve us food; and to have him look me in the eye and let me know that this day was meaningful to **him,** as well—it all made me feel as small as my dad's humor often had. This smallness wasn't a feeling of being insignificant or unworthy; it was a reminder of the feeling I had enjoyed as a boy when my dad would swing me around, then hoist me into the air and put me on his shoulders. I was small, but I was elevated.

As John Lewis brought me seconds of eggs and potatoes, I sat back and looked at him closely. I breathed deep and slow, quieting extraneous thoughts, fully in the moment. I **saw** him—every line on his face, his head bald like a monk's, the gentle grace that emanated from his eyes. I looked over at the pictures of civil rights heroes on the walls, pictures that captured the history that had so changed my present, black-and-white photos of faces I recognized and many I didn't. While I may not have known all their faces, I knew them. They were soldiers who had struggled in the years leading up to my birth—unimaginable sacrifice from black folks, white folks, Latinos, Jews, Muslims, Christians, old and young, gay and straight, Americans who challenged their country to live its truth. I breathed deeply, and I knew: I was sitting on their shoulders. My generation was born on higher ground, territory that our ancestors earned for us. I studied the faces on the wall, and felt gratitude. I looked at John Lewis. He was speaking to me of "the work still to do" and of his pride in my becoming a senator—the fourth black person ever to be popularly elected to our Senate, after Edward Brooke, Carol Moseley Braun, and Barack Obama. We posed for pictures on his balcony and shared smiles and hugs, before I was hurried off by staffers determined to keep me on schedule.

We walked through Congress's corridors, on our way to a meeting with Senator Reid before I would be officially sworn in. The grandeur of this place was not lost on me—the statues, the marble floors, the painted ceilings. Every inch spoke of majesty and splendor. But my mom wasn't distracted or lost in thought. She was full of spirit and inspiration from our visit with John Lewis, and knowing that I would be leaving her in moments to take my oath, she seized the remaining time. I'd been through this before: whether I was leaving for the first day of school, or heading off to a big football game, my mom would straighten me up, adjust my tie, and pepper me with wisdom. In my adolescent years I would squirm so much that I only half heard her words, but now, I savored these seconds and listened with gratitude. I wondered if those hallowed halls had ever heard this kind of lecture given to a Senator. Had Daniel Webster's and Lyndon Johnson's moms let them have it before they swore their oaths?

This is how I remember her words:

"Don't get carried away with all of this," she said. "Always remember why you came down here and who sent you. Remember, of he to whom much is given, much is required. Remember, the title doesn't make the man, the man must make the title. Remember, no matter what, I love you. **Remember.**"

On the afternoon of October 31, 2013, I was sworn in by Vice President Joe Biden to be America's 1,949th senator. I then immediately got laughed at.

My first official action in the U.S. Senate was a cloture vote on the nomination of Mel Watt to the Federal Housing Finance Agency. While I had taken time the day before to learn what a cloture vote was, along with some other procedural rules, I hadn't thought about something very practical: How does one actually vote in the Senate? Is there a lever to pull? A button to push?

So, moments after I took my oath, while I was distracted by shaking hands and greeting other senators on the floor, the presiding officer moved us right into the cloture vote. I had read up on Mel Watt and called him on the phone to discuss his nomination, but didn't know how to register my vote on the Senate floor. Suddenly, I heard my name being called by the parliamentarian. I looked around, feeling exposed. It felt like everyone on the Senate floor, everyone in the gallery, and all seven people across the country watching C-SPAN2 were staring at me. Then, in a show of true mercy, the senior senator from New Jersey, Robert Menendez, performed his senior duty—he leaned over and said, "Cory, just raise your hand and say 'Aye.'" I did as I was told, injecting as much confidence as possible into my voice as I cast my first vote. And a small group of friends, family, and staff watching from the gallery, including my minister and my mother, broke the protocol of silence and laughed. I often joke that I judge the closeness of my friends by how much they tease me, and those of my closest family and friends watching from the gallery got a lot closer at that inaugural moment of my Senate career.

My pathway to the Senate floor was highly unusual. In fact, the **Wall Street Journal** reported that I was only the twenty-first person since 1789 to ascend directly from mayor to Senator. It was certainly a jarring switch from Newark's city hall to the Senate floor.

But while my geography had changed, my mission had not. My mom had implored me to remember why I had come to the Senate; there was no chance I could ever forget.

Campaigning for the Senate had taken me all

over New Jersey, from shore towns to the beautiful old communities along the Pennsylvania border, from the Delaware Bay to the Palisades. But as I ran, my job as mayor continued to demand engagement and focus. Each long day spent campaigning for Senate and doing my job as mayor required a new level of endurance and grit, and making everything all the more difficult were my dad's health issues. In the final weeks of the campaign, Newark had a ten-day stretch with an equal number of murders, an alarming outbreak of violence. And so, in the final stretch of the campaign, I went back to where I had been in my earliest days as mayor: in a police car, doing night patrols and ride-alongs with police leadership on Newark streets.

It was September, weeks until Election Day, and I was riding with our police director, Sammy DeMaio, one of the most dedicated professionals I had on my team. We drove through the city, visiting high-crime areas, talking with patrol officers, stopping to chat with community leaders and residents. It was good to be on the streets; it was good to be in the community again, connecting. Between stops, Sammy was proudly telling me about his fourteen-year-old son, who had just started playing freshman football, which led to us sharing exaggerated stories about our fourteen-year-old freshman selves and our high school football glory days. Clearly the older we got, the better we had been.

Then, a call came in: another murder. The lights

and sirens went on, and we raced to Riverview Terrace, a public housing complex in the East Ward. A crowd had gathered, numerous police vehicles were scattered about, and officers worked to secure the area. Sammy and I were briefed by detectives on the scene. A fourteen-year-old named Ali Rajohn Eric Henderson had been shot dead. I walked over to his body and stared at him. I closed my eyes, breathed deep, and said a quick prayer for him.

Opening my eyes, I turned to my security detail and asked if they were sure this kid was only fourteen. Large and muscular, he looked like a man as he lay there in a pool of his own blood. I was a big guy who grew fast and was always larger than my peers, but I don't think I was his size at fourteen. Ali Rajohn Eric Henderson would have been the hottest prospect on any football team. Instead, here he was. And for the neighborhood—the children, families, and people looking down from windows on another bloody boy—this would be a night they'd never forget. Trauma is tenacious; wounds can heal, but the scars always remain.

I turned away from Ali and went to talk to Riverview residents. I listened to their concerns, hugged folks, encouraged people, and was encouraged by others. At some point, Sammy pulled me aside to tell me that when they searched Ali's apartment, officers recovered thirty bricks of heroin, a loaded

handgun, and a box of bullets from his bedroom—
just feet from his mother's room. I wanted to yell.
My thoughts immediately turned to the mom. Had
she known? How could she not? Did she realize her
teenage boy had descended into a dangerous world
of gangs, guns, and drugs? I couldn't help but feel
anger. I wanted to lay blame; this was on her, wasn't
it? Of course, this was also on us. I swallowed hard,
knowing that judgment would accomplish nothing
in that moment, and that there was work to do. I
conferred with the police about securing the neighborhood, talked to Sammy about our larger strategy to stem the spike in violence, and went back to
talking to residents.

Sometimes hours move slowly but days fly by. In
what seemed like a flash, Election Day had come
and gone and I was in Washington, D.C., getting
pats on the back and shaking hands with my new
fellow senators, many of whom I had been reading
about and seeing on TV for years. But Ali Rajohn
Eric Henderson was still on my mind.

During the campaign, I had benefited from the
fact that our triumphs during my years as mayor
were obvious to the eye: acres of new parks, new
high-performing schools for thousands of Newark
children, thousands of housing units, reductions
in crime, the city's population growing for the first

time in sixty years, and the biggest economic development boom in the city since the 1960s.

But the worst economy in over seventy years was like a hurricane-force headwind deterring our progress. New Jersey as a whole had one of the highest foreclosure rates in the nation, increased unemployment, stagnant or declining wages for many who still had jobs, and growing child poverty. These challenges were even more concentrated in New Jersey's cities, and Newark was no exception. Making matters worse was a unique American reality, something that deepened poverty, fueled unemployment, and contributed to crime, all while demanding egregious amounts of taxpayer dollars: mass incarceration.

In the 1970s, our nation's policy makers embraced a drug war and clamored to appear tough on crime—and the United States Senate helped lead the way. With bipartisan determination, federal laws were changed, punishments were put on steroids, and our prison populations exploded. Federal laws such as 1986's Anti–Drug Abuse Act and 1994's crime bill sent a flood of money into states to incarcerate more Americans and build more prisons to hold them. As a result, the federal prison population has expanded 800 percent since 1980. America has become the undisputed global leader in putting her own citizens behind bars—our nation is home to 5 percent of the world's population but incarcerates 25 percent of the world's prison population. In the land of the free, you have more of a chance of losing your freedom to incarceration for a nonviolent crime than anywhere else on the planet.

If you are born in America today and are white, you have a one in seventeen chance of spending time in jail; if you are Latino, one in six; if you are black, one in three. If you go to prison for a nonviolent crime, you will return to society as part of a growing group of second-class citizens—often denied basic citizenship rights such as being able to vote or serve on a jury. If you have a felony conviction, you face often overwhelming obstacles to getting a job, obtaining housing, receiving a license to start a business, being approved for a loan, getting a driver's license, having access to drug treatment, finding educational opportunities, receiving job training, or finding money for your next meal, as even food stamps are routinely denied to the formerly incarcerated.

Faced with diminished options, minimal support, and few models of success to emulate, many return to lives of crime. About 77 percent of all released prisoners are rearrested within five years.

In cities all over America, people without much hope of being able to reintegrate into society spiral downward until they are gone from society—they just vanish. A 2015 study showed that one in six black men simply disappear from American life; overwhelmingly, they are either murdered or incarcerated. In Newark, we found that 85 percent of murder **victims** had been arrested before, an average of ten times, and the person most likely to be murdered is someone who has just gotten out of prison in the past six months. Men and women without much hope, without the tools, skills, or opportunities to reenter society, get caught up in savage circumstances of their own making and of ours, get dragged down by their bad personal decisions and our horrible policy choices. And this all plays out on American streets, from sea to shining sea.

In a way, my entire professional life has been spent trying to deal with the jagged shards of our broken criminal justice system, trying to put them back together, all the while feeling like I wasn't fixing a failed system but just minimizing the damage. This broken system touches all areas of our lives, whether we see it or not—from the amount of taxes we pay to fuel a failing behemoth bureaucracy to dealing with the person in our life who has been touched by the criminal justice system directly. When I was mayor, much of my work was spent trying to change this reality. I spent day after day designing, implementing, funding, and checking in on interventions to achieve things our criminal justice system was not doing adequately: providing for the safety of our communities and expanding hope for the countless men at risk of disappearing from Newark for good. Scarcely a day went by in Newark when I did not face a resident who sought help in light of an arrest or past conviction. Thousands of people in Newark—those formerly incarcerated and those not—worked on this issue. From prison ministries in churches to struggling nonprofits to teachers and community leaders, we all worked to empower those looking for a way out of their second-class citizenship.

Over the years, our initiatives helped keep thousands of Newarkers from recidivating—and they cost a fraction of what taxpayers would have spent rearresting, retrying, and reimprisoning these people. The irony remains that money for efforts to put and keep people in jail and prison is far easier to come by than the scant funds we cobbled together to run these fledgling programs. In fact, my team spent enormous amounts of time chasing philanthropic dollars and putting together grant proposals to keep them operational. I went to great personal lengths to help ex-offenders, writing letters of reference, begging lawyer friends to represent people, or cajoling other friends to give someone a shot as an employee. But again, I always had the feeling that although we were making an important difference, we were not **fixing** the system.

Making matters even more complicated was the fact that I was in charge of the city's police department. Our dedicated officers did the job my administration asked them to do, so I knew that for every Newarker we were helping on his way out of prison for a nonviolent crime, we were arresting others and putting them into a machine that did not adequately reflect our most precious values of justice, fairness, and proportionality.

In my campaign for the Senate seat, I went all over New Jersey talking about my vision for federal policy. I talked about numerous issues, from job creation to college affordability, to homeland security, but no matter where I was or who the audience was, I almost always discussed reforming our nation's criminal justice system. It wasn't among the top issues that New Jersey residents listed as their most pressing concerns; in fact, I was warned that I shouldn't talk much about it. But I knew that from our state's cities to our wealthiest suburbs, this issue hurt us all and needed to be confronted head-on. It consumed an egregious amount of our collective resources, destroyed the lives of men and women who could easily have become productive and contributing members of our society, and deeply offended our common values as a nation.

And when I was asked what was perhaps the most common question I heard on the campaign trail—"In this climate of vicious partisanship, how can you make a difference in Washington?"—I would go right to criminal justice reform as an example of an issue I could work with Republicans on to get something done. I talked about conservative thought leaders such as Newt Gingrich and Grover Norquist, who shared my view that the system was broken **and** shared many of my ideas about what needed to be fixed at the federal level. In this context, the Republican senator I most often mentioned was Rand Paul. During the campaign, he had come to New Jersey, ripping me with his rhetoric, and yet he was someone I could work with to deal with one of our country's most pressing issues.

Years of bruising elections in Newark had taught me that when it comes time to govern, you have to let go of any hurt generated by the insults or dirty tricks of a campaign. If I'd carried a grudge, I wouldn't have been able to pick up an ally. Lincoln put it another way: "Do I not destroy my enemies when I make them my friends?"

I couldn't disagree with Rand Paul more on so many other policy issues, but that wasn't the point. That **couldn't** be the point if I was going to do what my constituents had sent me to Washington to do. When it came to criminal justice reform, I could find common ground with people like Rand, Mike Lee from Utah, Jeff Flake from Arizona, and Dean Heller from Nevada. Rand spoke openly and regularly about the broken system, the failed policies of the war on drugs, and even the racial disparities in incarceration. He discussed many of the same solutions that I did. To put it simply, he and a small group of my future Republican colleagues gave me hope—hope that the tide was turning and there was an opening to do something bipartisan in Washington that would begin to undo the damage done by decades of bad bills; hope that my journey from being a mayor to a senator wouldn't compromise my mission to make a difference on issues that mattered, but enable me to better fulfill it.

8

THE HIGH COST OF CHEAP LABOR

Anyone who has ever struggled with poverty knows how extremely expensive it is to be poor.

—James Baldwin

I SINNED, AND I LIKED IT.

It was one of the seven deadly ones, and I didn't just sin a little; I luxuriated in it, savoring my sinning. And I invited friends to witness it: my former chief of staff, Modia Butler; my longtime security detail, Kevin Batts; my 2014 campaign manager, Brendan Gill; and a young rising star from Delaware, then serving as my body man, Eugene Young. They were all gathered to see my descent into debauchery.

"Man down!" they joked.

I was at IHOP. I was indulging in my favorite of the deadly sins: gluttony. This would be my last non-vegan meal.

I had been a vegetarian since 1992—a lifestyle choice that had started as an experiment. I was heading off to Oxford on a Rhodes Scholarship, and I decided to make a bit of a Socratic quest of it. Socrates said the unexamined life was not worth living, so I went to England with the idea that I would spend those two years studying and exploring my ideas, my values, my choices, my actions, myself. I wanted to express my own authenticity, to be the best version of myself, to live with more integrity, striving to make my ideas and actions align as closely as possible.

At Oxford, I read deeply and widely. I became transfixed by Gandhi. In particular, I loved his autobiography's subtitle: **The Story of My Experiments with Truth.** The more I thought about it, the more I realized that I should do more experimenting with my own truth. In a free market, we vote every day with our dollars, but I had never asked questions about where the things I bought came from, and what I was actually endorsing with my dollars. The more I became aware of those choices, the more I wanted to align my choices with my values. It is an almost impossible task, and one that I knew would be a bit outrageous if I took it to an extreme. But could I make **some** changes that would simplify this quest for me?

I realized, for example, that there was a lot about food I could never fully pin down. After poring over data on health, the environment, and how industrial agriculture treated animals, I thought I should try to go without meat. Did I need it? Was I the master of my desires, or had my desires mastered me? I decided to try being a vegetarian.

Within a couple of months I was astounded by the results. Active as I was, when I went vegetarian my body felt supercharged. I felt energy like I hadn't ever had before. My sleep improved, my recovery after workouts improved, and I felt lighter, stronger, and more capable. I never looked back.

Twenty-two years later, after more reading, study, and self-examination, I decided to try another experiment for the same reasons: from the day after Election Day 2014 until the end of that year, I would try being a vegan. It, too, would become an experiment that would stick. This IHOP breakfast was my last hurrah.

Our server that morning was a young woman named Natasha Laurel. I am one of those customers who likes to talk to the waitstaff—a trait I get from my father, who loved to engage with people. So many times as a kid, I delighted as my dad and the servers would joke, laugh, and brighten each other's days. Plus I used to work at my parents' soul food restaurant in Teaneck, New Jersey. I have a feeling that if everyone had to wait tables at some point in their lives, the world would be a nicer place. I love what Dave Barry says: "A person who is nice to you but rude to the waiter is not a nice person."

I didn't know Natasha, but we began joking back and forth. If this was to be my last non-vegan meal, I'd be going out in style. "Look," I told her, "this may sound like I'm ordering for the whole table, but this is just me. Those guys can order what they want, but this is what I want, and if your hand cramps writing it all down, I'm sorry."

"Okay," she said. "I'm ready."

I ordered the pumpkin pancakes, two orders of eggs with extra cheese, stuffed French toast, and hash browns. Plus I decided to try another type of pancake that had some kind of fruit on top of it—fruit, after all, is healthy, right?

Natasha chuckled as I went on and on. "Is that it?" she asked.

"I think so, but leave a menu here just in case I change my mind."

Natasha and I kept joking and chatting as she did laps back and forth to the kitchen. I learned that she was thirty-two years old, a single mother of three boys living in Newark's West Ward in a public housing complex called Bradley Court with a reputation for drugs and violence. I asked her if she worked here full-time. Yes, she said. I asked her if this was what she really wanted to do. No, she said. I asked if she had another job in mind or if she had a dream for herself. This question made her smile; her dream was to be a counselor.

"A counselor?" I asked.

"Yes," she replied. She loved helping people in need, counseling folks, empowering them.

I thought, **Yes, she'd make a great social worker.**

Before long, our meal was over—it was Election Day, after all, and we needed to get back to work. But I was impressed with Natasha. We talked more as I was paying the bill and getting ready to waddle out. Surely, raising three young boys in Bradley Court had its challenges. The more she talked, the more I wanted to meet her kids. So I asked her if I could. She didn't seem surprised by my request, and I said that maybe some of my friends and I could take them to the movies so she could have an evening to herself. She agreed.

I found myself thinking about Natasha a lot that day. Part of me felt frustrated, because I sensed there were things she hadn't told me. I knew Natasha lived in Bradley Court because she couldn't afford to live anywhere else—which was because she made very little money waiting tables at IHOP. The minimum wage for workers who receive tips is $2.13 an hour, and it hasn't been increased for more than **twenty years**. While the regular federal minimum wage has been raised, a concession was made between the National Restaurant Association and Congress to increase the minimum wage but **not** the tipped wage. So while minimum wage workers have seen some increase in their income, tipped workers have not, leaving them dependent on each customer.

Natasha would later tell me that most people don't know that servers' income depends on tips and that, in a poor community, people don't always have extra money for a tip—something she understands in her heart and has compassion for:

> They be like, "Oh my goodness, we didn't know you get $2.13. I would of been tipping more." You just get some people who think you're getting a paycheck and they just don't give anything. You might have some people over here because of the poverty and everything they go through, some people just don't have it and they just make enough to go out and eat. We're dealing with different circumstances when you're serving. You're dealing with different circumstances.
>
> We have some servers who don't understand that and they get upset and they get aggravated. They don't know that, but when you come from a struggling situation you know other people have struggles.

Natasha was working full-time and picking up extra shifts; during good years at IHOP she was barely making enough to keep her family's head above water.

The food I ate that morning was especially cheap because taxpayers subsidize many of the ingredients that go into the food served at IHOP, from corn to sugar to meat products. But another reason why the food is so cheap is because of this cheap labor. IHOP, like many restaurants in our country, pay workers the $2.13 tipped wage—and then folks like Natasha, who work hard jobs for long hours, still have to rely on the taxpayer-funded social safety net. They are outsourcing the true cost of their food to all of us. Cheap food actually isn't cheap. In fact, it comes at a high cost.

Restaurant workers make up about 10 percent of the U.S. workforce and are one of the fastest growing parts of our economy. And yet for many workers like Natasha, the prospects for better-paying jobs are dim.

The idea that restaurant workers are all high school or college kids working part-time jobs to help pay for extras not provided by their parents is wrong. Sixty-six percent of tipped workers are twenty-five years or older. Half, like Natasha, are over thirty. About a third are parents. Between 40 and 50 percent earn less than a living wage, which means that they don't make enough money to maintain an adequate standard of living and have to turn to other means to make ends meet. These "other means" are often public assistance.

Ironically, about a third of restaurant workers are considered "food insecure" by the U.S. Department of Agriculture's definition. "Food insecurity" means that you don't have the ability to buy nutritional, safe food. Many of the people who put food on our plate actually—**literally**—can't afford to eat it or to feed it to their own families. Like Natasha, 20 percent of restaurant workers rely on food stamps—so says Restaurant Opportunity Centers United. According to its report, between 2009 and 2013 Americans subsidized the restaurant industry's low wages with nearly $9.5 billion of tax money through programs such as SNAP (food stamps), public housing and Section 8 housing subsidies, and Medicaid.

When Natasha was ten years old, she was raped by a twenty-year-old man and impregnated, and had an abortion. Her mother was in the hospital at the time of the assault, suffering from mental health issues and drug addiction. Hearing the news, she descended even deeper into mental instability.

Natasha's grandmother took her in and helped raise her. Natasha's mother eventually got out of the hospital and returned home. During her teenage years, Natasha went back and forth between her mother's home and her grandmother's. But life with her mother was unstable and dangerous. In her early teen years, Natasha was assaulted again—at which point her grandmother effectively removed her from that environment.

At eighteen, Natasha dropped out of high school with just months to go before graduation. She was struggling and says that this was the one period in which she rebelled. She hung out with friends and experimented with marijuana and alcohol but soon gravitated toward work. Her aunt had a store and she started working there, doing all different tasks, but because she was smart, she was soon helping her aunt with accounting and taxes. At nineteen, Natasha got pregnant and gave birth to a son on January 1, 2001. The father was a man who was staying in her building. She had two more kids in 2002 and 2004 with a man she was deeply in love with, though the relationship never resulted in marriage.

Both men are now involved with their sons' lives. The father of her oldest, though, has traveled a difficult road. He got caught up in drugs and served some time in prison. The father of her younger kids has been more of a constant in the children's lives and has had more steady work, but he, too, has faced challenges. He was sitting in his car one day when a shootout erupted, and he was shot multiple times in the crossfire—yet he still managed to drive himself to University Hospital's emergency room, which is right across from the IHOP Natasha now works at.

Most people don't realize that one shooting like this—barely mentioned in the newspaper—has ramifications far beyond what most people can imagine. It not only shatters a few lives but damages the larger ecosystem in which we live, having impacts on dozens of lives, if not hundreds or thousands.

Another example Natasha lived is a shooting that happened at IHOP, not long after she started working there in 2004. When you start at a restaurant like IHOP you don't walk into the best shifts; you have to pay your dues, so you start at night or as a hostess. The manager recognized Natasha's work ethic and knew that she had three children, so she allowed her to move quickly from hostess to server, and soon Natasha had more control over her schedule. The IHOP was a popular spot in Newark and was open twenty-four hours, which allowed the group of servers who worked there to do double shifts—often working the morning shift, which would end around three in the afternoon, then spending time with their families before coming back for the night shift. These were Natasha's best earning years. She worked many, many doubles— and even though it meant little to no sleep, she still got to spend time with her kids.

Childcare was not an option with Natasha's salary, but she organized her network of family and friends, working with each person's schedule, transportation, and meals so that every moment of her kids' days were filled with activities and adult supervision. When she walked me through her kids' schedules and the schedules of those watching the boys, where they were sleeping and how they were protected by caring, trusted adults 24/7, I felt certain that the Department of Defense could hire her to train people on how to run logistics and supply chains.

But critical to her plan was her ability to do extra shifts at the IHOP. With an accountant's attention to detail, she generously went through her expenses with me—rent (subsidized), food (including her allotment of about $400 a month for SNAP), car (bus routes couldn't accommodate all the moving around she needed to do), Wi-Fi in her home (for her kids' classes; this isn't a luxury anymore, it is a necessity for their education), and clothing for her boys (who seemed always to be growing). We even got down to cleaning products and her system for making a dollop of dishwashing liquid go a long way. As we talked, we shared stories about all the things that many Newarkers know about how to make ends meet. We talked about her rule not to shop at the beginning of the month—because many of the stores, knowing when paychecks and Social Security checks land, jack up prices at that time—and to avoid bodegas, because prices there can be higher for food staples than in a larger store. Now she was lucky to have transportation out to a Walmart and larger supermarkets, so she could buy there in bulk. We discussed those discount clothing places—like the old Valley Fair in Irvington, New Jersey—where you could get clothing far below retail prices, and how crowded those places could get with so many trying to make ends meet.

But Natasha also shared with me how even with her frugal practices, thrifty shopping, and insider knowledge about how to get the best deals, any unexpected occurrence in a month could set her back. A traffic ticket or a flat tire, a torn pair of sneakers—any one of these things was enough to damage her fragile financial well-being. And so was something not nearly so mundane—like a shooting.

At about 2:00 a.m. on March 23, 2013, two groups of customers walked into the IHOP where Natasha worked. She wasn't on duty that night, but some of her colleagues told her later that there was tension between these two groups as soon as they came in. Two ex-lovers—one in each group—were angry at each other, and arguments flared up.

Papa Khaly Ndiaye, the thirty-year-old night manager of the IHOP, tried to calm the tensions. He was friendly and well liked by the restaurant's staff, and had worked his way up from the kitchen to management. He was a recent immigrant from Senegal, having come to America to prove he could make it. He was newly married.

The IHOP was almost always crowded, even at this late hour. People liked it because the restaurant was clean, friendly, and safe. In fact, a year earlier the management had decided not to continue the presence of an armed security guard. But that night, yelling and screaming between the two groups soon gave way to shoving and pushing. Ndiaye, a cook, and other waitstaff tried to get the crowd to leave. At some point, a man wearing a hoodie came to the door, seemingly having been called by one of the groups. He challenged one of the most aggressive men to "come outside."

As the **Star-Ledger** reported:

He seemed to be baiting him, repeating over and over again, "Come outside; come outside; just come outside," the waiter recalled. Instinctively, and fearing the worst, the waiter said he, Papa Khaly Ndiaye, and a cook all tried to hold the man back.

But then "he pushes my hand down," the waiter said of the man from the group of 13, "and then he's like, 'I got this, I got this'— and then he starts walking out. I go to open the door . . . and I hear 'pop, pop,'" said the waiter, speaking of gunshots he believes the man in the hoodie fired in turn.

The waiter added that he believes the man who stepped outside got hit with a bullet but survived. At the same moment, though, Papa Khaly Ndiaye, still struggling with the man who forced his way out of the doors into danger, apparently got caught in the gunfire, too, the waiter said. But he was not as lucky.

"I looked back and just see [my manager] sliding down the door and onto the ground," the waiter recalled, his voice choking now. "And I heard three more shots. But it looked like he [the shooter] wasn't even looking at who he was shooting at. He just put his hand over the rail, and he was shooting."

Police say two people, in addition to the manager, were also shot, but officials would not identify them.

Ndiaye's murder shook Newark. It definitely shook me. According to Natasha, it shattered the staff as well: "It took a drastic toll on everybody here," she said. "Some people couldn't shake it and just said they couldn't stay here because of what happened."

At the time of the shooting, I didn't fully grasp the destruction that would ripple out from the pull of that trigger. Not only would many of the workers leave to find other jobs—most of them moving to other jobs in the restaurant industry, starting again at the bottom with the worst shifts—but the IHOP's business would tail off dramatically as regular customers went elsewhere. I didn't notice until years later that they eliminated the night shift. Natasha walked me through the decline that resulted—in her own income and that of her coworkers. For most, it was a financial crisis.

The stories of people in the service industry are routinely tough. Many face tremendous challenges in their work environments, including wage theft, where restaurants use complicated and exploitative processes to distribute tips; break violations, where workers are denied meaningful breaks or denied breaks completely; sexual harassment; and unstable schedules, where they don't find out their work hours until shortly beforehand, making juggling kids' schedules nearly impossible. Survey after survey and study after study show that these practices are widespread in the restaurant industry. These abuses in the industry happen daily. According to a report in the **Wall Street Journal,** "A 2014 study by the U.S. Department of Labor found that wage violations—concentrated mostly in the hospitality industry—result in between $10 million and $20 million of lost worker income a week in New York state."

Natasha is all too familiar with what goes on in the restaurant industry. She also knows that many people are starting to organize to fight for better wages, better working conditions, and an end to abuse—but she let me know how hard it is to get people who have difficult lives, and jobs they can't afford to lose, to organize. "If you talk to them about it, the questions come back: 'Are you crazy? Are you going to help me get a job? Who's going to pay my bills?'—things like that. It's all about adapting, dealing with it, and going on, just hoping and praying."

Natasha didn't leave the IHOP after the shooting and she wasn't content just to hope and pray. Like always, she worked. While Natasha didn't want to risk leaving and ending up in a worse situation, she didn't simply surrender to her situation, either. She and some co-workers appealed to area clergy, who understood the crisis and began bringing their churches back to eat at the IHOP again. It worked to some degree, and business has been slowly coming back—though not enough to merit a return to a twenty-four-hour schedule. In the meantime, Natasha has tried to put herself in a situation to get a better job in the future. She doesn't have much time beyond work and family, but she has been able to get a license to be a security guard. She doesn't have a license to carry a firearm, which reduces her potential pay, but she figures it could open her up to opportunities down the road.

For now, Natasha makes the best of her work. In fact, she doesn't see it purely as work. She sees it as a mission to connect with people every day. She is one of those people who lives to serve and believes that no matter where you are or what you are doing, you can make a difference.

> **That's why I like being here, too, because I interact with people. I see older people. You'd be surprised how a smile and having a conversation could brighten somebody's day. Somebody could sit down, you'd never know they were so sad, and then you talk to them. I hear their stories. Some people come in here, they'll be like, "Oh, I just lost somebody," and then when they leave they're like, "You know what? You made me feel better today."**

This is the Natasha I met on Election Day, when I was nervous about my big day and was dealing with it by devouring enough carbohydrates to fuel the offensive line of the New York Giants. She made me feel better. She lifted me with her light.

Our society claims to value children, but struggling mothers like Natasha get no paid family leave. The U.S. is the only developed country that doesn't offer government-sponsored paid family leave. Almost all of the world's nations—from Afghanistan to the Democratic Republic of Congo—offer this kind of support, but we don't. Natasha's son had a case of asthma that sent him to the hospital regularly. In an industry that offers workers no sick days (in which people regularly come to work ill and as a result spread their germs on our food because they can't afford to stay home), where people have no paid family leave, or vacation days, a child's illness is so much more than the minor stress and inconvenience my mother endured when I got sick. There is the added stress of how to pay a doctor or a co-pay, how to make rent if you miss a day's work to stay home with your child, how to cope with not being there when your son, hospitalized for asthma, calls for his mother.

It is not a **free** market when industry reaps the benefit by passing on its costs to us. When it comes to the service industry, we pay billions of dollars to help support families like Natasha's, but that doesn't account for the full costs to our society of kids growing up in poverty. Poor children face staggering challenges: increased risk of low birth weight, negative impacts on early cognitive development, higher incidents of childhood illnesses such as asthma and obesity, and greatly reduced chances of attending college (only about nine out of every one hundred kids born in poverty will earn a college degree). On top of this, poor children deal with greater degrees of environmental hazards from pollution, noise, and traffic, as well as other stressors harmful to their well-being. In a competitive and global knowledge-based economy, a nation's most valuable natural resource is its children. And yet we are reckless with this treasure.

But there is hope. I see it in how more and more Americans are waking up to challenges low-wage workers face, and in how many in the industry are actually—if sometimes reluctantly—beginning to change their practices. Perhaps my greatest source of hope comes from the fact that on every step of my journey, I have encountered people who understand that we are all in this together, and who act accordingly. As Gwendolyn Brooks once said: "We are each other's harvest: we are each other's business: we are each other's magnitude and bond."

In my conversations with Natasha, I learned that people call her "Mama Tasha" at the IHOP. This came up when she was telling me a story about a young girl, twelve or thirteen years old, who came in with her grandmother. Natasha noticed that the girl had a hickey on her neck. She overheard some of their conversation and grew concerned, because the girl seemed not to be listening to her grandmother. When the girl stepped away from the table, Natasha checked in with the grandmother; she was frustrated with her granddaughter and asked Natasha to help. Natasha told me that when she looked at the young girl, it took her back to her own childhood—to her traumas, to her challenges, to her getting lost and dropping out of school.

I looked at her and I saw her, and when I looked at her I saw me. . . . I said, "Let me tell you something. Enjoy your childhood,

because you don't get that back. Don't rush nothing. . . . That same boy that's trying to influence you to do the things that you're doing, he isn't going to take you nowhere but through trauma, headache, and heartache. While you're still a child, enjoy it. You've got parents. My parents are not here."

I had a nice little talk with her. Her grandmother was sitting there and she said, "Thank you," and the little girl looked at me and she said, "I'll listen." Whatever I said to her inspired her, but I went into the bathroom and I cried.

One of my co-workers came in, she said, "Mama . . . ?" Everybody calls me Mama Tasha here. She said, "Why you crying?" I said, "Because if somebody took that time out to talk to her just the way I did, I probably would've been better off. Who knows what I just showed her? That talk right there could've changed her life. If somebody would've took that time out with me . . ."

Her grandmother came back and said "I thank you," and she gave me a hug. Sometime when people talk to you, when it's coming from family, you a knucklehead, you don't listen; what they know? When you get somebody from a different aspect or somebody you don't know, you've got to look at them and be like, "Maybe they've got a story to tell, maybe they're telling me this for a reason."

It's crazy, because I used to pray and ask, "What is my purpose in life?" but I see it, because I could be anywhere—I could be in the supermarket, anywhere—somebody just start talking to me. I give them the insight of what I've seen and what I saw because I saw a lot as I was growing up. Even though I'm thirty-three and I'm still young, my insides and my soul feel old.

As old as her soul might be, Natasha is tireless in her pursuit of an American dream—one that, for her, isn't just about **her** children, but about all children. And she continues, every day, doing the best she can, where she is, with what God gave her.

9

LAW, ORDER & ACCOUNTABILITY

Not everything that is faced can be changed, but nothing can be changed until it is faced.

—James Baldwin

A POLICE OFFICER WAS YELLING COMMANDS. I couldn't hear him clearly, but what it sounded like to me was, "Stop! Don't move!"

I did move. I ran.

The officer's voice was loud enough to rise above the noise of the street. I could hear his authoritative tone, tense and focused, as the crisis of the moment grew.

His gun was drawn. His two hands grasped the weapon as he shouted commands.

Years of informal training from parents and family members—as well as my own experiences—told me to obey police officers or, when they were engaged in police activity, to steer clear or to back away. But this time, I ignored what I had known and I gambled.

I gambled that the officer wasn't going to shoot. That he knew doing so presented a host of risks. It was a summer afternoon in Newark's downtown, and on a street crowded with cars and sidewalks full of people, the risk of firing a weapon was too high.

The officer yelled again, louder now. I could hear him clearly. "Stop! Drop the knife!"

The officer, Michael Lopez, wasn't yelling at me. He was yelling at a man brandishing half of a pair of long scissors. Officer Lopez had just tussled with the man, who had slashed at him with his weapon, catching his shirt but missing the flesh underneath. At that point, Officer Lopez pulled his weapon and, with some distance between him and the man, began yelling at him to stop, freeze, and drop the weapon.

About two weeks earlier, I had been sworn in as Newark's mayor. On my way out of my new office in city hall, walking toward Broad Street to climb into a city-issued SUV, I had heard the officer yell.

I looked up to see Officer Lopez standing, gun drawn, and then I saw a man with what appeared to be a bundle in one hand and a knife in the other.

I made an instant—and, I would learn, woefully incomplete—calculation: (1) the man wasn't bigger than me, and (2) I could catch him.

So I threw off my suit coat, yelled as loud as I could—"Hey! Stop!"—and then, with something between imprudence and reckless bravado, I sprinted into Broad Street. I was gambling the officer wouldn't shoot. I was betting that if the knife-wielding man saw a six-foot-three, 250-pound man sprinting at him, he wouldn't stand his ground. I was wagering that—given my charge and the armed police officer—he would turn and run. Plus I knew I wouldn't be charging alone; two officers assigned to my security detail were right there with me. My sprint caught the two detectives off guard, but I yelled at them as I entered Broad Street, "Let's go!" The two officers, Kendrick Isaac and Billy Valentin, and I worked our way through the street, zigging and zagging through traffic. And the man did as I hoped: seeing the three of us charging at him, he turned and ran.

My security detail probably should have tackled **me,** as their job was to protect me, even when I did stupid things like put myself between an officer with a gun and a man with a knife. But they did as I had hoped they would, and gave chase with me. Though I had a head start, Detective Valentin soon passed me. Easily catching up to the suspect first, Valentin dove at him, hitting him in the small of the back and knocking him to the ground. Detective Isaac was on him in an instant, and I yelled at them to secure the hand with the weapon as I tried to step on it with my foot. Other officers joined in, and they had him immobilized in seconds.

Angry and full of adrenaline, I looked at the man. He was probably in his late fifties. He looked even more frail up close, and seemed much less of a threat now that he was in custody. He had the appearance of someone mentally unstable or addicted to drugs. As my fury subsided, my compassion for him began to rise. I turned around; in the heat of the moment, I had forgotten that we were on Broad Street in the middle of the day. People were watching us. With my last bit of rapidly diminishing bravado, I exclaimed, "Not in our city! Not anymore!" People applauded.

It was one of the more overblown and inaccurate statements I've ever made.

Our challenges in Newark—like the massive challenge of crime across our nation—would not be ended by a single arrest or a chest-pounding politician. In that moment, I deeply believed the words I'd spoken. But my administration was only days old. We were just beginning a journey of facing the complex challenges of crime fighting; we were struggling with a range of issues that aren't confined by city limits; we were taking on challenges that are interrelated with factors and causes beyond the reach of a local government. We had our work cut out for us—and I had a lot of hard lessons to learn.

One thing I didn't need to learn was what our campaign pollsters told us: the top issue in the minds of Newarkers was crime. The polls showed there was new universal concern about crime, safety, and security, but this was no revelation. After about a decade in Newark, I knew this at the core of my being.

I had conversations about crime every day, all across the city. Living in Brick Towers, I knew how concerns about crime weighed on the lives of so many people, bringing stress and strain. I knew firsthand how crime affected people: the day I moved into the city, I had my things stolen from my friend's car, and over the years I dealt with plenty more problems like that. Car break-ins were a frustrating inconvenience—I had to deal with smashed windows, replace popped door locks, install all kinds of antitheft systems—but for others, who worked hard but made less than I did, such inconveniences were much more serious setbacks, expenses that might be unbearable. The smallest things could trigger a spiral into the deeper distress of debt.

But far more destructive than property crime was violent crime. Victims of violent attacks could find them to be destabilizing events. Beyond the physical injuries, beyond the financial nightmare of losing much of the little you have, there are emotional consequences that are hard to measure but are every bit as real and damaging.

Because we are connected to each other, these incidents don't happen in a vacuum; they occur in neighborhoods, in communities, in cities. Each violent crime reaches far beyond the immediate victim. Violence is ultimately an assault on an entire community: it wounds general well-being, leaving scars that can't be seen but which also can't be ignored or denied.

In community meetings and tenant meetings, at block parties, in conversations with nonprofit and business leaders, with principals and teachers, and even with my neighbors and friends, person after person insisted to me, when I was mayor, that reducing crime was critical for our city. They didn't need a poll to tell them this; they knew the impact of crime on their lives and the lives of their neighbors. I carried into the job of mayor thoughts of friends and neighbors who had been victimized by crime, lives that had been upended by violence.

In the run-up to the 2006 mayoral election, I was approached by a worried mother. In the basement of a building on Spruce Street, after a tenant meeting, a mother who assumed I would be mayor walked up and demanded that I do something about the situation in the neighborhood, and started telling me about her traumatized child. She described what was happening with her son in a way that made me think that he was suffering post-traumatic stress from having to dive for the ground when a shooting happened or when he heard gunfire at night. She told me how even innocent loud noises, like the pop of a balloon, now made him panic and grow anxious. She described how her once-outgoing boy had become withdrawn, quiet, and fearful of leaving her side.

It is profoundly unfair that too many Americans, like this boy and his mother, who work hard but make little, who are stuck with limited housing options, who don't have access to the kind of mental health professionals that the more affluent have, must live in neighborhoods where they regularly experience trauma. This is not normal, but somehow we behave as if it is. We accept it. If anything, we think it is "their" problem.

When fear becomes the norm, it stalks your life relentlessly, lurking and casting shadows over your daily routine. Fear changes you. Fear changes us. My parents worried about me, but they never had to deal with an ever-present fear that violence could erupt at any moment and consume their child in an instant, affecting him or her in ways that no hug or loving assurance could heal.

This mother on Spruce Street made it clear that **it was not fair,** that we live in America, a nation that promises better. Shouldn't our collective outrage at the challenges faced by our fellow citizens inspire more action, engagement, and passion?

Crime makes for simplistic generalities, easy finger-pointing. It's tempting to wash your hands of responsibility and just blame the "bad guy." If we could just capture all the bad guys and lock them up, put enough cops on the street, create enough deterrence with strict penalties, then wouldn't everything be okay? Now, bad guys **do** need to be locked up. We need more cops. Deterrents properly placed can help. But that is not enough. We are one society, and as Dr. Martin Luther King Jr. said, what we will have to repent for is not the "vitriolic words and violent actions of the bad people," but the "appalling silence and indifference of the good people."

In one of my first major meetings on crime in Newark, a law enforcement officer reinforced King's message. The meeting took place at the FBI's Newark field office. The concrete, glass, steel, and cement block building was built on our waterfront, and as a city council member I had railed against its construction. When cities across the country are opening up their waterfront to parks, river walks, and restaurants, who uses that land for an FBI bunker? I lost that council vote 8–1.

But now we were sitting around a big conference table in that very building along the Passaic River. The FBI agents were eager to talk with my police leadership and me, to try to forge a strong relationship with our team. It was a constructive meeting—and for me, a learning session.

That day, I got a solid introduction to the many things the FBI did for our city and state. They reviewed with me a considerable amount of data on everything from gang crime to terrorism. As they rolled through the data on violent crime in and around our city, I said to the then special agent in charge, Les Weiser, "How do we solve this problem?"

I was looking for answers, a strategy we could pursue to produce real results in reducing crime.

Agent Weiser looked at me. "Mayor," he said, "we **don't** solve this problem. We just attend to the symptoms of the problem." I knew that by "we" he wasn't just talking about the FBI; he was talking about law enforcement.

I swore my oath of office with a sense of mission for the city: to expand economic development and opportunity in the city; to improve the quality of life for children and families; to bring needed reforms to government; and to reduce crime. But when I raised my hand at my inauguration, crime was foremost on my mind. I hadn't wanted to wait for the formal ceremony to get started; though we told few people, that official swearing-in in front of thousands was just a reenactment. I wanted to begin dealing with the city's urgencies right away, so in a private ceremony, I'd been sworn in at midnight. And the first orders I gave involved the police department.

I hit the ground running. I began working around the clock, going days with just a few hours of sleep, testing my endurance and that of my senior team, who in many cases matched my pace or exceeded it. Beyond our challenges with crime, which had been spiking in 2005 and '06, crises were breaking out all around us.

We had a massive budget shortfall with a structural budget deficit and seemingly no way to close it; the city had been spending at levels way beyond its recurring revenue for years, and the nonrecurring revenue streams were drying up as we entered office, leaving us with no good options. The structural deficit was about $180 million on a roughly $600 million general fund—which meant that if we were to eliminate our debt, we would have to develop or attract new housing and businesses that could generate tax income, identify other sources of revenue, or cut our government by one-third.

We knew immediately that the gap couldn't responsibly be closed in twelve months, and thus we had many years of unpopular financial decisions ahead of us. But even then we didn't foresee the global financial meltdown or having a new governor in a few years who—with his own priorities—would cut many of the streams of revenue that could have lessened the pain of our decisions.

Amid all of these challenges, the murder rate was rising. In every community meeting I went to, every neighborhood I visited, the plea was for more public safety, usually articulated as a call for more police presence. People wanted walking patrols, dedicated officers assigned to their neighborhoods, a police substation, or simply increased police visibility. But I knew, as Agent Weiser had said, this wasn't just a police problem.

I told all my departmental leaders that we needed their help in fighting crime. All hands on deck. Departments tasked with inspections, sanitation, and neighborhood services were now to see themselves as playing an active role in crime reduction. We targeted high-crime areas with efforts to board up abandoned housing, clean vacant lots, fix signage, and increase the brightness of streetlights. I created a multi-department task force—we called it "the Task Force with No Name"—to coordinate across departments and with the police in addressing conditions that attracted crime.

We focused not just on cleaning up neighborhoods but on doing right by them. Newark was one of the worst cities in America in terms of usable park space per person—an unfortunate distinction, given that parks elevate the quality of life for residents and improve the safety of neighborhoods. When we redid a baseball field in Newark's South Ward, I remember a parent thanking me, saying it was about time we demonstrated to our kids that we love them as much as other towns that had nice facilities love their kids. We were soon investing in acres and acres of new and refurbished parks all around the city, transforming open fields known for criminal activity into community centers. Before we knew it, we had done more to expand and improve city parks in Newark than had been done in our city for over a century.

On top of this, we focused on looking after people who were being released from prison or who had previous convictions. We knew it was critical to help ex-offenders, because without opportunity men and women go back to prison at alarming rates, while with help—often just in finding a job—they were far more likely to stay out of trouble. We had little money to run these programs, but we got creative, and I sought private donations and foundation grants for them. Seeking grants for city initiatives, in fact, would become an increasingly large part of my efforts as mayor.

My team engaged in dozens of other strategies to reduce crime, from court reforms that provided alternatives to detention for low-level offenders to expanding youth activities during the summer. But what made me feel even more encouraged was how eagerly Newark residents stepped up to help. The activities of Newarkers all around the city were inspiring. Community members led cleanups of abandoned lots, activists stepped forward to help with prisoner reentry programs, and one neighborhood in the South Ward even began nightly citizen patrols.

The clergy of Newark also helped in significant

ways. At the beginning of my term I put a call out to the city's religious leaders and asked them to join me in a hotel for twenty-four hours of fasting, prayer, and planning. Out of this meeting came a clergy not just engaged and selfless—they already were that—but, crucially, more coordinated with our efforts. We formed clergy police patrols; some religious leaders assisted us in enforcing our youth curfew; others helped with our prisoner reentry work; many worked to foster more dialogue between police and the community by hosting public safety town halls in their churches. Knowing that seniors are often the eyes and ears of the community, we formed a Senior Citizen Police Academy. We put classes of seniors through a program mirroring parts of our police training process; most popular for the seniors was when they learned about guns and went to the firing range. The end goal was to foster a closer relationship between them and officers and to get their help in identifying, responding to, and preventing crime.

Amid all of the activity, I found it invaluable to be out and about as much as possible, in community and tenant meetings, visiting businesses and churches, and walking blocks in neighborhoods all over the city, particularly ones that were known for high crime. I enjoyed being out on weekends the most, especially at night. I rolled up on kids out in violation of our city curfew and either encouraged them to go home or saw them to the door myself.

If I saw guys out in areas known for drugs, I got out to talk with them. I'd ask if the guys needed work, if they were interested in a job that was safe and reliable. I'd hear excuses about how they had tried and failed, and I would invite them to let me help them find a job.

"Show me you're serious," I would say. "Come to my apartment first thing in the morning and my team and I will try to help you find a job." Most wouldn't show, but I was impressed by the dozens who did. We couldn't always find them work, but we almost always managed to set them up with some training, at the very least.

Newarkers wanted to help; we just had to find ways to let them. To better incentivize getting tips on crime, we formed an anonymous gun hotline where we offered people $1,000 if they called with a tip that led to the recovery of an illegal weapon. We even received tips from people calling from prison. This program resulted in getting many weapons off our streets—and I believe it saved lives.

In my first years on the job, perhaps my favorite activity in the warmer months was just going around the city and playing basketball or hosting other events—often late at night and in neighborhoods known for high crime. We would get the crime-scene lights—huge lights that could illuminate an entire street—and we'd play basketball and enjoy other games with kids in the community. My police detail often played with me. I had fun talking smack when young folks couldn't beat a mayor many years their senior, and I swallowed a lot of pride when we did get beaten. I savored those games and the other activities we would do with our kids—usually Simon Says, or, as I called it, "Take the Mayor's Money," because I'd give the winners cash prizes. Years later I still have people coming up to me in Newark insisting that they beat me in a basketball game—to which I reply, "That's because I let you."

In my years as mayor, I served with two police directors. Both men were sons of police officers. Both grew up inspired to serve by fathers who dedicated themselves to law enforcement. Well before they went to the police academy, they learned about policing through observation and dinner table conversations. They witnessed the honor, the courage, and the challenges of the job from men for whom it wasn't a job but a mission.

My first police director was Garry McCarthy, who told me the compelling story of his father, who served in the New York City Police Department—but first served in the Marine Corps during World War II. Garry would speak of how his father was wounded three times, earned a Bronze Star, and fought in critical battles at Guadalcanal and on Iwo Jima. On Iwo Jima he and all but two of his forty-four-member platoon were wounded. His platoon was part of the division that raised the famous American flag on Mt. Suribachi.

Garry rose through the ranks of the NYPD and was assigned tougher and tougher details, where he made a considerable difference. Eventually he was named to run Comstat (a law enforcement management system that increases police accountability and better enables effective strategy through the use of computer-generated data) for the whole department during a period of crime reduction in New York City. I hired him in the months after I took office, and he went to work with a sense of urgency that reflected mine.

He and I were immediately concerned about the physical condition of the Newark Police Department. All aspects of the department's physical plant, equipment, and vehicles were in a significant state of disrepair. When I first visited the West Precinct in the city, I was so shocked at what I saw that I invited members of the media to come see the conditions for themselves: mold covering walls, nonfunctioning bathrooms, sections that were closed off because the ceilings seemed to be caving in. The fact that our officers showed up to work in these conditions and still did their jobs with dedication and commitment was a testament to them. I wouldn't let budget problems stop us from doing right by the men and women serving, and so we set out to give the department an upgrade. I quoted Hannibal to my first mayoral chief of staff, Pablo Fonseca: "We will either find a way or make one."

Beyond the deteriorating buildings, our police vehicles were a wreck, and many of the cars and motorcycles were operational only because officers were so dedicated to the job that they kept them running themselves, paying for parts and tools out of their own pocket. Even worse, the internal systems in the department were paper based—critical information was kept in handwritten logs, and arrest reports were done on **typewriters.** Typing forms in 2006 made no sense and also meant that processing one arrest could keep a police officer off the streets for hours. And because it was so hard to find typewriter ribbons, some officers would actually carry spares around with them, as if the essential parts of a Newark police officer's gear were handcuffs, radio, gun, and . . . a typewriter ribbon.

We went to work on the physical plant, computers, and other technology. We formed a police foundation to raise philanthropic dollars for critical police needs, and I spent increasing amounts of time seeking donations. We created an adopt-a-precinct program to help with improvements to the buildings. We bought computers with city money and eventually got many more donated; by placing them in cars, we could give our officers on patrol access to critical information and the ability to write reports without coming back to a precinct.

Through philanthropy we eventually had the resources to embrace more cutting-edge technology, from hundreds of public safety cameras installed in communities to gunshot-detection and -location audio technology.

All the while, Director McCarthy continued to make key policy changes in the department, including moving more police from administrative positions to patrol, and directing scarce resources already in the field.

For example, he changed the Gang Enforcement Unit's schedule from working daytime during the week to covering weekends and evenings—as gangs, of course, don't take nights and weekends off.

During these early days, I was intent on leading from a place of knowledge, so I virtually embedded myself with the police department. For hours each day I was with officers, learning from them, developing a deeper understanding of their job, and talking with Director McCarthy and members of his team. At all hours I visited officers on patrol, supervisors at precincts, and special task forces as they prepared to go out on duty. I attended Comstat meetings, got real-time police reports on my BlackBerry, observed police in the field, inspected equipment, and did everything I could to let officers know what I expected from them and also how much I believed in and appreciated them.

Many nights I would go out on patrols. This made for long days. I would finish my workday, try to take an hour or so to nap and eat, and then go ride with police officers from ten o'clock until early the next morning—often until three or four. I wanted to be out during the times and in the places where serious crime most often happened. Not only did I seek to observe our officers at work, but also I wanted them and the community to know how high a priority I placed on the work they were doing.

The closer I drew to officers, the more I was struck by the humble heroism of the men and women of the Newark Police Department and some of the other law enforcement agencies we cooperated with on the federal, state, county, and local levels. I got to know them and their families. I saw their professionalism on the job; I saw how they were willing to take extraordinary risks, often putting themselves squarely into life-threatening situations to carry out their duties.

I also saw how we as a city and as a larger society were demanding more and more from them every day. Police officers, like teachers, have seen their roles expand. They are now called to do things that go well beyond the job description. The police officers who served in Newark, like many other American police officers, are societal problem solvers—they are mediators, psychologists, grief therapists, relationship counselors, child welfare specialists, and more. In addition, they must wrestle with all that they see, often the worst attitudes and behavior we have to offer. At times they endure abuse from those they encounter: aggressive language, derogatory remarks, insults. Further, police officers get glimpses into many of the most difficult moments of our lives—they are called to witness and deal with things that we wouldn't show or share with our closest family or friends. Too often they witness us at our worst, our most vulnerable, our most broken; they see our failures and our most unthinkable traumas. On a regular basis, I bore witness to the resiliency, character, and bravery of the men and women of the Newark Police Department as they made extraordinary efforts to try to save the lives of people in our community.

I'll never forget the day Director McCarthy called me about a hostage situation. Just blocks from where I lived, there was a distressed woman with a gun, holding her child and threatening to kill the infant. The woman had already shot at her boyfriend, who managed to escape by jumping out the window. He was wounded but stable enough to alert police to the crisis. Within minutes police were outside, trying to negotiate with her. As the director and I began to discuss options, I heard what sounded like gunfire through my phone, and then I heard our officers yelling, "Go! Go! Go!"

The officers ran up the steps and into the apartment without hesitation, but they were too late: the woman had shot her child and then herself. The professionals there tried to save the baby's life;

they tried to save the shooter's life as well. But they couldn't. What does a baby who's been shot to death look like? The gruesome reality of the whole incident was described to me. A part of me crumbled in pain just hearing it. But what happens to people who witness this kind of horror all too often?

I've heard too many such incidents from our officers, and heard how they cope and continue. These resilient men and women have seen human failings, depravity, cruelty, and evil laid bare before their eyes; they have witnessed the most heinous of crimes. Yet they still go home from work to be with their families, only to come back again the next day and dedicate themselves to the job once more.

In my first term as mayor, our city lowered crime significantly. In 2008, Newark experienced its longest stretch of time without a murder since 1961, and in 2010, it experienced its first calendar month without a murder since 1966. Making clear that this was not a statistical anomaly, the **New York Times** reported that Columbia economist Dan O'Flaherty placed the odds of Newark going 43 days without a murder at 1 in 111,482. Even with setbacks in my second term, the average crime rates over my time as mayor compared to the year I took office would be marked by double-digit percentage drops in murder rate, aggravated assault, theft, auto theft, and shootings. The reductions were a credit to our whole city, not least to the activism of residents, the partnerships of organizations that built parks and helped men and women coming home from prison, and the dedication of our police force. Even so, reducing the number of murders didn't mean that there weren't still people getting killed; we still had crime, too much of it. And while the data showed us that there were far fewer incidents of crime in our city those first four years, that doesn't do much to comfort a family reeling from the murder of their child. We had much more work to do, and this sense of urgency never abated.

With Director McCarthy's success, he was soon hired by Rahm Emanuel to lead our nation's second-largest police department in Chicago. In 2011 I asked Sammy DeMaio to replace him. Director DeMaio was the fastest-ascending police officer in the modern history of our department, a man who had earned the respect not just of his fellow officers but also of people in the community. Even many of my worst critics respected him, trusted him, and supported his appointment.

As it happened, he was stepping forward just as I was about to face some of the toughest challenges in my time as mayor.

When the looming budget challenges finally crashed down upon us, Newark and other New Jersey cities had to make major cuts to first responders. Some were able to cut their numbers through attrition, but most of us had to lay off members of our departments. Trenton laid off 33 percent, Paterson 25 percent, and we in Newark were forced to cut our police department by 12 percent. As hard as we tried to insulate the department from cuts, it became an unsolvable math problem.

Almost immediately we saw crime rise from our historic lows. Director DeMaio, new to the job, pulled together his team and did a great job of stretching dwindling resources and trying new, effective strategies to stem the increase. Thanks to his leadership, we were able to keep overall crime in my second term below where we had started in 2006, though higher than the lows we had achieved in my first term.

Around the time of the layoffs, when our police department was severely down in manpower, when we were cash-strapped and pulling people from desk jobs, supervisory roles, data collection, and more to put them on the streets, we were hit with a lawsuit by a citizens' group represented by the American Civil Liberties Union. They filed a complaint with the federal Department of Justice and asked them to investigate police treatment of citizens, alleging a long pattern of abuse and claiming that the culture of our department was toxic, engaging in routine violations of the constitutional rights of our citizens, particularly blacks.

At first I was infuriated, and I made my displeasure known. I had believed the ACLU was willing to work with us to address some of the issues they

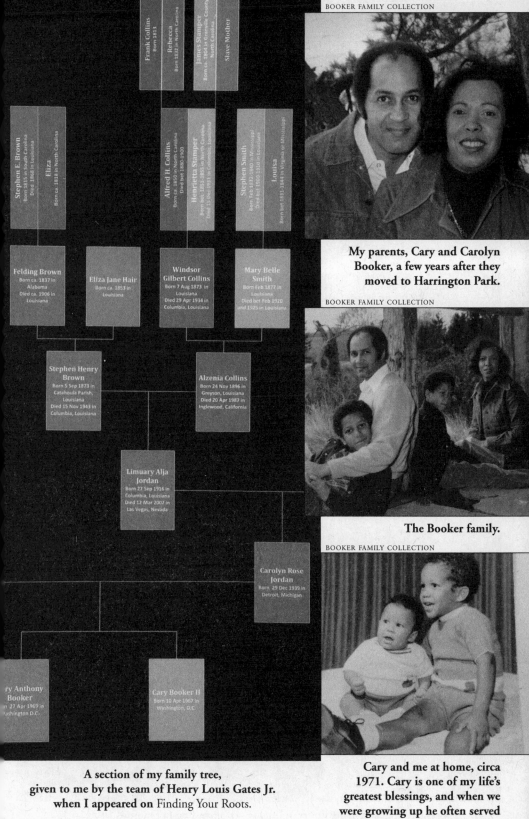

Frank Collins
Born 1813

Rebecca
Born 1832 in North Carolina

James Stamper
Born ca. 1824 in Granville County,
North Carolina

Slave Mother

Stephen E. Brown
Born 1815 in South Carolina
Died 1868 in Louisiana

Eliza
Born ca. 1838 in North Carolina

Alfred H. Collins
Born ca. 1850 in North Carolina
Died bet 1880-1900

Henrietta Stamper
Born bet 1851-1855 in North Carolina
Died 15 Dec 1931 in Columbia, Louisiana

Stephen Smith
Born Feb 1832-1840 in Mississippi
Died bet 1900-1910 in Louisiana

Louisa
Born bet 1831-1844 in Virginia or Mississippi

Felding Brown
Born ca. 1837 in
Alabama
Died ca. 1906 in
Louisiana

Eliza Jane Hair
Born ca. 1853 in
Louisiana

Windsor
Gilbert Collins
Born 7 Aug 1873 in
Louisiana
Died 29 Apr 1934 in
Columbia, Louisiana

Mary Belle
Smith
Born Feb 1877 in
Louisiana
Died bet Feb 1920
and 1925 in Louisiana

Stephen Henry
Brown
Born 5 Sep 1873 in
Catahoula Parish,
Louisiana
Died 15 Nov 1943 in
Columbia, Louisiana

Alzenia Collins
Born 24 Nov 1896 in
Greyson, Louisiana
Died 20 Apr 1987 in
Inglewood, California

Limuary Alja
Jordan
Born 27 Sep 1916 in
Columbia, Louisiana
Died 12 Mar 2007 in
Las Vegas, Nevada

Carolyn Rose
Jordan
Born 29 Dec 1939 in
Detroit, Michigan

ry Anthony
Booker
n 27 Apr 1969 in
ashington D.C.

Cary Booker II
Born 10 Apr 1967 in
Washington, D.C.

My parents, Cary and Carolyn Booker, a few years after they moved to Harrington Park.

The Booker family.

A section of my family tree, given to me by the team of Henry Louis Gates Jr. when I appeared on Finding Your Roots.

Cary and me at home, circa 1971. Cary is one of my life's greatest blessings, and when we were growing up he often served as a third parent.

So much of who I am was forged in athletics, starting with youth soccer in Harrington Park.
Over the years, my coaches have been some of my great life teachers.

Sports have opened many doors in life for me, including to Stanford University.
I've often said that football was my ticket, but not my destination.

One of our proudest accomplishments in my time as mayor was to bring about the greatest period of economic development since the 1960s. In the midst of the worst economic downturn since the Depression, we were able to put Newark on a new economic trajectory.

From a movie theater to new parks, am proud of how much Newark has nsformed in my time. Perhaps most telling was that for the first time in most sixty years, the population was growing again—with more people taking part in the resurgence of New Jersey's largest city.

Innovations taking place in Newark generated international interest. British Prime Minister David Cameron came to Newark to learn about our strides in helping people reenter society after time in prison, as well as other advances in social service.

In 2011, Newark hosted the Newark Peace Education Summit, which included talks by three Nobel Laureates, including the Dalai Lama.

Friends and family gather together to celebrate the birth of Ms. Virginia Jones. While I help blow out the candles, to the left of her sit Newark Housing Authority Executive Director Keith Kinnard and one of Ms. Jones's daughters.

Pictured here at the Garden Spires campout are two great Newark activists: Nancy Zak (left) of the Ironbound Community Corporation and the HUD Tenants Coalition, and Elaine Sewell, president of the Garden Spires Tenant Association.

Day one of the campout at Garden Spires. To my left are Elaine Sewell and then-Assemblyman Craig Stanley.

With Mayor Sharpe James in the Garden Spires housing complex in August 1999, just after the hunger strike ended.

One of my intense conversations with friend and mentor Frank Hutchins, circa 1998.

Months after Frank's death, city officials joined together to name a street after one of Newark's legendary tenants' rights activists.

While often trivialized, I have found that social media— the sharing of photos, experiences, and ideas— helps us to meaningfully connect to one another, to understand one another, to see one another.

Sitting with Carl Sharif, one of my great mentors who commanded wide respect in New Jersey politics.

Keith Williams giving me a tour of the Greater Newark Conservancy's garden.

Natasha Laurel at the IHOP in Newark's Central Ward, one of my favorite pre-vegan breakfast spots.

On October 31, 2013, I was sworn in as a United States senator by Vice President Joe Biden. My father had died earlier that month and this would always be one of my most precious moments with my mother.

New to the Senate, I've been fortunate to have many friends and mentors as colleagues. Here I am with one of them, Kirsten Gillibrand of New York.

I've been blessed in all of my campaigns to have friends and family to work, volunteer, and help in my efforts—from childhood friends to college classmates, from teammates to teachers. That said, of them all, my most persuasive campaigners have always been my mom and dad.

had raised, so this felt like a stab in the back. Instead of collaborating with me to solve a problem that had roots that went back decades in our department, they went to Washington, D.C. Beyond feeling betrayed, I felt like this wasn't productive—it was terrible timing, and would undermine our efforts to protect our residents.

Which isn't to say that I didn't believe there were problems.

I wasn't satisfied with the state of police-community relations. I saw signs that some of my officers needed to improve their conduct; for example, arriving at the scene of a shooting, I once watched an officer escalate the tension, acting in a disrespectful way toward residents. But, in one of my biggest mistakes as a manager, I had established no reliable analytics on these types of issues. Instead of finding ways to independently assess our progress in police accountability, I clung to the general understanding of our efforts to improve police conduct and community relations. At a time when I was fond of using that old saying, "In God we trust, but everyone else bring me data," I was making the critical mistake of not looking at good data on police-community relations and misconduct. I was confusing activity with progress.

And now the DOJ was investigating our department. My chief of staff, Mo Butler, greeted the news differently than I did. He heard me about how any other city in the state merited this investigation as much as ours did, and about how the ACLU was singling us out. Mo was sympathetic to my sentiments, but after consulting with the U.S. attorney, Paul Fishman, he came to see that we didn't have adequate clarity on the issues they were bringing up. He realized that while we had shifted much of our city to a far more transparent management system, we lacked the transparency in our police department that any one of us would want, not just as managers but as citizens. Furthermore, he saw that we didn't have the capacity to collect the needed data. In other words, he believed that we **did** need help. My complaints about our cash-strapped police department were proof that the feds could play a constructive role in helping us achieve our own goals of accountability and transparency. Mo pressed me gently but persistently, continuing to remind me of my own values, my own governing ideals, and our past conversations. He even reminded me of my own problems with the police in the years before I became mayor. He was a constant source of reasoned counsel—and he saw little here besides upside.

And so on an afternoon when I was on a high from an economic development win that would create many jobs for Newarkers, Mo stepped into my office, pulled up a chair, and sat in front of my desk. He had mastered his approach to me, knew when to have the tough conversations, and just by his tone of voice, I knew I was about to be hit with well-prepared, wise thoughts.

These were Mo's points:

1. We owed it to our residents to know the full truth of our police department. And we were about to get—at the DOJ's expense—millions of dollars' worth of free consulting.

2. This was important for the community, for our neighborhoods, friends, allies, and fellow activists. There were indeed allegations of police misconduct in Newark, around New Jersey, and across our nation. We now had a pathway that would allow us to confirm or dismiss a number of those concerns. This was an invaluable gift to police-community relations, and that trust between the police and the community was a critical element in making our neighborhoods safer and stronger.

3. If they found little, we would learn from the experience, improve on the things they pointed out, and move on. If they found real problems— well, we wanted to know about them as soon as possible.

4. Although I now had a number of twenty-four-hour police details assigned to me and my house, if I stepped out of my crime-fighting bubble and was once again just another young black guy, I would not only embrace a comprehensive investigation, I'd be demanding it. He told me that if I had so

quickly forgotten my own life experiences, I had my head up my large black posterior region.

His counsel was humbling, but it was also correct.

Issues of police-community relations had been festering in Newark since well before the 1967 riots. In fact, those issues were a principal reason the riots had happened in the first place. Since then, there had not been a major investigation into our police department by independent authorities. The more I reflected on it, the more absurd it seemed that city or police leaders had not called for some kind of major independent audit or investigation years ago. The more I reflected on it, the more I wished that the investigation had happened at the beginning of my first term instead of in my second term. I should have been the one who called for it then—and I needed to embrace it now. After reacting against the investigation publicly, I changed my tune.

It didn't take long for the investigators to begin pointing out problems—from our failure to collect critical data (lacking even the right technology to do so) to our failure to implement our own policies. I ordered my team to pounce on every flaw they pointed out—in fact, I didn't really have to order, because Director DeMaio, working closely with the DOJ, was proactive at every step. The DOJ conducted themselves with professionalism, and I appreciated the oversight of Paul Fishman, the U.S. attorney, who was more interested in solving problems than in elevating his reputation. He never tried to score cheap points in the press and instead dug in deeper to help advance our department.

When the final report was written, it pointed out serious problems in our department. Among the most significant were:

• The Newark police department failed to establish sufficient legal basis for the majority of our police stops.

• The Newark police department stopped blacks at a much higher rate than whites and Latinos—and while this divergence could be explained in part by crime patterns, calls for service, and suspect data, it clearly meant that when officers lacked sufficient stated or recorded justification for those stops, they potentially were violating the constitutional rights of citizens, with blacks bearing the brunt of such stops.

• There was wide evidence of retaliation against individuals who questioned police actions or who were guilty of simply being rude and argumentative to police. Such behavior is not grounds for arrest or detention, but often Newark officers justified arrests and detentions based on those reasons alone.

• Using officers' own accounts and justifications, the DOJ pointed to a clear and compelling pattern of excessive use of force against Newark residents.

• There was a lack of internal controls to prevent theft of property from detained or arrested citizens, and complaints of theft were not properly investigated.

Many people don't realize that police can't stop anyone they want just because of a generalized suspicion. There are clear legal standards. Officers may briefly detain a person for investigative purposes only if the officer has "reasonable suspicion" that criminal activity is occurring. Reasonable suspicion is a step below the "probable cause" necessary for an arrest. "Reasonable suspicion" requires more than being in a high-crime area or acting furtive in front of police.

The Department of Justice, using our own records, showed that our officers were not justifying reasons for stopping individuals. In the sample they examined, they found that for 15.8 percent of our stops, there was no record of any justification whatsoever; of the remaining stops, officers failed to articulate reasons that met the "reasonable suspicion" standard in 75 percent of them. The report noted that the reasons for stops were often minor, such as an individual "reacting negatively" in the presence of a police officer.

Another significant issue that surfaced in the

report was that we were not providing the necessary oversight to officers or training them to ensure that we would protect constitutional rights. Perhaps many of the stops did have a justifiable reason behind them, but we failed to adequately train officers to articulate their reasoning. And our supervisors were instead allowing for a climate in which police, instead of developing an organizational culture in which policing practices could affirm citizens' rights, were instead creating a climate in which those rights could be violated without adequate accountability. Police are granted extraordinary powers; the power to detain, the power to suspend someone's freedom, and the power to use force, even deadly force. Without sufficient basis to justify the exercise of that power, we were undermining police legitimacy and eroding community trust.

The report also challenged a type of police stop in which I had put great faith—our quality-of-life stop, which stemmed from George Kelling and James Q. Wilson's "broken-windows" theory of policing. The idea is that if you focus on minor infractions that disrupt the quality of life, things that might seem small in the context of more serious crime, you can actually undermine the more serious crime. Kelling and Wilson's theory was widely adopted and is credited by many with playing a role in New York City's success at reducing crime in the 1990s. But they also gave fair warning about how quality-of-life enforcement could undercut the larger goals of a department if there was a lack of legitimacy and equity.

Kelling and Wilson were concerned with the treatment of poor and minority communities as well. The poorest communities were often subject to policing practices that had a disproportionate financial impact. As Udi Ofer, the ACLU of New Jersey's executive director, wrote me in an email:

> Quality of life enforcement in Newark has only led to increased disharmony, as the idea of cracking down on minor offenses has only pushed people in communities subjected to this form of policing—mainly low income communities of color—into being entangled with the criminal justice system. While an arrest or a summons for a minor offense may not seem like a big deal, it can have serious consequences, including a warrant out for your arrest if you fail to show up in court or pay a fine (which can be significant), and a criminal record that makes getting a job and back on your feet so much harder. And while New York City did see a big drop in crime while this philosophy was being implemented, the fall in crime rates actually began during the Dinkins years, and other cities across the nation also saw crime fall without relying on such heavy-handed policing tactics. To me, this issue fits

well with your leadership on ending mass incarceration, and in speaking out against the collateral consequences of an aggressive, and in many ways ineffective, criminal justice system.

Decades after these practices were documented, judicially upheld, and implemented across our nation, the DOJ alleged that our use of stop-and-frisk and quality-of-life summonses were not, on the whole, helping us drive down crime. They argued that the way we deployed these tactics actually worked, in many cases, to undermine the quality of life for residents.

Now that I was mayor, I was responsible for the problem no matter what its source or how far it went back. More than this, even as I had strived my entire life to be a force for equity, fairness, justice, and opportunity, it was obvious that some of our police practices, **on my watch,** were undermining not only my own values but my life's mission.

My administration had done a thorough job of developing accountability systems for inspections, motor vehicles, sanitation, recreation, and numerous other departments and divisions that allowed us to survive the tsunami of the global financial collapse and provide better service to residents. Yet with all the emphasis on data and measures, we failed to gather sufficient data on police accountability.

The ACLU did not examine only Newark; it also reviewed the arrest practices of four other major

New Jersey cities, specifically looking at low-level offenses: disorderly conduct, loitering, defiant trespass, and marijuana possession. They found that these problems with policing are not Newark's alone. They are a New Jersey problem; they are an American problem.

The fact is, poor and minority communities disproportionately bear the brunt of crime. But they also bear the brunt of policing practices that punish their communities—for minor offenses or no offense at all—in ways that wealthier communities simply don't experience.

The irony is that communities that are crying out for more police often end up getting a type of policing they aren't seeking and not enough of the police work they need. In a world of budget cuts, we aren't adequately investing in local law enforcement and the strategies that can work, such as community policing, but instead are allowing practices to proliferate that don't reflect our common values.

As William J. Stuntz writes in his book **The Collapse of American Criminal Justice**:

> Bottom line: poor black neighborhoods see too little of the kinds of policing and criminal punishments that do the most good, and too much of the kinds that do the most harm.

I had to find ways to ensure that our police department delivered the kind of services that our community truly needed. To that end, I learned from my time as mayor that leaders have an urgent need for accurate data and data transparency. Data, especially in a time of constrained resources, can help drive desired changes. What we needed to ensure effective policing were systems of accountability. And critical to true accountability are metrics of police integrity. Without them, declarations about police conduct are only rhetoric.

There was much work to do, and Newark's police department couldn't do it alone. We needed oversight, partners, and help from the community. Before the DOJ's report was completed, I turned my attention to reforms.

To this day I am grateful for the assistance of ACLU of New Jersey's Executive Director, Udi Ofer. With humility and grace, Udi sought to partner with us to implement best practices. He wasn't looking for cheap publicity for his organization, but instead sought to fix the problems. He shared my belief that Newark could be a model for reforms on issues that were being talked about from New York City to Los Angeles.

So while the DOJ was hard at work finishing its investigation, we began to work on substantive and meaningful reforms. One of the points the DOJ identified again and again was Newark's lack of data collection, analysis, and review. More than this, there was a lack of transparency: the public didn't know what the police were doing on issues of great concern. We turned to Udi and the ACLU to partner with us in making improvements on those fronts.

We first focused our attention on the problems with stop-and-frisk and agreed to work toward having the highest possible level of transparency in relation to these practices. We agreed to post our stop-and-frisk data on the city website once a month and began working toward a policy that the ACLU would call "one of the most comprehensive in the nation." The policy called for collecting and posting data on who was being stopped beyond what was being done elsewhere, including data on youth and students as well as people who had limited English proficiency.

Another important step was establishing more departmental accountability. So while Director De-Maio worked on internal systems of accountability, I focused on establishing a Civilian Complaint Review Board for the police department; it was long past time for such a move. I announced in my last State of the City address that we would be establishing such a board and that we would begin gathering community input. We turned again to the ACLU to begin this process, which was advanced by my successor, Newark's current mayor, Ras Baraka. Mayor Baraka not only instituted the board but is further strengthening it.

Accountability reforms were just beginning in Newark, and there is a long way to go. From body cameras to management systems that provide real-time reviews of officer conduct, accountability is a critical trend that must continue in Newark and is urgently needed across our nation. It protects both our officers and the communities they serve. In the same way that I didn't appreciate the extent of the challenges in Newark, too many don't see the extent of our policing challenges in America— nor do they see how they endanger public safety and compromise our values. When it comes to our American values and ideals of fairness, justice, and equality under the law, we are seeing only the tip of the iceberg, not fully understanding the magnitude of the peril that lies beneath.

Even with the emergence of dash cams, body cams, training, and accountability, there is a stunning lack of urgency to address these problems. We may see snippets of video that capture tragic glimpses of the problems with police conduct, but many still discount the severity, gravity, and prevalence of the issues. Perhaps this is because we just have no way of measuring it adequately, since we don't demand the data and we aren't performing the needed audits and investigations. We often end up in national conversations that are akin to arguing about what the temperature is in a room without looking at the thermostat. What we need is a collective call to the common good based upon indisputable facts and the broader aspirational ideals to which we all ascribe.

But my experience in Newark gives me hope.

I now know that some of the most important work we need to do to reduce crime has nothing to do with police. I am proud that more people are realizing the failure of mass incarceration and how lack of opportunity after returning from prison can send too many of our fellow Americans spiraling back toward crime. I am proud that more people are realizing the importance of giving addicts treatment instead of longer sentences behind bars. I am proud that there is a growing awareness of America's unmet mental health needs.

We are also coming to realize how essential it is to dismantle the school-to-prison pipeline—the ridiculous policies that have criminalized kids instead of nurturing them, helping them, and healing them. There is a growing body of research that shows we can lower crime rates by better dealing with childhood trauma and investing in policies such as Nurse-Family Partnerships, where at-risk mothers get home nurse visits that are proven to reduce the cost to taxpayers of everything from kids' emergency room visits to teens' encounters with the police.

Clearly our country knows that many of the things we can do to reduce crime go far beyond the call for more police action, stiffer criminal penalties, and fewer opportunities for redemption. The question now is not **can** we do it, but whether we have the collective will to pursue these strategies and implement more enlightened policies.

I am also growing more hopeful about issues of race and the criminal justice system. We can't achieve our ideals of safety and security in our country without confronting the persistent realities of race in our criminal justice system. When it comes to policing, the attention being paid to videos of minorities being treated badly by police is good—**if** we learn from them. I am inspired by the police officers and police leaders I know around our country of all races who are coming to understand the urgent need to address issues of accountability and integrity.

In what the **New York Times** called an "unusually candid speech," FBI director James Comey spoke of the pressing challenges we face. Comey is from a law enforcement family: his grandfather, the child of Irish immigrants, was a New York City cop.

With the death of Michael Brown in Ferguson, the death of Eric Garner in Staten Island, the ongoing protests throughout the country, and the assassinations of NYPD Officers Wenjian Liu and Rafael Ramos, we are at a crossroads. As a society, we can choose to live our everyday lives, raising our families and going to work, hoping that someone, somewhere, will do something to ease the tension—to smooth over the conflict. We can roll up our car windows, turn up the radio and drive around these problems, or we can choose to have an open and honest discussion about what our relationship is today—what it should be, what it could be, and what it needs to be—if we took more time to better understand one another. . . .

Much research points to the widespread existence of unconscious bias. Many people in our white-majority culture have unconscious racial biases and react differently to a white face than a black face. In fact, we all, white and black, carry various biases around with us. . . .

But if we can't help our latent biases, we can help our behavior in response to those instinctive reactions, which is why we work to design systems and processes that overcome that very human part of us all. Although the research may be unsettling, it is what we do next that matters most. . . .

A mental shortcut becomes almost irresistible and maybe even rational by some lights. The two young black men on one side of the street look like so many others the officer has locked up. Two white men on the other side of the street—even in the same clothes—do not. The officer does not make the same association about the two white guys, whether that officer is white or black. And that drives different behavior. The officer turns toward one side of the street and not the other. We need to come to grips with the fact that this behavior complicates the relationship between police and the communities they serve. . . .

Perhaps the reason we struggle as a nation is because we've come to see only what we represent, at face value, instead of who we are. We simply must see the people we serve.

Director Comey and other law enforcement leaders are now speaking more openly and honestly about implicit racial bias and how it affects policing in substantive and measurable ways. In fact, many departments around the country are beginning to realize that with appropriate training and awareness, we can significantly lessen the impact of this bias.

In addition to training, we must collect better data. I am still astounded at how little data on police accountability and integrity we collect and analyze. You can't have accountability without standards, a way to measure those standards and consequences, or changes that are made when those standards aren't met. I introduced legislation in the Senate for better data collection on the federal level, and was encouraged when Director Comey also made that call:

Not long after riots broke out in Ferguson late last summer, I asked my staff to tell me how many people shot by police were African-American in this country. I wanted to see trends. I wanted to see information. They couldn't give it to me, and it wasn't their fault. Demographic data regarding officer-involved shootings is not consistently reported to us through our Uniform Crime Reporting Program. Because reporting is voluntary, our data is incomplete and therefore, in the aggregate, unreliable.

I recently listened to a thoughtful big city police chief express his frustration with that lack of reliable data. He said he didn't know whether the Ferguson police shot one person a week, one a year, or one a century, and that in the absence of good data, "all we get are ideological thunderbolts, when what we need are ideological agnostics who use information to try to solve problems." He's right.

The first step to understanding what is really going on in our communities and in our country is to gather more and better data related to those we arrest, those we confront for breaking the law and jeopardizing public safety, and those who confront us. "Data" seems a dry and boring word but, without it, we cannot understand our world and make it better.

I am grateful to the activists who refuse to let issues of police accountability slip from the attention of policy makers, leaders, and the public at large. I am grateful that they are expanding awareness and disturbing the false comforts of indifference and privilege. Their cause is not one of self-interest; rather, they seek to make our democracy stronger, more just, and more united. Sometimes we need to be shaken into awareness and awakened to the vital need for more empathy and action in a nation that still has a long way to go on matters of racial reconciliation.

Police officers are different from many others in our society. In cities and communities across America, most of our law enforcement officers demonstrate persistent professionalism, unwavering bravery, an almost irrational willingness to sacrifice for their community, and a profound and inspiring love of neighbor and country. For the sake of their work, our safety, and the integrity of our nation, we must train them even better and hold them to higher levels of accountability. And we must remember that police can't solve the problems of crime in America alone. We must take much greater responsibility upon ourselves to do that. We must take much greater responsibility for each other.

10

INCARCERATION NATION

It is said that no one truly knows a nation until one has been inside its jails. A nation should not be judged by how it treats its highest citizens, but its lowest ones.

—Nelson Mandela

I N 1994, DURING MY FIRST YEAR AT YALE LAW School, I went to prison. More specifically, I went to Green Haven Correctional Facility, a maximum-security prison in upstate New York, as part of a program at the law school. The premise of the Green Haven Prison Project was that "those who aspire to work in the field of law, and those whose lives are most intimately impacted by those laws, have much to learn from each other."

This premise was true, but it was an understatement. I was twenty-five at the time and, like most Americans, I knew the basics of how prisons worked and what purpose they served, I had heard about people being sentenced to prison terms, caught some news programs about them, and I had seen **The Shawshank Redemption**. But I didn't **know** America's prisons. To me, prisons were like our landfills: I had an abstract understanding of them but had never visited one, and I didn't give them much thought even when I was putting my trash in waste baskets or plastic bags. Landfills were just **away**—the place where we sent our trash.

Now that I was confronting the truth about my relationship with American prisons, it didn't sit right with me. Perhaps one reason for this was my faith. In the Bible there are many mentions of prisoners and our obligations to them, and it was clear to me that I wasn't fulfilling them. It is written that Jesus tells his followers that in the end He will separate the righteous and set them at his right hand. He continues:

Then the King will say to those on his right, "Come, you who are blessed by my Father; take your inheritance, the kingdom prepared for you since the creation of the world. For I was hungry and you gave me something to eat, I was thirsty and you gave me something to drink, I was a stranger and you invited me in, I needed clothes and you clothed me, I was sick and you looked after me, I was in prison and you came to visit me."

Then the righteous will answer him, "Lord, when did we see you hungry and feed you, or thirsty and give you something to drink? When did we see you a stranger and invite you in, or needing clothes and clothe you? When did we see you sick or in prison and go to visit you?"

The King will reply, "Truly I tell you, whatever you did for one of the least of these brothers and sisters of mine, you did for me."

On the drive to Green Haven, leaving Yale's Connecticut campus and heading north to Dutchess County, New York, I realized I had no idea where I was heading. Sure, I knew the location on the map, but I had no reliable gauge for my expectations. It was as if I went sailing forth on a cloudy night with no compass, no stars, and no sight of the horizon. My ignorance embarrassed and disconcerted me.

A few months earlier, as I was arriving at law school for my first year, a broad bipartisan group in Congress passed the Violent Crime Control and Law Enforcement Act—often called the "crime bill." This was the largest piece of criminal justice legislation enacted in U.S. history. It had elements worth applauding, from more funding for communities to hire police to resources and protections for victims of domestic violence. But the bill also increased federal mandatory minimum sentences, incentivized harsher criminal punishments at the state level, took away inmate education resources, and provided funds for building new prisons. The overall effect was to turbo-charge the already surging momentum of the tough-on-crime movement that was sweeping across America—and which pushed for more and longer punishments, swelling our jails and prisons.

The irony is that before the bill was passed by Congress, crime rates had already begun what would be a long and continuous decline. Data analyzed by Pew Charitable Trusts, the National Research Council, and others show no correlation between our massive increases in sentencing and imprisonment and this decline.

While in retrospect it seems clear that the increase in harshly punitive sentencing did not substantively affect crime rates, back in 1994, some well-positioned researchers knew we were heading down an expensive, wasteful, and dangerous path. Our approach had begun in the 1980s, with the domestic war on drugs and a succession of legislation at the federal and state levels that increased penalties, established mandatory minimums, and filled our jails and prisons with nonviolent offenders. In 1994 the research agency for the federal courts, the Federal Judicial Center, wrote:

> There is substantial evidence that the mandatory minimums result every year in the lengthy incarceration of thousands of low-level offenders who could be effectively sentenced to shorter periods of time at an annual savings of several hundred million dollars, and that the mandatory minimums do not narrowly target violent criminals or major drug traffickers. The statutes have unintended consequences that compromise the basic fairness and integrity of the federal criminal justice system. Moreover, the benefits of mandatory minimums could be achieved at a lower cost and with fewer negative side effects through application of the federal Sentencing Guidelines.

In 1994, Nick Turner was a second-year law student at Yale. He was assigned as my "big brother" to mentor me as I adjusted to law school. Nick is a wonderful guy, fun to be around, with a great sense of humor that counterbalances his serious sense of mission. He was the perfect "big brother" in that he, too, was struggling to figure out what to do after law school that could make a difference. Our journey to Green Haven Correctional Facility was also his first time in an American prison.

Nick and I had come of age in the 1980s and early '90s, during the era of mass incarceration—one of the more significant shifts in American criminal justice in over a century. This wasn't a policy shift championed by one party over another; legislators who supported the changes didn't come from one particular side, ideology, or region of the country. This was more than anything a product of a time when fear and demagoguery ruled, and public opinion was calling for harsher and harsher punishments. Twenty years later, Nick and I are now working to reverse the rise of hyperincarceration in our nation. Nick is the head of a leading criminal-justice nonprofit called the Vera Institute of Justice; through research and innovative pilot projects, the group works to make the U.S. justice system fairer and more effective.

In the spring of 2015, Nick asked me to join him for a forum at George Washington University to discuss the current state of affairs and our mission to change it. The data on our criminal justice system is striking, and revealing it before audiences like that at GW always gets a reaction. Here are some of the key points:

• The federal incarceration rate has increased 800 percent and state incarceration rates have increased 500 percent since 1980.
• Our nation is now the undisputed incarceration capital of the world. America has roughly

5 percent of the globe's population but about 25 percent—one out of every four—of the imprisoned people on the planet.

• Roughly one-third of all adult Americans have an arrest record.

As we rolled out these statistics to the people in that auditorium, I saw looks of surprise and faces full of disgust. Most Americans don't know the extent of our incarceration explosion, and hearing about it sparks feelings of disbelief. As was the case for me on my first trip to Green Haven in 1994, we just don't think about our prisons. And not thinking about our prisons means that we don't invest ourselves in this part of our society; we segregate ourselves from it in thought and understanding. But while we perceive ourselves as separate from the world of jails and prisons, in reality we are more intimately connected than we know. Incarceration affects all of us, daily.

Because New Jersey and our nation as a whole have a serious problem with crumbling infrastructure, I often make the point that, in the years between 1990 and 2005, a new prison opened in the United States **every ten days**. The astonishing rate of construction draws precious public resources away from other priorities. At the same time, America—which once had the top-ranked infrastructure, from roads to bridges to airports, seaports, and electrical grids—has slipped to twelfth place. Our global competitors in Asia and Europe outpace us in infrastructure investment, devoting to it more than double the percentage of GDP that we do. We are the land of the free, but these other countries enjoy a liberty dividend that we do not.

To further illustrate how mass incarceration affects us all, I often talk about the cost of college, the quality of public universities, and America's historical global leadership in education. We used to be tops in the percentage of population with a college degree; now we are in danger of slipping out of the top ten. Again, compare this with the trajectory of our exploding prison population. As the **Washington Post** reported, "We have slightly more jails and prisons in the U.S.—5,000 plus—than we do degree-granting colleges and universities. In many parts of America, particularly the South, there are more people living in prisons than on college campuses."

Beyond this draining of resources, what is increasingly disturbing is whom we incarcerate. This explosion of arrests is disproportionately focused on the most vulnerable of Americans. It was almost as if our mighty nation has said, "Give me your tired, your poor, your huddled masses yearning to breathe free, the wretched refuse of your teeming shore, send these, the homeless, tempest-tost to me: **because these are the people I will incarcerate at rates never before seen in modern history**."

When you look at America's prison population,

that is generally who you see: the poor, the sick, the tempest-tost.

- More than 80 percent of Americans charged with felonies are poor and deemed indigent by the courts.
- Between 25 and 40 percent of all mentally ill Americans will be jailed or incarcerated at some point in their lives.
- Sixty-five percent of all American inmates meet the medical criteria for the disease of addiction.
- There is profound evidence that alarming numbers of victims of childhood sexual trauma are routed into the criminal justice system at an early age, in what is called the "sexual-abuse-to-prison pipeline." As one study states: "Sexual abuse is one of the primary predictors of girls' entry into the juvenile justice system."

Furthermore, the overwhelming majority of our incarcerated population have been found guilty of **nonviolent** crimes: 74 percent of those in state prisons and 87 percent in federal prisons. Jails—which hold people awaiting trial, and which have nine times the admission rate of our prisons—hold about 75 percent nonviolent offenders.

At law school, I became acutely aware of the glaring injustice of all of this. Taking constitutional law, torts, civil procedure, and other classes, I began reading actual cases for the first time, seminal cases with names I had heard thrown around for years: **Dred Scott v. Sandford**, **Plessy v. Ferguson**, **Brown v. Board of Education**, **Miranda v. Arizona**, **Gideon v. Wainwright**. As I looked at more modern cases, however, I could see that our legal system was shifting. Right before my eyes, major shifts had already begun that made places like Green Haven more crowded, that called for the building of prisons, that changed the culture of criminal justice. Case after case tested the new harsh laws of the land, and most of them failed. Legal appeals for mercy, common sense, and pragmatism couldn't gain any purchase in the face of laws that not only affected the fate of millions but also changed the roles of lawyers and judges, turning them into political pawns as the legislative branch launched a major offensive in the drug war.

Legislatures enacted mandatory minimum sentences and three-strikes-and-you're-out laws, a one-size-fits-all approach to sentencing that prevented judges from exercising their discretion. Judges were trained to assess the facts and circumstances surrounding a crime and craft a sentence proportional to the offense, but the new laws took them out of that role. And many of the legislators who were seizing this power from judges bragged on the stump about the implementation of these policies. Some used fear tactics to attack their opponents, casting them as soft on crime.

This was, importantly, the era of Willie Horton. Horton became a household name while I was in college during the 1988 presidential campaign, when George H.W. Bush seized on the fact that while his opponent, Michael Dukakis, was governor of Massachusetts, Horton had been allowed out of prison on a furlough and failed to return, going on to commit robbery, assault, and rape. Bush's campaign manager, Lee Atwater, determined to use Horton as a tool to sow fear and depict Dukakis as dangerously soft on crime, said, "By the time we're finished, they're going to wonder whether Willie Horton is Dukakis's running mate."

As I read these cases in law school and began to see the larger context surrounding these massive changes in our legal system, I also saw how unprecedented sentences were being upheld by the Supreme Court. The nation's highest court saw these sentences as neither cruel nor unusual. The formative texts I encountered in law school were echoed powerfully years later by Michelle Alexander in her book, **The New Jim Crow**:

In 1982, the Supreme Court upheld forty years of imprisonment for possession and an attempt to sell 9 ounces of marijuana. Several years later, in **Harmelin v. Michigan**, the Court upheld a sentence of **life imprisonment** for a defendant with no prior convictions who attempted to sell 672 grams (approximately 23 ounces) of crack cocaine. The Court found the sentences imposed in those cases "reasonably proportionate" to the offenses committed—and not "cruel and unusual" in violation of the Eighth Amendment. This ruling was remarkable given that, prior to the Drug Reform Act of 1986, the longest sentence Congress had ever imposed for possession of any drug in any amount was one year. A life sentence for a first-time drug offense is unheard of in the rest of the developed world. . . .

In law school, when I first confronted these realities, they were an assault on my naivete regarding issues of law and justice. I had thought that our criminal justice system was fueled by an abundance of criminal trials and that my fellow citizens at least always had their day in court. But I learned now that I was wrong. New harsh penalties presented criminal defendants with tragic choices and perverse incentives not to go to trial. In fact, trials were becoming virtually extinct. As Jed Rakoff writes in "Why Innocent People Plead Guilty":

One thing that did become quickly apparent, however, was that these guidelines, along with mandatory minimums, were causing the virtual extinction of jury trials in federal criminal cases. Thus, whereas in 1980, 19 percent of all federal defendants went to trial, by 2000 the number had decreased to less than 6 percent and by 2010 to less than 3 percent, where it has remained ever since.

Judge Nancy Gertner, who served on the federal bench for seventeen years, stated that of the approximately five hundred sentences she handed down, "80 percent I believe were unfair and disproportionate." She wrote:

True, we have a federal plea system, not a trial system. True, to call the process "plea bargaining" is a cruel misnomer. There is nothing here remotely like fair bargaining between equal parties with equal resources or equal information. The prosecutors' power . . . is extraordinary, far surpassing that of prosecutors of years past, and in most cases, far surpassing the judge's. . . . As a result of the prosecutor's decision to charge the defendant with an offense for which there is a mandatory minimum sentence, no judging was going on about the sentence. The prosecutor sentenced the defendant, not the judge, with far less transparency and no appeal.

Before long, I began working in Yale's legal clinics because I felt compelled to get to work addressing a system that seemed so utterly broken. Though decisions such as **Gideon v. Wainwright** had given poor people the right to counsel, this applied to criminal cases. In civil proceedings, which still hold great consequence, particularly for poor people, this is not always the case. I was motivated by the fact that having a lawyer—or even a law student—stand up for a person in the court system could make the difference between homelessness and housing for that person, between security for that person's children and having them taken by the state.

Prominent criminal defense attorneys came to speak to us at law school, and they were some of the most powerful speakers I heard there—or anywhere else, for that matter. People such as Bryan Stevenson of the Equal Justice Initiative and Stephen Bright of the Southern Center for Human Rights and a professor at the law school documented how, in reality, my notion that because everyone was entitled to legal counsel they would get it was flat-out wrong.

Most people who enter our criminal justice system are poor, and they face profound challenges in acquiring adequate counsel. Public defenders routinely have unconscionably large caseloads. Thousands of poor people are going to jail or pleading guilty to crimes every year after barely talking to a lawyer. In the face of overwhelmingly long and harsh penalties, defendants are spending woefully inadequate time in discussion with counsel before making perhaps the most consequential decision of their lifetime: whether or not to enter into a plea bargain. As was reported by the Constitution Project:

> Frequently, public defenders are asked to represent far too many clients. Sometimes the defenders have well over 100 clients at a time, with many clients charged with serious offenses, and their cases moving quickly through the court system. As a consequence, defense lawyers are constantly forced to violate their oaths as attorneys because their caseloads make it impossible for them to practice law as they are required to do according to the profession's rules. They cannot interview their clients properly, effectively seek their pretrial release, file appropriate motions, conduct necessary fact investigations, negotiate responsibly with the prosecutor, adequately prepare for hearings, and perform countless other tasks that normally would be undertaken by a lawyer with sufficient time and resources. Yes, the clients have lawyers, but lawyers with crushing caseloads who, through no fault of their own, provide second-rate legal services, simply because it is not humanly possible for them to do otherwise.

An investigation by the American Bar Association further documented the problem: preposterously high caseloads are crippling the ability of lawyers to provide anything close to an adequate defense. As one public defender reported to the ABA:

> I started this job in August of 2007. The first time I counted my open cases, I stopped at 315. A few months later, it was up to roughly 330–340. The most painful and infuriating aspect of this is the impact on the defendants. Where do I even begin? People are going to jail because of my inability to devote enough time to their case.

It was my trip in 1994 to Green Haven Correctional Facility that brought all these truths home to me. In that maximum-security correctional facility, I was forced to confront my naive assumptions, and to shine a light on an area I had allowed to stay dark for too long.

After going through security, through heavy doors that always seemed to be slamming, after metal detectors and loud buzzing sounds that put me increasingly on edge, we finally arrived in what looked like a large classroom—save for the heavy doors and bars. Our "meeting" was a group conversation, and as I sat there among the inmates, I had time for some individual back-and-forth. Many of the men there were in for life. The discussion was about legal issues and society, and what struck me was how similar this talk was to the ones I'd had in the law school cafeteria with my classmates. The men were sharp and sophisticated. What struck me was how normal they seemed to me; they seemed like guys I knew. By no means did I lose sight of the fact that some of them had committed horrible crimes, but it was also clear that these human beings were much more than the crimes they had committed. To paraphrase Bryan Stevenson, they were much more than the worst things they had done.

One of the men, Charles Hamilton, seemed like the leader of the group. (Later, classmates of mine would work to help him get parole.) He had been incarcerated for the first time as a teenager and had spent decades—the majority of his life, all his adult years—in prison. Charles ran the Green Haven–Yale program from the prison side. He and a couple of the other guys sitting near me made me comfortable enough to ask questions.

What is it like, living this existence? How do you keep yourself going?

A few of their responses stick with me to this day. One of the men in for life told me he found purpose in helping other inmates, especially those who weren't staying long and would soon be going back to the streets. He told me he tried to mentor them, that he made it his mission to help them to leave and never come back.

"Anything that goes on out there goes on in here in one form or another," he said. Another man told me, "Just because we are behind these walls doesn't mean we're cut off from the world." What he meant was, the bad stuff out there went on inside the prison, too—alcohol and drug abuse, prostitution, and so on. But so did the good things— honor, friendships, self-sacrifice, and, if you chose to take them, opportunities to make yourself better. I pressed the inmates on the first part and was surprised by some of the stories of illegal activity in prisons. They also shared with me examples of guys doing right by each other. Listening to them, I saw that some of them were examples of men taking responsibility for each other and boldly acting in service of others. In fact, for Charles's parole application he had incredible testimonies from guards, other prison authorities, and visitors like us all attesting to his character.

Before I knew it, our time at Green Haven was over; it had flown by. We said goodbye with warmth and a sense of connection. As I was walking back out into the world I knew, I had the same feeling of discomfort, but now I didn't need to question it. I still couldn't explain the emotions I'd felt going in, but now I could begin to sort through them. As I got into my car I looked out at the walls of the prison and felt the solace that came from knowing why I was feeling so much tension and anxiety, and being aware that I could use that energy as fuel.

There was the obvious feeling: "There but for the grace of God go I." I could walk out of that place instead of remaining not just because of my own choices but also because of the abundantly privileged environments in which I had lived. But there was more to my discomfort than that. **I** was responsible. People were being put into this massive, expanding facility in my name, and until now I had given it too little thought. In criminal cases, it is "the People versus . . ." or "the United States versus . . . ," and I realized now that **we** are the people and that **we** are the United States. People's liberty taken away, their freedom seized, prison after prison built, filled and filled again—now I knew, and I couldn't deny it. I'd marched right in and seen a key part of the whole: the good and the bad, the truth and the lies, how our system works and how it fails.

I walked out of that prison free, and yet I was shackled to what I now knew. I was implicated. I couldn't take my full measure of pride in our greatness as a society if I was not willing to take responsibility for our failures.

I remembered what that man had said to me: **Just because we are behind these walls doesn't mean we're cut off from the world.** Their connection to us had not vanished. No matter how high the walls, how thick the steel bars, or how heavy the doors, we still were part of the same whole. We send men and women to prison, but they aren't cast out of existence.

In the summer of 2015, twenty-one years after my first visit to Green Haven, I was walking around Newark with Shane Smith, co-founder and CEO of Vice Media. Vice was shooting a documentary for HBO about the failures of the criminal justice system. As part of the special, they wanted to interview me about the criminal justice system and its impact on our communities. I had thought I would talk to them about the children of the incarcerated. (After all, there are now more than 2.7 million American children with one or both parents currently incarcerated, and approximately 10 million children with a parent who was at one point incarcerated. One in nine black children is growing up with a parent behind bars.) But as I walked with Shane around the low-income neighborhood I'd lived in as mayor, trailed by cameras, I began stopping men we saw on the street and talking with them. We must have spoken with a couple of dozen men. And we asked them if they had ever been arrested and sent to jail or prison.

I don't remember a single one saying no.

One night, several years ago, frustrated by what I perceived to be an instance of hypocrisy, I wrote something that to this day I find myself turning to:

Before you speak to me about your religion, first show it to me in how you treat other people; before you tell me how much you love your God, show me in how much you love all His children; before you preach to me of your passion for your faith, teach me about it through your compassion for your neighbors.

Now, whenever possible, I lend my voice to the growing chorus of Americans who want to confront the fact that though we often speak about our principles as a nation, we are not, in fact, living our truth as a nation—not when it comes to our broken criminal justice system. Our failure to address this problem diminishes us all. It imperils the common ideals we cherish as a country: freedom and fairness, justice and redemption.

This issue is not a divisive one. In recent years it has become clear that reducing the burdens of mass incarceration appeals to people of all backgrounds and ideologies: liberals, conservatives, Democrats, Republicans. Those who want a smaller government and lower taxes, those who want safer streets, those who care about racial and socioeconomic justice, and those who want our policies to reflect the values of compassion and forgiveness so foundational to their religion. In this fight, I have found allies in the Koch brothers, as well as the Clintons; I have partnered with Republican senators, including Ted Cruz, Rand Paul, John Cornyn, Mike Lee, and Chuck Grassley, as well as Democratic senators Dick Durbin, Patrick Leahy, Al Franken, Chuck Schumer, Sheldon Whitehouse, and Chris Murphy; I have worked not only across the aisle but across the Capitol with Republican House member Jim Sensenbrenner and Democrat House member Elijah Cummings, Republican Darrell Issa and Democrat Sheila Jackson Lee; I have connected with John Legend and Grover Norquist, Alicia Keys and Newt Gingrich. Indeed, this issue stands out to me as one on which the people of our nation are increasingly aligned. Which only makes inaction all the more inexcusable.

We must act.

We must end this legal, fiscal, public safety, and moral nightmare. We are implicated, we are responsible: all of us, together. We must change and work toward a criminal justice system that demonstrates our collective values. As Langston Hughes wrote, "To save the dream for one / It must be saved for ALL."

11

MY BROTHER'S KEEPER

I onward go, I stop,
With hinged knees and steady hand to
    dress wounds,
I am firm with each, the pangs are sharp
    yet unavoidable,
One turns to me his appealing eyes—poor
    boy! I never knew you,
Yet I think I could not refuse this moment
    to die for you, if that would save you.

—WALT WHITMAN, "The Wound-Dresser"

THE SMALL BASEMENT ROOM OF THE WILLIE T. Wright Apartments in Newark's Central Ward was standing-room only, packed with men of all ages, from guys barely in their twenties to men in their fifties and sixties. I scanned their faces and saw looks of hope and humility. A few seemed beaten down by circumstance but definitely not broken. If they'd been broken, they wouldn't have been there. They were there because they believed they could find a way; they were there because they still had hope, a resolve wrestled from trials and circumstances I would never know.

As they walked in, some eagerly shook my hand. Men older than me called me "sir" or "Councilman," treating me with a level of deference that made me feel uncomfortable. I didn't want any man to elevate me in even the slightest way—and especially not under these circumstances. **I** owed **them** humility and respect. What's more, I felt an uneasiness bordering on shame about the circumstances of our meeting. But here we were, a bunch of men in a basement, hoping to defy the odds in a fixed game.

I loosened my tie, took it and my jacket off, rolled up my sleeves. As people flowed in, the room became more and more inadequate; we were packed in close, and for some reason I thought taking off my jacket and tie would narrow the distance between us. It probably just made me feel more comfortable. I took folding chairs out from behind the table and offered them to a few of the older men so that they could sit down; my staff and I would stand. Several more men streamed in, lining up along the sides of the room and soon reaching all the way to where we were standing.

How could I have so badly miscalculated the size of the room we needed? Given what I knew, I should have booked a gym at one of the local schools.

I was twenty-nine. I had just been elected to the

Central Ward council seat in an upset. I had beaten an incumbent who was more than forty years my senior and had held the seat for sixteen years. I was a year out of law school, where I had spent a lot of time sitting in classes—but **not** like this one. Those classes were in ivy-covered buildings, modern and comfortable, with very few black men. Those classes did not fully explore how our broken legal system damages communities such as Newark. I felt that every law school student should see rooms like that one in the Willie T. Wright Apartments; that America should see.

I was holding the free clinic to help men learn how to expunge their records. Expungement, in the criminal justice sense, means to clear one's record. Some states, like New Jersey, have narrow laws that allow certain people who made a mistake to petition after a number of years to have that mistake removed so that it won't appear in criminal history searches. I hoped to help give the men in that basement a clean slate, to help them break out of what Michelle Alexander calls the American caste system, in which they were judged by their criminal past. Rather, I wanted them to be judged only by their promise and their determination to work hard and play by the rules.

At last, it was time to begin. I opened the clinic with introductory remarks. We had no microphone, but I spoke loud enough for people out in the hallway to hear. I thanked our hosts and my dear friends, the Cole family, who were resident leaders at this apartment complex; I introduced my staff, and then the lawyers. I spoke in a serious tone. I acknowledged that the men were there because they wanted to get jobs, to provide for their families, and to move on with their lives. I acknowledged how hard it was for anybody with a criminal conviction to get a job, and explained that expungement was one way to help change that.

Too many people give up, I said, and in order to make money some go back to doing things that get them arrested again. I promised to all, those who might qualify for expungement and those who might not, that we would try to help beyond this clinic. This was only a first step. We were calling employers and looking for ones that were willing to hire the formerly incarcerated.

I thanked them for not giving up. And standing there in front of that packed room, my mind flashed back to the man who had given me the life-changing assignment that led me here, to this moment.

I am a Jersey boy, but not from Newark. I had moved to the city in my last year of law school, and when I announced my intention to run for the Central Ward seat, many in Newark's political establishment attacked my electoral ambitions with ferocious condemnation. The thrust of their criticisms was that I wasn't from the city, that I was a "carpetbagger." (There were a host of other attacks I hadn't expected, like the one that alleged I was with the CIA and was bringing drugs into the community.) My opponent was particularly colorful with his attacks. He spoke in a folksy way with a sense of humor that I might have found endearing if I hadn't been on the wrong end of it. **His initials are CB. What do you think that stands for? Carpet Bagger!**

My mentor in Newark electoral politics was a man named Carl Sharif. Carl, born and raised in Newark, had been active in politics since high school and had earned a reputation as a man of conscience in the political class. Handsome and charismatic, he was interested not in being an elected official but in making the politics of Newark work. Carl believed that leaders should be connected to the community, should recognize the dignity and strength of the people, and should help leverage that strength to expand opportunity—particularly educational and economic opportunity. Carl believed that Newarkers were struggling in an increasingly globalized economy; the city needed servant leaders who could reengage people in politics and, through that activism, shape the economic realities of the coming century to the people's benefit. He believed that Newark sat on some of the most valuable land in the Northeast and that its politicians should leverage assets to expand opportunity for all.

In Newark, particularly in the black community, few had more legitimacy than Carl. Of course, not everyone liked him—in Newark, as in life, you probably aren't accomplishing all that much if everyone likes you—but he was most certainly respected by all. Carl wasn't in anyone's political camp; he wasn't a mercenary for hire, though he did often get paid for his services. Instead, he was more of a political idealist, part Malcolm X, part David Axelrod. Carl and his team were purpose-driven and chose candidates who they hoped would reflect what they stood for. And he won elections. His reputation for effectiveness grew with each political victory, and his constant efforts on behalf of people—helping them get jobs, start businesses, find housing, build housing, and achieve elected office—earned him a following of loyal friends and allies.

To paraphrase Mark Twain, you should never confuse someone's schooling with his education. Carl did not have a college degree, but he was one of the wisest men I had ever met. He spent hours questioning me and listening to my plans, my passions, and my dreams before he committed to helping me. Once the decision was made, he took me to school.

Carl gave me a master class. He taught me many of the basic things I still rely on in campaigns today, critical elements of political strategy and tactics. He also gave me spiritual counsel, encouraging me to be myself; in this he built upon my parents' foundation. Carl advised that the world doesn't need imitation. Despite the attacks against me pointing out that I wasn't a born and bred Newarker, Carl argued that we don't need candidates who try to contort themselves into what they **think** people will support. **Be who you are, Cory, nothing more,** he told me. **You will be surprised. You will earn people's trust—and if you trust them back, people will give you a chance.**

It was a shock to many that Carl embraced me and invested his reputation in me—a twentysomething little known in Newark beyond tenants' rights activists and the buildings in which I worked. When word got around that Carl was with me, my candidacy gained legitimacy and I became a threat to the incumbent and the city's political status quo.

I often say I got my BA from Stanford, but I got my PhD from the streets of Newark. I say this because some of my best life professors were people like Frank Hutchins, Virginia Jones, and Carl Sharif. And probably the best assignment I ever received came from Professor Sharif; without it, I never would have won that first campaign and probably wouldn't be in elected office today. Beyond its strategic importance, his directive gave focus to my mission. The assignment: go on a quest to knock on every voter's door in the Central Ward of Newark, and be boldly, fully, and unapologetically myself with every person I met. **Don't deny your suburban roots,** he told me. **Don't pretend**

you know what you don't know, and don't pander. Listen to them, learn from them, share your ideals and heart.

In retrospect, I think he had two agendas with this assignment—one he stated, and one he kept to himself. The stated one was to get me to introduce myself to people in the ward. Amid so much rumor, with Central Ward residents being hit with a barrage of hate flyers calling me, among many other things, a member of the KKK, he knew that if people met me, if they heard from my own mouth what I stood for, I would get their vote.

The other reason I suspect Carl wanted me to knock on every door was because he knew it would shape **me.** He knew that this quest would leave an indelible impression on me that would be the foundation of my political career as a council member and beyond. He knew that not only would residents feel me but I would feel them, too, that I would more deeply believe in them, that I would bond with them.

When I formally announced my candidacy, I gave up my post–law school public interest fellowship and lived off my credit card, my savings, and lots of free food from friends. I spent the winter of 1997 and the spring of 1998 in laundromats, at bus stops, in bars, and in front of schools and daycare centers talking to parents as they dropped off and picked up their kids. I knocked on thousands of doors across the ward, from the decades-old high-rise public housing of Stella Wright to brand-new condos in a section called Society Hill.

There was no filter between me and the people, and so I received a whole lot of honesty. I heard pride of place, love of city, bitterness, strength, frustration, anger, humor, hopefulness, fears, and dreams. I was invited into living rooms, and I held a good number of conversations through screen doors while standing in the bitter cold. Thanks to Carl's advice, I made lifelong friendships and gained dozens of incredible campaign volunteers.

My volunteers were courageous, dedicated, and generous of spirit. They came from varied backgrounds. They were high school students, college students, and senior citizens. They were community leaders, tenant leaders, and activists. They joined me after long days at work and gave up their weekends, early mornings, and late nights for our campaign. Perhaps the most persuasive volunteers I had were my mom, my dad, and my brother, Cary.

We encountered a wide range of responses to our knocks. There were slammed doors and many people who grumbled, "I don't have time." More than once people opened doors in various states of undress, and I had challenging encounters with my share of dogs, including two bites. But Central Ward residents, for the most part, engaged with me, and I cherish those conversations. Many of them weren't even aware that an election was approaching. Many didn't know who their Central

Ward council member was. Many had never met a city official and were impressed that I was on their doorstep.

Those thousands of direct conversations worked. At the end of them, I got commitments. People pledged their support and committed to go out and vote on Election Day. I would take their names, phone numbers, and contact information and we would stay in touch with letters of gratitude and phone calls to remind people to vote.

We won the election, but not necessarily by taking votes away from our opponent. He received roughly the same number of votes as he had in his past election victories. We won because we brought hundreds of new people to the polls, people who were willing to take a chance on me.

So in the summer of 1998, just days after swearing my oath of office, there I was, standing in the basement meeting room at the Willie T. Wright Apartments, the room overflowing with black men. And I realized that I should have known; I should have better estimated the demand for what we were trying to do. I should have known because every day on the campaign trail, I heard two things from hundreds of men I talked to: **I can't get a job** and **I have a record**. Many were candid about what they had done. Some had committed violent crimes; most had been convicted on nonviolent drug offenses.

Many times a woman would speak up for a man—a mother, sister, girlfriend, or wife would walk me through the man's saga. She would detail how many job applications he had filled out, how many certificates he'd earned in job training courses that went nowhere, how he couldn't even get a fast-food restaurant to give him a chance. They detailed how the rejections were taking their toll. Some agonized about how it seemed like the system wanted them to do something wrong because it was providing no options for them to do something right.

Every day of that campaign, I had learned that my ward, which was upwards of 90 percent blacks and Latinos, housed thousands of men desperate to go to work, to contribute to their family, to assert their dignity through a job—desperate for an opportunity even if it was minimum wage and manual labor. But these men were being limited by previous convictions, many of them minor.

What frustrated me was that I knew, from living in the relatively privileged communities I grew up in, that the drug war wasn't waged in those places like it was in Newark. I was coming from college campuses and suburban towns where marijuana, ecstasy, cocaine, and other drugs were widespread and often used openly, with little fear of the police. Witnessing drug use wasn't a rare occurrence in my life. Yet few Yale or Stanford students worried about being stopped and frisked on campus or having their homes or dorms raided by the police—in fact, I never knew of it to happen. Nor did I know of the DEA or local police raiding homes in Harrington Park or Old Tappan; there was drug use there, but the enforcement of the law was clearly different.

The war on drugs has turned out to be a war on **people**—and far too often a war on people of color and the poor. Marijuana use, for example, is roughly equal among blacks and whites, yet blacks are 3.7 times more likely to be arrested for possession than whites; in some states they are six times more likely. In the states with the worst disparities, across all offenses blacks were ten, fifteen, or even thirty times more likely to be arrested than white residents in the same county.

Further, there is no difference between blacks and whites in dealing drugs. In fact, some studies show that whites are more likely than blacks to sell drugs, even though blacks are far more likely to be arrested for it. Today, about one in ten Americans has been arrested on drug-related charges, but—despite blacks and Latinos committing drug offenses at a rate no different than whites—Latinos are incarcerated in state prisons at nearly twice the rate of whites for the same offenses, and blacks are incarcerated at a rate six times greater than whites.

The sheer scale of the issue had sunk in as I knocked on those doors throughout the Central Ward. These weren't statistics. These were men from families and neighborhoods ravaged by mass arrest.

Those who had been arrested were facing penalties for their nonviolent drug involvement way out of proportion to any that befell people in the places where I had lived before. What I saw as the inconsequential actions of some of my peers at Stanford and Yale and the suburban towns of northern New Jersey were crimes that had life-altering consequences for people in Newark.

The American caste system is far more extensive than most of us realize. People with an arrest record teeter on the edges of this caste system: Americans who have been arrested feel its effects, they experience the symptoms even though they don't have the terminal disease. They live in a world where the principle of innocent until proven guilty is a fundamental value in our justice system. However, thirty-six states legally allow employers to deny jobs to people who were arrested but never convicted of a crime, leaving an innocent person with no recourse in the face of this legal discrimination.

For poor Americans, an arrest alone is enough to block them from accessing the American dream—or at least a more secure American reality. The arrest reduces employment opportunities. For example, according to the National Employment Law Project, "the likelihood of a callback for an interview for an entry level position drops off by 50 percent for those applicants with an arrest or a criminal history." And the arrest effectively reduces a person's earnings, which minimizes his or her ability to provide for a family.

To make matters worse, when it comes to the nearly seventeen million background checks done by the FBI each year for employers, approximately **half** of those records contain incomplete or inaccurate information. So even if a person is innocent, wrongfully arrested, or simply arrested by mistake, that mitigating resolution might not show up in a background check. And when such a mistake is not corrected, an employer is likely to pass that person over or disqualify him for employment. In fact, studies show that, as a result of inaccurate FBI records, nearly half a million Americans are in jeopardy of not obtaining a job that they would otherwise be offered, or of losing the job they already have.

The American Bar Association analyzed the many barriers imposed on people who were convicted of a crime—the so-called collateral consequences. They identified more than forty-five thousand collateral consequences affecting the formerly incarcerated in our nation. Of those, about 70 percent are related to employment. These Americans are no longer full citizens. Their stay in prison might have been short or might not have happened at all, but their sentence lasts a lifetime.

The economic impact on these men and women, on their children and other family members, is momentous and hurts America dramatically. It is a significant factor driving the high levels of poverty in our nation. A Villanova University study concluded that had the explosion in mass incarceration not occurred, poverty in America would have decreased by more than 20 percent.

Then there are the children of the formerly incarcerated. The punishing economic reality that comes from our repressive collateral consequences has a transgenerational impact. Not only do we impose punishments on adults well beyond their prison terms, but we impose those punishments on their **children** as well. This of course only ensures that more American children grow up in crisis, with poor kids being disproportionately affected. Because formerly incarcerated parents face a bar from public housing, food assistance, and other crucial elements of the social safety net, kids with incarcerated parents are more likely than other children to experience higher rates of food insecurity and homelessness.

While campaigning on a cold day in early 1998, I was invited into a small low-rise public housing apartment. I sat on a couch and listened to a story I was finding increasingly familiar: a woman telling me of the stress of her husband's long-term unemployment and its effect on their family. Her husband echoed the pain and frustration of his job search. He had been released from prison years ear-

lier, and he detailed to me all the things he was trying to do to earn money for his family. He could
occasionally find odd jobs or be picked up for some
manual labor, but he couldn't find steady work.

While they were talking, they intermittently
apologized for their two adorable boys—maybe
four and six years old—who were grabbing for
my campaign cards, asking for buttons, reaching
for my extra pens; one even climbed on my lap,
where I held him and bounced him gently on my
knee. This couple made me think of my parents.
My brother and I were also two years apart, and
how many times had our mom apologized for our
curiosity and playfulness?

But there was tension in the room. I could see
that the woman was overworked and had a beautiful face eclipsed with worry and strain. I could
hear the pain in the man's voice as he confirmed the
circumstances his wife had laid bare before me, the
stranger at their door. I wondered how that stress
visited upon their kids, what it would mean for two
boys to see their dad struggling. I wondered how
they would fare in a criminal justice system that
set the odds so strongly against young black boys,
especially given the data now showing that one in
three black boys born today will be arrested in his
lifetime.

Looking around the apartment, I could see it
was not in great shape; it was barely adequate for
a family. They made it clear they wanted to live

elsewhere, that they'd be happy to get out of their apartment if only they could afford to—if only the father had a shot at getting a job.

All I had to give them was an ear, a bunch of campaign material, and my pledge that I would try to do something if elected.

In this basement at the Willie T. Wright Apartments, I was making my first attempt at doing something substantive. But when the lawyer began to speak, it didn't have the effect I had hoped for. Anguished faces greeted his words. Many heads dropped, and guys started to get up and leave. They couldn't afford to waste more time in yet another dead end.

The lawyer had announced what the qualifying requirements were to get your record expunged. To begin with, the charge had to be nonviolent. Even if you had an assault charge from a bar fight with no serious injuries—fights like ones I had seen growing up—the charge could not be expunged. You could expunge only possession of drugs—but if you had an amount that was too large or if you were caught trying to sell drugs, your record could not be expunged. If you had been caught with possession more than once, your record could not be expunged. And if five years hadn't passed since the end of your time in jail or on probation or parole, your record could not be expunged.

The room was emptying out. I quickly moved

over to the door and backed into the hallway as people were slipping past me and leaving. I told the men that we would reach out to them. I repeated that we were seeking employers that might hire people with convictions. Some stopped and talked to me. One man had a large binder, and he opened it, showing me all the letters from people who would vouch for him. There were letters from clergy, one from a police officer, one from a former employer. I saw certificates of service and commendations from organizations he volunteered with. There were probably thirty pages in all.

He was angry—not at me, but his voice was full of frustration.

I remember him asking, "What is it going to take? It's been over ten years; what is it going to take for me to get a second chance?"

Nearly 70 percent of nonviolent offenders will return to prison within three years of their release, only to be released again and find themselves in the same dire circumstances. That means that most of the guys who come out of prison will end up going back. And when they do, it costs society billions. There are police costs, court costs, jail costs, prison costs, and most of all, human costs: families broken, neighborhoods scarred, children affected. These costs will be paid for generations. Their failure is on us, too.

People have themselves to blame for their decisions; that is undeniable. But don't we have a legal obligation to structure a system that is balanced, not savagely slanted against minorities and the poor? Don't we have a fiscal responsibility to take a commonsense approach to reducing the cost to taxpayers? Don't we have a moral responsibility to offer redemption to someone who has paid his debt instead of unyielding retribution against him and his family? For a crime, there is a debt owed to society, and there must be a proportionate punishment. But the man with the binder full of references was asking the right question. Aren't we a nation that believes our fellow citizens deserve, at some point, a second chance?

The obvious answer to that question permeated Newark. When I began in politics in the 1990s, it wasn't an answer that had been arrived at by most of our state or federal policy makers. Yet from my neighbors in Brick Towers to the first doors I knocked on when running for City Council to the beginnings of my first term as mayor, Newark spoke as one: **We must address the ravages of our criminal justice system, a system that is putting more and more people in prison and then releasing them into our community ill-equipped to provide for themselves and their families, ill-served by the reality of thousands of collateral consequences.**

Eight years after my election to the Central

Ward council seat—and my first anemic expungement clinic—I was elected mayor of Newark. That
May 2006, we scrambled to put together a transition committee before my July 1 inauguration.
We invited all of Newark to participate, and I was
thrilled that thousands volunteered. We separated
our transition into four committees: child and
family well-being, public safety, government reform, and economic development. We brought together experts and community leaders to head each
committee and invited all who wanted to participate to join in large work sessions to hammer out
recommendations.

These sessions produced a consistent recom-
mendation, the only theme that was present in
every meeting and in every report: Newarkers
wanted ex-offender reentry to be addressed by our
administration.

I swore my oath of office with the community's
clear directive in mind, and I am grateful that I
had a team of people inside and outside city hall to
help launch our city's initiatives. Despite decreasing
resources—and, soon, a global economic crisis—a
large group of willing advocates accomplished a
number of things of which I'm particularly proud:
organizing many of New Jersey's private lawyers
into a pro bono legal service project called Reentry
Legal Services, or ReLeSe, that helped men and
women through the complicated administrative issues and legal challenges they face upon returning

home; forming New Jersey's first municipal office of reentry; establishing a city-wide Clean & Green program to engage ex-offenders in jobs greening our city while providing them with training for better future employment; and working with a nonprofit to start a fraternity of men called Delta Alpha Delta Sigma (DADS) that offered men mentors, parenting classes, job preparation training, and more, all of which helped to reduce the rate of recidivism. I'm also proud of all the work we did to see that our state's expungement laws were expanded, allowing more people a shot at a clean slate.

Some of the people who inspired me most were the leaders among Newark's reentry advocates, who themselves had been to prison. Many of these men and women had been addicted to drugs, had been homeless, had known depths of poverty, had been shot, had been the victim of sexual or physical abuse as children, and had experienced an array of other traumas in their lives. As Zora Neale Hurston wrote, many of them had "been in Sorrow's kitchen and licked out all the pots." These men and women came out of prison, found their pathway to physical recovery and spiritual restoration through extraordinary service to other people coming home from prison or jail. Many could have moved on, could have gotten themselves together and gone about their own business, but because they'd been through a broken system, they felt called to help others piece themselves back together.

Some were pastors, some worked with me in city hall on my staff, others led organizations with names like Prodigal Sons and Daughters, Stop Shootin' Inc., and the Fatherhood Center. Others weren't part of any organization. I would connect with them as they ministered in the streets, giving of the few dollars they had or hustling for help from me or anyone with resources to keep one more kid coming home off the street and into something positive.

In totality, these citizens accomplished much good in Newark. Their work was practical—they were paragons of common sense amid systemic madness—and through their relentless hard work, they lit up some of the darkest corners of our nation with the light of their love. They exhibited greatness in perhaps the most important way—not in how high they rose, but in how many people they lifted.

In my years as mayor, thousands were lifted by our collective reentry efforts. But thousands more than that came falling back to the streets of Newark—about two thousand a year were released from prison and even more from our jails. So for every one who was helped, there were so many more who needed it. We were bailing out our leaking boat with tablespoons in a rainstorm. And there was no great rescue coming, no cavalry to back up those men and women working in the trenches. The initiatives we ran in Newark were underfunded, held together with philanthropy and trickling streams of government dollars. I spent more and more time running around, trying to raise philanthropic dollars for Newark initiatives.

I also tried to get more investments from the state and federal governments. One of the conversations I most regret in my term as mayor was when I lost my temper—something I rarely do—at a member of Governor Jon Corzine's staff when I found out that, because of their financial constraints, they weren't able to offer more support. I was rude and disrespectful, letting out months and months of frustration on a guy who truly didn't deserve it. Shooting off my mouth was just shooting the messenger. Though I would continue asking, if not begging, people for money for our reentry programs, I grew increasingly frustrated that my economic argument failed so often with government leaders. It often seemed like when it came to criminal justice expenditures—just as is the case in infrastructure development, early childhood education, and countless other areas—our society would much rather pay an obscene amount of money on the back end of a problem than pay a relatively small amount up front on evidence-based programs that would prevent the problem from happening in the first place.

It was clear to me that the money we were investing in reentry in Newark was creating a significant savings for state and federal taxpayers. But it didn't give stability to many of our programs. In fact, my overreliance on philanthropy would jeopardize the long-term security of the programs. This was not a sustainable strategy. We wouldn't run our police department, courts, jails, or prisons on philanthropy, yet another vital component of our criminal justice system was being run on generous yet unreliable charities.

When I was first elected, I was a poor manager of myself. I often mistook the urgent for the important. I tried to meet the demands of the city personally, as opposed to focusing on building systems and a structure that would meet those demands more efficiently. I struggled with how best to deal with the constant flow of people caught up in the criminal justice system who turned directly to me for help. At many events I attended, in many neighborhoods I visited, I would encounter formerly incarcerated people asking for help—and I didn't handle it well.

In those days I lived in Newark's South Ward, on the top floor of a three-family home. One reason I picked this neighborhood—after Brick Towers closed—was because it had one of the highest rates of shootings in the city. I knew from watching the former mayor that Newark's chief executive had twenty-four-hour protection, even at his house when he wasn't home. I figured that if my home was going to have round-the-clock police presence, why not live in a community that could benefit from all that security? This decision sparked heated debate among my staff and police leadership, but given that I was coming off eight years of living in Brick Towers, no appeal about my safety or "quality of life" was persuasive. I insisted that I would live in the section of the city that reflected many of the urgencies that had inspired me to run for office in the first place. (I did make one concession to security, though; the police department would rent out the apartment below mine and use it as my detail's perch.)

When formerly incarcerated men asked me for assistance with employment, I would give them information about our job placement center downtown. Guys would look at me cynically, doubting they would find help, believing that they would encounter yet more hoops to jump through. So I began to counter that cynicism with a challenge: "If you are really serious about getting a job, then come to my home at 6:00 a.m. and I will meet with you personally about it." I'd often tell them to feel free to bring friends. Many wouldn't show. But quite a number did come, and to those who did accept my offer I gave $20 for their time.

Much to the irritation of my chief of staff and police director, I held some of these early-morning sessions with people on the second floor of our building. My police leadership felt this compromised my security and that of the officers, as those visiting job seekers saw our cameras and other security elements. But I persisted and found the early-morning sessions productive. I occasionally had job placement staff come to my house, as well, and take people through the established processes.

One day, two guys I'd met showed up for career help. After counseling them I realized they had no place to sleep, no money for food, and not much more than the clothes on their back—a situation not all that uncommon in Newark. I was particularly touched by the sincerity of these two men, so I offered them one of the spare bedrooms in the second-floor apartment. They stayed there for a week or so as we tried to get them on their feet.

For my staff, this was a bridge too far. They insisted it was potentially a violation of a host of rules and regulations, put me and the police department at a serious risk of legal liability if anything happened, endangered my security and that of the officers who now had to keep an eye on these men as well as the security of the building—not to mention that it possibly violated the lease the city had with the landlord.

I had to admit it: I was wrong. While nothing consequential happened beyond two men getting an opportunity, the lectures I got from staff members were correct. With the exception of the aftermath of Superstorm Sandy, I would never again invite people to stay in the building, and I reduced my morning invitations for people to meet me for jobs but never fully stopped; instead of meeting in my apartment, we met outside the house.

In communities like Newark, brave, loving people tend to those in a broken system. They are grassroots leaders, nonprofit heads, volunteers, and activists with a seemingly inexhaustible source of grace and mercy. They help thousands of others, trying to rescue them from a plight that is both of their making and of ours. Exhausted and determined, they work. But they need help, a lot more help. It's not just about more effort, however. To fix this problem we can't simply attend to the effect—we need to address the cause.

To that end, I have often been reminded of the following parable:

There was a man walking beside a river. His mind was elsewhere but he heard a troubling sound and looked into the water: a child was drowning in the river. He dove in to save her. Just as he pulled her to the safety of the riverbank, he turned and saw another child floating down the river. He jumped back in and saved that child. Exhausted, he placed the second child on the riverbank—but even as he did, he saw yet another child. He dove in again. This continued, one helpless child after another, and he summoned all of his physical strength and endurance, diving in again and again.

At last, mired in his struggles, he saw another man walking along the river. He desperately called out, "Friend, please! Come, jump into the water! Help me save these children."

The younger man moved on, accelerating his pace.

The man in the river screamed again, "Help me! Get into this water, there are children to save!"

The younger man kept moving, now sprinting away.

Finally the man in the river screamed at him in anger, "How can you be so cruel? There are children drowning here! Don't be such an evil man, come help me!"

Now the younger man did stop. He turned to face the man in the river and yelled at him, "No, I won't come into the water with you. I'm going upriver to find out why these children are in the water in the first place so I can stop it."

I am a senator now. I am not running city departments, not crisscrossing the nation to raise philanthropy to support grassroots efforts, not holding meetings at my apartment with men and women who want a shot at redemption. I sometimes miss the daily work in Newark, side by side with people who made me better just through witnessing them. But I know there are a host of federal laws that need to be addressed, and I am proud to be working with new allies to change them.

On the state and federal levels, this coalition of actors is emerging from all parts of the political spectrum and we are fighting to fix this broken system, to roll back draconian laws, and to stop so many of our fellow citizens from being unnecessarily dumped, like scrap, into a poisoned river.

With all that is at stake, with the urgencies of this crisis, I have become a prisoner of hope. I believe common sense will prevail over senselessness. I believe enlightened economics will win out over the gross and wanton waste of collective treasure and human potential. I believe that calls for compassion will trump fear-fueled demands for more and more retribution. I believe that we are not a nation of fear, but a nation of love—a love that heals, not hurts, a love that affirms the dignity and humanity of all, not diminishes the poor and the marginalized. I believe that this broken system, which afflicts us all, will be repaired. It must be if we are to hold true to our most precious ideals of liberty and justice for all.

12

THE LAW OF
THE COMMONS

"The Holy Land is everywhere."

—BLACK ELK

PROFOUND CONNECTIONS EXIST BETWEEN all; interdependency so manifest that perceived separation is a delusion. Like a great pool containing millions of drops of water, introduce a stone and all are elevated, poison a part and all are ill affected. You can't connect more or less; the connection exists no matter what our perception. But ignore the connection, deny it, and consequences come. Yet still we too often obscure the truth of our interconnection; we insult our bonds with indifference; and through self-inflicted blindness to connection we curse the whole and damn ourselves.

The law always is: you reap what you sow; for every action there is an equal and opposite reaction; cause and effect. Humble people teach us this and more. They are great masters, the best of whom I have found are not on television, not at a university, and not elected to any office. They do not preach sermons, give lectures, or dispense orders. They do. Without fanfare, they do the best they can, with what they have, where they are. They themselves are often the ignored and marginalized, and often they are the redeemed or the prodigal child come home repentant. Whatever their journey, they humbly manifest the truth preached by Dr. King: "Injustice anywhere is a threat to justice everywhere; we are all caught in an inescapable network of mutuality, tied in a common garment of destiny."

A stimulus check arrived in the mail for Mr. Leroy Edwards.

Retired from thirty-five years working a government job, Mr. Edwards lived in a high-rise building across the street from a vacant lot overgrown by weeds, strewn with trash, and used by young men to sell drugs. The lot and the daily dealings of these men cast a shadow over the community, darkening the lives of the families living in his building.

The check delivered a considerable sum for a

man on a limited fixed income. He went off to Home Depot and used it to buy a lawn mower. And then he began. He walked into the lot and began to work the land. People watched him, feared for him. Would the drug dealers retaliate? Would they hurt the elderly man?

Mr. Edwards continued, unafraid.

He tended the earth, working a little each day. He cut the lawn, trimmed the edges, filled bag after bag. Slowly, beauty was revealed: plastic, broken glass, and cans were removed, bagged, and sent away. By his hands, the earth was exposed and people saw its magnificent nature.

Gradually, the shadow dissipated. The men who sold drugs left of their own accord. A corner lot became a community green; embarrassment, indifference, and frustration turned to pride. Those who never had done so before ventured into the space, sat and lay upon the ground, embracing their inheritance.

Mr. Edwards embodies an ideal that is at the core of American identity, and of civilizations beyond, an ideal of reverence: stewardship of the public trust, guardianship of the commons. This ideal is the deeply held recognition that if we are mindful of our abundant natural gifts, we all benefit.

In a larger way, Mr. Edwards was embodying a Justinian ideal. The Roman Emperor Justinian codified the Corpus Juris Civilis around AD 530, which became the basis of the public trust doctrine in modern jurisprudence. It acknowledges the ideal that nature is part of the public trust, that each of us is responsible for it and also entitled to it. Nature is indeed an essential element of our humanity and an intrinsic aspect of citizenship. One of our most fundamental common traits is that we all inhabit the earth. We are all dependent on nature, so we all have a stake in the preservation of our environment.

In the call to respect the commons and uphold the public trust, there should be no partisanship. In fact, this is one of the most inclusive of our American ideals. Our respect for the commons is celebrated in our most patriotic songs, from Irving Berlin's lyrics in "God Bless America"—"From the mountains / To the prairies / To the oceans / White with foam"—to Woody Guthrie's challenging response in "This Land Is Your Land": "From the redwood forest to the Gulf Stream waters / This land was made for you and me."

Our rightful, long-cherished veneration of individual freedom and self-reliance and our faith in the free market must not be accepted as excuses to fail in our individual responsibilities to preserve our communal treasures. These American ideals, despite a history that too often exhibits evidence to the contrary, can and must coexist. The idea that each of us has an absolute right to get all we can get has led to the devastation of our commons. It has violated the Justinian ideal as well as the American dream; it has diminished us all and impoverished our children.

In 1968, the American ecologist Garret Hardin wrote a seminal essay describing what he called the "tragedy of the commons":

> The tragedy of the commons develops in this way. Picture a pasture open to all. It is to be expected that each herdsman will try to keep as many cattle as possible on the commons. Such an arrangement may work reasonably satisfactorily for centuries. . . . Finally, however, comes the day of reckoning. . . . At this point, the inherent logic of the commons remorselessly generates tragedy.
>
> As a rational being, each herdsman seeks to maximize his gain. Explicitly or implicitly, more or less consciously, he asks, "What is the utility **to me** of adding one more animal to my herd?" This utility has one negative and one positive component.
>
> The positive component is a function of the increment of one animal. Since the herdsman receives all the proceeds from the sale of the additional animal, the positive utility is nearly +1.
>
> The negative component is a function of the additional overgrazing created by one more

animal. Since, however, the effects of over-grazing are shared by all the herdsmen, the negative utility for any particular decision-making herdsman is only a fraction of −1.

Adding together the component partial utilities, the rational herdsman concludes that the only sensible course for him to pursue is to add another animal to his herd. And another; and another . . . But this is the conclusion reached by each and every rational herdsman sharing a commons. Therein is the tragedy. Each man is locked into a system that compels him to increase his herd without limit—in a world that is limited. Ruin is the destination toward which all men rush, each pursuing his own best interest in a society that believes in the freedom of the commons. Freedom in a commons brings ruin to all.

For Hardin, the free market ideal undermines the broader ideals and benefits of stewardship and conservation. The impulse to take more than your share seems rational, but in reality the consequences can be catastrophic. The unchecked cumulative effect of selfish actions is the loss of the commons—which is, in turn, an immeasurable opportunity lost for generations to come. The overgrazer is not only taking an irresponsible share but also closing out the chance that others may benefit from the land in the future—including his own children, grandchildren, great-grandchildren, and so on.

This is environmental irresponsibility in a nutshell: stealing from the future and calling it profit in the present.

We are all now paying for past theft in ways most Americans don't realize. We are struggling—unsuccessfully—to pay the debt that has been shifted onto us by a perversion of free market capitalism. It is why our nation spends billions of taxpayer dollars annually cleaning up everything from rivers and lakes to Superfund sites and brownfields. It is one of the reasons we pay billions of dollars in medical expenses and lose out on billions of dollars more in present-value economic productivity.

For me, this tragedy only deepens when illustrated not with a fictional pasture but with a real river.

Years ago, Newark residents and people from all over New Jersey, rich and poor, had access to the Passaic; this great American river and all its bounty was theirs. The city of Newark was founded thanks in part to the Passaic River and the rich bay into which it flowed. People could go to the river or the bay and gather clams, fish, or crabs. Within the Passaic's waters lay an abundance that could help provide for a family.

The founders of our country knew and enjoyed the Passaic. On July 10, 1778, not long after their valiant efforts against the British at the Battle of Monmouth, George Washington picnicked at the Great Falls in the then-town of Passaic with the Marquis de Lafayette and aides Alexander Hamilton and James McHenry. The falls were, after all, one of the natural wonders of the colonies, the second largest waterfall by volume in the United States east of the Mississippi River. The men sat and ate and marveled at the falls and the mighty river that flowed forth, down through Newark and into the bay. James McHenry, who would become President Washington's third secretary of war, wrote:

> After viewing these falls we seated ourselves round the General under a large spreading oak within view of the spray and in hearing of the noise. A fine cool spring bubbled out most charmingly from the bottom of the tree. . . . Then we chatted away a very cheerful half hour—and then took our leave of the friendly oak—its refreshing spring.

Alexander Hamilton is often credited with the vision to harness the power of the falls for manufacturing. The force of the river's waters was indeed employed, and manufacturing boomed in New Jersey in the nineteenth century as inventors, engineers, entrepreneurs, and hundreds of thousands of laboring hands helped fuel the American industrial revolution.

As manufacturing grew, however, so did the practice of polluting the river.

But it would be in the twentieth century that the lower Passaic would be dealt its mortal blow. In 1961, President Kennedy authorized Operation Ranch Hand—the name for the U.S. herbicide program in Vietnam. During that war, the American military sprayed an estimated nineteen million gallons of chemical herbicides and defoliants in Vietnam and surrounding nations. Most of the chemicals used went by the now notorious name Agent Orange. These herbicides killed plant life and also brought death and suffering to many Vietnamese and their unborn children. American soldiers, too, were exposed to the toxins, and thousands suffered deadly health effects, some of which were passed on to their children.

Here at home, some plants that manufactured Agent Orange also poisoned their surroundings— the environment and the people. One American chemical company, Diamond Alkali, started producing Agent Orange in a factory along the Passaic River located at 80 Lister Avenue in Newark—and reportedly dumped "bad" batches of Agent Orange directly into the river. At the same time, the chemicals at the factory site leached into the earth below the factory. Installing catch basins and properly disposing of the chemicals would have added hundreds of thousands of dollars to the business costs; pouring them into the river was the cheaper route for the company—even if far more expensive for the commons.

In 1983 the EPA confirmed what was already known—that the extreme levels of contaminants at the Diamond Alkali plant and in the lower Passaic River posed a grave threat to human life. The EPA added the site to its National Priorities List of Superfund sites around the country, making it eligible for taxpayer-funded cleanup. Hundreds of millions of dollars were spent to clean up the site, but eventually it would take billions of dollars of public resources to fully address the problem.

The destruction of the Passaic River is an example of the perversion of the free market. In theory, goods and services are to be priced according to the actual costs of production with an addition of incremental cost for profit. What actually happened in Newark and communities around the country—and continues to happen today—is that key costs of production were shifted onto society while the profits were kept by the enterprise. With their costs externalized, the enterprise's profits increase. In the case of the Passaic River, and in the cases of so many other national treasures, these externalized costs are paid for over and over again by one generation after another.

This was my environmental awakening.

It is hard to go through schools like Stanford and

Yale without gaining an ecological consciousness. When I lived on those campuses, stories of animals suffering, loss of species, and the destruction of habitats stirred serious concern. And those concerns, in turn, stimulated small forms of activism like a personal commitment to recycling, and also a broader awareness that we needed to do more to protect our planet. I entered my twenties believing I was an environmentally alert and engaged person. But I wasn't—not really. I lacked the urgency that our crisis demanded. More than anything, I was focused on issues such as equality, justice, and lack of opportunity, but I had yet to realize that pursuing justice without addressing environmental injustice was like trying to treat a knife wound with a Band-Aid.

The lower Passaic was killed and the people who lived along its banks were poisoned. The old Diamond Alkali factory has now been declared a Superfund site, and the more I learned about the Passaic River from activists in Newark's East Ward, the more I felt that we should encircle the site in yellow crime-scene tape.

One type of toxin found in the river, dioxins—the most dangerous by-product of the Agent Orange manufacturing process—cause cancers, reproductive problems, and damage to the hormonal and immune systems. The EPA also found that the river contained high levels of PCBs (which are linked to learning and behavioral problems as well as damage to the immune system) and mercury (which is linked to developmental and reproductive problems as well as adverse effects on the brain, nervous system, and kidneys).

Nancy Zak has spent a good part of her life in Newark's Ironbound fighting against these pollutants. Born in 1948, Nancy has been an activist almost from the beginning. In college she was deeply involved in the protests against the Vietnam War and has dedicated her life to issues of justice, from fairness in education to quality housing. In the 1970s she came to Newark as a public school teacher and soon joined the Ironbound Community Corporation whose mission is to bring people together to create a just, vibrant, and sustainable community.

One of the earliest conversations I had with Nancy was about the Diamond Alklar site, the Agent Orange Superfund site. She and her organization worked in the East Ward, but she didn't care that I represented the City's Central Ward. As she later told me, "Well, there's no boundaries on air, and this kind of pollution affects everybody." She was angry, impassioned—talking to her was an education. She told me stories about the government sending people out to Newark's Ironbound neighborhood in 1983 to test for contaminants; those workers walked around the neighborhood wearing hazmat suits, and the message was clear: where families were living and children were playing, government officials were afraid to tread. And those government officials had reason to be afraid. According to Nancy, they found that the highest levels of dioxins in any community in the United States were in Newark's Ironbound. It was so bad that the government sent people—again, in hazmat suits—out to the affected communities, in parks, neighborhoods streets, and by schools to vacuum up barrels and barrels of dirt, trying to remove dioxins that residents had been exposed to for years.

Nancy pressed me to fully understand the seriousness of the situation to **all** of Newark. She had no patience for the idea that we didn't all bare responsibility to alleviate the suffering of those who might not live in a certain political district. She spoke with emotion and demanded action—she helped to kick my consciousness into gear.

Nancy and a core group of activists—her husband, Arnold Cohen, fellow ICC members June Kruszewski and Joe Nardone, and a host of others across the city—were determined that the slow poisoning of a community had to be exposed, that they had to rally as much support as they could to a cause that was threatening children in Newark and beyond. The ICC understood that it wasn't just the Agent Orange site in question—their mission was to rectify past harms and protect against ongoing threats.

The vigilance of the ICC and the constant work they do to raise awareness and engage the community to stand against environmental threats is needed not just in Newark's East Ward. The crisis in our country extends far beyond the borders of the Ironbound, and poor and minority Americans are disproportionately at risk from the dangers of environmental contaminants. In our country, it is estimated that eleven million Americans, including approximately three to four million children, live within one mile of a Superfund site. Researchers at Princeton, MIT, and Berkeley, after reviewing hundreds of thousands of birth records, found that babies born to mothers living within one mile of a Superfund site prior to site cleanup had a 20 percent greater chance of being born with birth defects.

In the United States today, there are more than thirteen hundred Superfund sites. They are in every state and the District of Columbia. New Jersey, however, has the most. But the mechanism used by Congress to pay for Superfund cleanup—last reauthorized with bipartisan support in Congress and signed by Ronald Reagan—has expired, and cleanup has slowed to a dangerous pace. In 2014, along with Senator Barbara Boxer, I requested that the Government Accountability Office report on the downward funding trend and its impact on the effectiveness of the Superfund program in eliminating these ongoing threats to American health and safety. Their report found that the decline in funding for the program has predictably affected the pace of cleanup. In fact, it pointed out that from

1999 to 2013, the number of Superfund sites has actually been increasing in the United States. The problem is getting worse.

In Newark, the Passaic River's multibillion-dollar cleanup has been announced—with much credit due to tireless efforts of activists like Nancy Zak. In my first year as a senator, I was one of the politicians who gathered on its banks, with city and East Ward activists, to introduce a significant phase of the work. Toxic sludge will be removed from the riverbed and transported to sites where it will be disposed of safely. But with limited funds and an utter lack of urgency among too many elected leaders, the progress on this multiphase project will be slow, taking years, if not decades, depending on congressional funding. And unless real pressure is applied, I do not see Congress moving on the necessary funding. But Nancy and other activists are determined to demand more rapid action, and I, and others in Congress, will do our best to honor their passion for justice with our own.

Leaders from Newark's Ironbound were not my only environmental teachers. Arriving in Newark in the mid-1990s, I joined with people who were engaged in fights for quality housing, economic opportunity, high-performing schools, public safety, and more. The early leaders I worked with were also environmental activists, in a way, fighting against not only a polluted river but also dangerous air. I worked with Frank Hutchins, for example, to improve conditions in low-income housing, from Brick Towers to Garden Spires. Frank alerted me to problems I had never considered: children were being poisoned by the air they breathed; they were being poisoned by lead and were afflicted by asthma at stunning rates.

Most Americans do not appreciate the degree to which our children suffer from lead poisoning. Each year, more than half a million children under the age of six are diagnosed with lead poisoning. The long-lasting effects of lead on a child's brain are by now well documented: it results in learning disabilities, speech delays, hearing and memory problems, and reduced motor control and balance. According to the Green and Healthy Homes Initiative, children with lead poisoning are seven times more likely to drop out of school and six times more likely to become involved in the juvenile justice system.

The effects continue into adulthood, with a 46 percent increased rate of early mortality and increased risk of cardiovascular disease, hypertension, depression, reproductive problems, and complications related to osteoporosis. In some families, lead poisoning is now in the third generation, and scientists say it is possible that lead poisoning may be passed on from mother to child during pregnancy.

Through Frank, I began to meet children who were poisoned by lead. As a city council member, I met families and activists who needed help. So many of the parents I met played by the rules, working long hours for little pay, believing in the promise that if you give your children love and attention, they will thrive. But sitting in the conference room in city hall, hearing activists and families tell their stories, I could see that their belief in that promise had been shattered.

The numbers that these activists presented overwhelmed me; the scale of it all was hard to fathom. In 2001, an article in the **Star-Ledger** made the horror of the situation plain:

> Nine out of every 10 houses in the city are tainted with lead. In any given year, 30 to 50 percent of the state's childhood lead poisoning cases are in Newark. . . . Consider the numbers: There's proof that 3,770 housing units contain lead, but it is estimated that the true figure is 94,000. Last year alone there were 374 known cases of childhood lead poisoning, although estimates are that as many as 12,600 children are affected. . . . One Newark school principal says 10 percent of the students in her classrooms are incapable of learning because of lead-induced brain damage. Lead experts suggest the number may be much higher.

Then there is asthma.

In recent years, childhood asthma rates have skyrocketed, especially in inner cities. Poor Americans are at least 50 percent more likely to have the disease than those not living in poverty. Because of asthma, children miss approximately thirteen million school days per year; poor children, already at risk for failure, are therefore more likely to fall even further behind in their schoolwork. Asthma is the single most prevalent cause of childhood disability in the United States. The cost to taxpayers is more than $50 billion per year in healthcare expenses, missed school and work days, and early death.

The causes of asthma are not always natural: scientists link them to the conditions in low-income housing and the practices of industry. Which means the problem is often man-made—and, consequently, largely fixable.

As people come to understand the environmental damages being caused by carbon and industry pollutants, there is a call for "full-cost accounting." This is an effort to include the adverse environmental costs of manufacturing and other production in the price of producing those items—from the cost of cleanup to the health impacts of carbon pollution. Currently, companies' profit-and-loss statements don't account for these and other costs, which are paid for by us all, and disproportionately by the poor and vulnerable. By failing to pay for the real cost of production, by misrepresenting or ignoring the vast consequences of some of their work, certain businesses and corporations have pursued paths that are at odds with the interests of society. A greater movement toward full-cost accounting is critical if we are going to align business decisions with what is in the best interests of future generations—and that movement is already under way.

One of my fondest childhood memories is of working with my grandfather in our backyard, planting a garden. My grandfather went to an agricultural college in Arkansas and prided himself on his farming skills. Over the course of a few months, he helped me dig up a patch of ground to plant seeds. The conversations I had with my grandfather as we worked, me watching him and following his instructions and then witnessing how our dry seeds exploded to life, affected me deeply. It was so gratifying to see how our little garden could produce so many pounds of vegetables: squash, zucchini, tomatoes, carrots, potatoes, and more. This garden didn't simply make me marvel at nature; it helped me realize my connection to it, my dependence on it.

More than twenty years later, I was mayor of Newark. In the years in between, I had realized that my childhood access to nature was the privilege of a middle-income family. Digging into the soil to plant seeds, enjoying spontaneous family hikes, buying fresh fruits and vegetables, and breathing clean air should have been a matter of American right, a basic inheritance of every American, including the urban poor, but I had come to see that was not the case. In Newark, residents had had much of their inheritance stolen.

In city hall, my team and I worked with activists to reclaim our environmental strength. From creating new parks to investing in environmentally focused retrofits of public buildings, we began our work with the conviction that we couldn't succeed in our economic, community, and health goals for the city unless we addressed environmental challenges.

One of our most fruitful partnerships was with the Greater Newark Conservancy, a small nonprofit focused on improving Newark's natural environment. The conservancy and other activists approached us to create an "adopt-a-lot" program so that more residents could produce urban gardens. I credit this early work with leading to our larger urban farming movement, which transformed acres of Newark city ground into farmland that produced thousands of pounds of produce annually.

The very experience I had enjoyed with my grandfather was the Conservancy's vision for kids in Newark—and it had become mine, too. There was a rebelliousness in the environmental movement that ignited a fire in my administration as we continued to learn about and then embrace the possibilities. I came to believe that a garden in a city is a revolutionary expression, an act of righteous insubordination.

My administration worked in conjunction with nonprofits and grassroots activists to increase community gardens, begin large-scale urban farming, and bring in farmstands and farmers' markets. We also eventually had success bringing in the first supermarkets to some communities in Newark that hadn't had them for decades. From the ShopRite on Springfield Avenue to Newark's first Whole Foods, soon to be opened on Broad Street, I worked to convince companies to come to Newark, engaging in every type of persuasion that was legal.

In our efforts to green our city, we ended up having many discussions about trees. Before these conversations, trees to me were often sources of constituent complaints—fallen branches that needed to be cleared, dead trees that needed to be removed, roots that were pushing up sidewalks. But Newark's activists and leaders educated me on the benefits they provide, and soon we set out to find every way possible to plant more of them. Trees cool a city, provide oxygen, and help clean and filter the air of particulate matter, helping to combat respiratory problems. Trees help reduce storm water runoff, reducing erosion and the pollution that is carried into waterways. They even increase property values, adding beauty and character to a block.

But when my staff told me that tree planting could actually help in our efforts to reduce crime, at first I didn't believe them. So they provided the data: evidence from studies that there may in fact be a causal link between more trees and less crime and violence. In fact, beyond trees on the street, parks and green spaces all were associated with safer communities.

What are the consequences when that natural environment has been stolen from a community, robbed by those past and present? What are the consequences when the soil is poisoned and fresh food is scarce? What happens to a people when the air is full of particulate matter that threatens children and the elderly? What happens when the water flowing past your city isn't fresh but toxic—when a river is a place not of public possibility but of poison? Science can document what it does to our bodies—but what does it do to our spirits?

Richard Louv, in his book **Last Child in the Woods: Saving Our Children from Nature-Deficit Disorder,** writes that "time in nature is not leisure time; it's an essential investment in our children's health (and also, by the way, in our own). . . . In our bones we need the natural curves of hills, the scent of chaparral, the whisper of pines, the possibility of wildness. We require these patches of nature for our mental health and our spiritual resilience."

Estrangement from nature affects the soul in ways that are hard to measure. The importance of nature—of free, unfettered access to earth's public trust—is more a matter of Justinian-inspired juris-prudence than of modern-day market analysis. Access to and engagement with nature are an essential part of what makes us human.

These are the ideas that flourished among grass-roots activists in Newark. There was an urgency to confront those who stole our children's inheritance, to fight to undo the crimes of the past and those who foisted their costs on our children in the present. But environmental activists in Newark knew also that we need to establish the good, to assert the ideals and practices so needed by our children and families. These activists knew that the spirit of our city was not just wounded by environmental assaults but weakened by a lost appreciation of our interconnectedness with the natural world.

This idea helped to ignite tremendous change during the years I was mayor; it awoke in me a personal dedication to environmental activism that I had never felt before. I had come to Newark to confront poverty and inequality; I had sought to advocate for justice in economics, housing, education, and politics. Environmental activism had not been a cause of mine. Now that had changed; I came to realize there is no strength in communities if there is not human health—mental and physical—and environmental health as well.

• • •

In the mid-1990s, Robin Dougherty was living in the suburbs of New Jersey and working for a statewide environmental organization. But she had begun to have misgivings about her job. "It was a land preservation organization," she told me. "I mean, I enjoyed preserving land, but when I thought about it, it was really preserving land for people not to use, for more affluent suburban folks. It wasn't really my soul."

In 1998 she came to a crossroads in her life. She had two job offers: she could work for the Pocono Environmental Education Center, which is on tens of thousands of acres of national forest, to conduct environmental programs, or she could come to Newark and run a small organization called the Greater Newark Conservancy. The conservancy was focused on reclaiming and preserving green spaces in Newark, and sought to reconnect the city—especially its children—to the environment. Robin recalled:

> My husband said, "Well, of course you're going to go to the Pocono Environmental Education Center." I said, "Actually, I think I'm going to go to Newark." He looked at me like I had two heads, like, "Are you kidding? Why wouldn't you go to PEEC? It's safe. It's all this really cool environmental stuff." I said, "Yeah, that's exactly the point. They already have ev-

erything. Newark doesn't have that and it needs that. It needs some more focus on its environment." I decided to come to Newark and that was that.

In January 1999, she joined the conservancy and took the space that was available to them in Newark's downtown, in what she called "this tiny little awful office on Washington Street . . . where the ceiling was caving in and the roof was leaking. . . . Nature was coming into the building." Before long, the conservancy realized that their priority should be to get away from the city center and out to where people lived—into Newark's neighborhoods. They found a site—an old synagogue that had become a black church in Newark's Central Ward on historic Prince Street. The conservancy was able to buy the building with a grant, but it was in horrible shape. The roof was leaking, the windows were rotted out, and the structure was unsound—in fact, it was more a shell than a structure.

The onetime synagogue was in one of the sections hardest hit by the 1967 riots. Fires had raged up through the Central Ward and along Springfield Avenue, which intersects with Prince Street. In 1999, when the conservancy made the purchase, the area still featured large swaths of vacant lots and abandoned buildings. The conservancy pieced together grant after grant, including New Jersey Historic Preservation money, and was able to restore the building to some of its old glory. The Greater Newark Conservancy, in the center of the Central Ward, finally had a foothold. They had created what was perhaps New Jersey's first urban environmental center.

Walking the building and grounds today, you sense that there is something sacred about the place—and not just because of the past religious purposes of the building. Through force of will, from empty ground and broken buildings, determined people summoned forth a resurrection. This urban space, once destroyed by riots, was now a thriving oasis of life. It became a sanctuary for those who yearned for a reconnection; it became a center of education and discovery; it became a source of fresh food for families, and even a place where trash and scraps are composted and turned into soil that now helps grow plants, flowers, and food in planters and beds all around the city.

I got to know Robin well when I went to Garden Spires to camp out against the crime, violence, and conditions of those buildings and she and her team turned out to help. This determined woman was standing with me, making her message known: a focus on the environment meant a focus on the **whole** environment, plants and people, air and individuals, our earth and our communities.

During that campout, she and her team worked with the community, helping them to address the issue of access to fresh and healthy food. She impressed me because she was an activist who wasn't afraid to get her hands dirty. She had an authentic love of all living things—soil, plants, people—and she was offended when anyone trashed, degraded, or disregarded anything.

For her, there are no throwaway things in nature. **Nothing** is disposable, especially not people. Everything has a purpose, and just as you can reclaim an old synagogue, you can restore, recycle, redeem anything—or anybody.

Robin's mission involved the idea that kids in all communities deserved to have an experiential connection with nature. And she and her team went to many schools to engage with them in planting trees, growing vegetables, and through other activities interacting directly with the environment. Her work only fueled her convictions as she witnessed the impact of nature on kids and how the innate wisdom of children grew as they experienced the natural world around them:

> **We've always focused on how do we get kids outdoors to interact with nature because we know that it's a learning experience, it's an experience you can't mimic by reading about a butterfly in a book. You need to see it. You need to see the life in it. There are so many life lessons that occur in nature that you can use nature as this incredible teaching tool that does mimic**

life. An example of that is, we were working at McKinley School years ago, probably twelve, thirteen years ago. There was
a child that had been killed at the school
in a very bad car accident. Had to do with
a stolen car. There was another child that
had died from asthma. We were planting
trees at the school and putting yellow ribbons around the trees for the children that
had died at the school.

As we're planting these trees, this one
little child said—because we had talked
about why we were doing this—this one
kid said, "Yeah. My brother was shot and
killed a few months ago." Almost as if you
had said, My brother went to the dentist
and got a filling, or He went to the store
and bought a candy bar. . . . It began to
open up a conversation about nature and
all of the things about nature that we like
or that we don't like, right?

We like trees, but maybe we don't like
insects. Even if you don't like insects, they
have a purpose. If you see an insect and
you don't like the look of it, what should
you do? Should you hurt it, or should you
accept it because it plays an important role
in nature?

It just began to open up this whole
conversation about the same thing about

people. We don't all like how each other look. Maybe we don't like how each other acts, but that doesn't mean we need to hurt people. This is something that kids can easily relate to.

The Greater Newark Conservancy now serves thousands of kids in Newark and gives them avenues to an experiential education that goes beyond just learning about the science of ecology—they also learn about the wisdom of life, recognize the diversity of existence, and develop a reverence for nature, others, and themselves.

Robin understood that it wasn't just children who needed to learn, connect, and experience the natural world. She saw the healing power that adults experience when reconnecting to nature as well.

When I was mayor, I joined with the Greater Newark Conservancy and other activists to create an urban farming movement in Newark. We were able to transform a number of lots, encompassing almost two city blocks, into farms. The first year we produced about five thousand pounds of fresh vegetables; eventually, our production grew to some sixty-five thousand pounds of healthy plant-based food. The farms made fresh food available to our communities, provided opportunities for schools and kids to learn, and also served a purpose beyond what I expected with adults in the community.

Newark's urban farms became popular community centers in our city. The urban farming movement not only helped get people access to fresh foods but also reinvigorated a lost connection to nature **and** the connections between people.

And the farming—working the soil, planting, growing life, and harvesting the bounty—offered an unexpected opportunity to address a key mission for our city and my administration: helping those men and women coming home from prison. My staff came up with the idea of offering those men and women jobs on our farms or on other greening projects around the city, a program we called Clean & Green. They were minimum-wage jobs, but the program gave them an immediate source of income, some training, and help with improving their soft occupational skills. We knew this program could lead to longer-term employment and reduce recidivism, but we had no idea how successful the program would turn out to be. As Robin recalled:

> **The first day when we have orientation for the program, these men and women show up and they're all completely disengaged. They are feeling and looking hopeless. They sit in their chairs and their heads are down, they're not looking at anyone. They're just thinking, "Okay, I'm here in another place. I'm going to have to do something to get some money. Got to get**

through it, whatever it is." They have no sense of hope.

I had all these guys out there working. I was right there with them planting. Here I've got some of these big burly guys that have just come out of prison, right? They're big and they're not sure what this is all about. I'm handing them these little tiny seeds that you can barely even see, right? They look like a piece of dandruff in your head. It's like, "Okay, we're going to plant these seeds." They're just looking at me like, Crazy white woman. Who are you? What is this all about?

They're looking at me, shaking their heads, but they do it, right, because "Hey, we're getting paid, so we're going to do this job. Whatever we've got to do." They're just not confident about it. About three weeks later, they look over and they're like, "Hey, there's some stuff coming up here out of the ground." They're looking and I'm like, "Well, that's what we planted." They're like, "Really? It's growing?" I'm like, "Yeah. That's what we were doing." Clearly, all the time I spent telling them what we were doing they weren't listening at all. They were still thinking, Crazy white lady.

They began to watch it and it was like all of the sudden it was theirs. It was their idea and it was theirs. Every day they wanted to go where they had planted their stuff and make sure it was watered and no one was standing on it, no one was hurting it. Then, they were asking their friends to come in and see what was happening. When the food began to grow, it was unbelievable the number of members of the community that would come by and thank the participants for growing all this food. I'd swear it's the first time in their lives they ever had any self-esteem about anything. Just to watch them glow over what they had done.

And this was what I appreciated most about Robin: she realized that working with those coming home from prison wasn't simply about charity or some one-sided act of mercy. Her whole conception of our interconnected natural environment gave her clarity to see that injustice anywhere is a threat to justice everywhere—and to reach out to others is very much in one's own self-interest. The transformation that occurs isn't limited to the person who is "helped." Instead, all involved are helped. All are transformed.

What made me even more excited about Clean & Green was that many of the men and women who entered it became the program's supervisors and leaders. Many joined the Greater Newark Conservancy's staff. Theirs are stories of personal transformation and community transformation.

The office manager, for example, is Naimah Evans. A woman who has faced tremendous challenges in her life and found strength and stability at the Conservancy, she brings a tremendous spirit to the Conservancy, she is in many ways the glue that keeps the community united in mission and purpose. Robin tells her story:

> **Naimah's mom died of AIDS, Dad was not in the home. Bounced from foster home to foster home. Got kicked out of high school. Went to a girls' home. Ended up in prison for a few years for drug sales.**
>
> **She started five years ago and we just promoted her to office manager. She was working in the field. She was doing greening, helping people with their community garden. About nine months ago, we promoted her to be our office manager because she's just made so many changes in her life. Her word and my word is "normal." I keep saying to her, "Naimah, your life needs to be normal." That's her password for her computer: "normal."**

The Greater Newark Conservancy, the Trust for Public Land, the Weequahic Park Association, and so many other groups in the city of Newark and beyond focus on the environment, but really they focus on rehabilitation, redemption, and connection. They seek to restore the glory, grace, and abundance of the commons, as well as our right of access to it—to that which binds us all together, whether we realize it or not. They face seemingly insurmountable odds, they deal, every day, with the damage done to the natural world around them—yet they are ceaseless in their determination to restore it. These are people who seek to repair the broken and return us to greatness.

There is an old rabbinical idea that if you hear the Messiah has come, first plant a tree and then go and see if it is true. The salvation of our nation, and indeed of the world—the reclamation and preservation of the commons—is on us. As James Baldwin wrote in **The Fire Next Time**: "Everything now, we must assume, is in our hands; we have no right to assume otherwise."

We are making choices every day, with action or with inaction; we are helping or we are contributing to the destruction of the commons. We can be thankful that the idea of the tragedy of the commons is a cautionary tale, not a preordained destiny. Speak to Mr. Edwards or Robin, or Naimah. With a mustard seed, some good soil, and hard work, we can reclaim the wonders of the commons and redeem ourselves. In this interdependent world, we can help make a more hopeful reality for all, in all spaces. I've seen it, in the midst of the harshest conditions; I've watched glory grow and farms flourish. I've witnessed the seeds of miracles sprouting in a city by the Passaic called Newark, New Jersey.

EPILOGUE
GO FAR TOGETHER

Interdependence is and ought to be as much the ideal of man as self-sufficiency.

—MAHATMA GANDHI

THERE IS AN OLD AFRICAN PROVERB THAT I keep close at hand for whenever I need reminding of the urgency of our time: **If you want to go fast, go alone, but if you want to go far, go together.**

This is a question, to go together or go alone, that each of us has to answer. The destiny of our country will surely depend on how many of us choose to join forces and fight the battles of our time, side by side. Cynicism about America's current state of affairs is ultimately a form of surrender; a toxic state of mind that perpetuates the notion that we don't have the power to make a difference, that things will never change. This idea is not only wrong, it is dangerous. I learned this firsthand in New Jersey, where problems like violence festered and exploded because, while many condemned what was going on, too few took **responsibility** for it—too few realized that their neighbor's tragedy was a tragedy for them as well.

The heroes of my life—my parents and teachers, colleagues and mentors—have taught me, above all, that individuals **can** have a profound impact on our communities. We, each of us, manifest our power through our daily actions: the depth of our empathy for others despite lines of division, the strength of the kindness we extend to those outside of our circles of comfort, and the sacrifices we perform in service to the greater good. The story of America has always been a celebration of our connections.

In 1825, Senator Daniel Webster, while dedicating a monument on the fiftieth anniversary of Bunker Hill, spoke eloquently of his generation's obligations to one another—and the obligations of generations to come. He cast his eye toward the future:

Let the sacred obligations which have devolved on this generation, and on us, sink deep into our hearts. Those who established our liberty and our government are daily dropping from among us. The great trust now descends to new hands. Let us apply ourselves to that which is presented to us, as our appropriate object. We can win no laurels in a war for independence. Earlier and worthier hands have gathered them all. Nor are there places for us by the side of Solon, and Alfred, and other founders of states. Our fathers have filled them. But there remains to us a great duty of defense and preservation; and there is opened to us, also, a noble pursuit, to which the spirit of the times strongly invites us. Our proper business is improvement. Let our age be the age of improvement. . . . [L]et us . . . see whether we also, in our day and generation, may not perform something worthy to be remembered. Let us cultivate a true spirit of union and harmony.

Webster was a giant of the legislative body where I now serve, a senator for the ages. But you don't have to be a lawmaker or politician to make a difference—in fact, if we were to leave everything up to the public sector we will surely fall far short of perfecting our union. To succeed in this new America, we need senators and shopkeepers, natives and immigrants, young and old, Republicans, Democrats, and everyone in between. We need **us**.
We are now generations past our nation's found-

ing, past the crisis of the Civil War, and the Great Depression, past two world wars, the civil rights movement, and a cold war, but the call of our country still abides; the dream of our nation still demands. There is much work to do to ensure that we are a nation which lives up to its promise of fairness, security, and ever-increasing opportunity. Both history and our own lives tell us that the fulfillment of potential takes steady action, hard work, and the love of many. To meet our most daunting challenges, at home and abroad, we must come together, work together, and recognize that our nation will rise or fall together—for we are truly an interdependent people.

In the pages you have just read, I have tried my best to share my own story and the stories of the people who shaped me, in what I hope is a worthy and motivating tribute to this ideal of interdependence. But these are, in the end, just a handful of stories pulled from our much larger, much richer national narrative, a great work that's constantly unfolding. With so much at stake, we now, together, must write the next chapter in our American story.

ACKNOWLEDGMENTS

> When you get to the end of all the light you
> know and it's time to step into the darkness
> of the unknown, faith is knowing that one
> of two things shall happen: either you will
> be given something solid to stand on, or
> you will be taught how to fly.
>
> —EDWARD TELLER

I have been advised many times that every day we
should do something that frightens us. The process
of writing a book, something I have never done before, was exciting—but it was indeed, with all the
work it would entail, a frightening prospect.

I am indebted to a host of people who helped
me, again and again, to choose confidence over
doubt; to choose courage over fear, stress, and perhaps one or two bouts of dread; to choose hope
that my words would prove a worthy contribu-

tion to the broader ideals I most cherish, instead of despair that they would fall flat. Through the process, I was a student: learning to be a better writer, I found many great teachers, mentors, and fellow learners with whom to share notes.

I must first thank my editor, Mark Tavani. Beyond my own labors, no one worked harder in service of this project. Incredibly, I think he believed in this project well before I even thought of writing a book. Throughout the process, he served as collaborator, experienced guide, and patient instructor, and on more than one occasion he talked me out of frustration and back toward productivity. Mark is a man of seemingly fathomless kindness and generosity of spirit; possessing a wisdom that I found fortifying, he was a perfect partner for me in this endeavor. I am forever grateful to him, and to his family, who tolerated the enormous amount of time—at all hours, day and night—he invested in this book. Publishing is of course a team sport, and I want to thank the whole team at Ballantine/Bantam Dell. Gina Centrello, Jennifer Tung, Richard Callison, Susan Corcoran, Michelle Jasmine, Quinne Rogers, Denise Cronin, Toby Ernst, Rachel Kind, Joseph Perez, Pam Alders, Shona McCarthy, Carole Lowenstein, and everyone in sales—thank you for making this book possible.

As Mark moved on to another job, I was blessed to also have Andy Ward as an editor. Andy stepped into the project and in short time proved to be an essential partner in finishing the project and making sure it was in the strongest possible form. Andy's contributions are on every page of the book, and his professional expertise not only significantly elevated the final product but for me constituted a graduate level course in writing.

I am also deeply grateful to Veronica Chambers. Veronica is herself a truly accomplished writer and for months worked with me to shape a collection of thoughts into a cohesive structure upon which to build a book. More than this, she was my partner in what was perhaps one of the most gratifying parts of the process: the dozens of interviews we conducted with people I have known throughout my life. She exhibited an abiding manner, connecting with people who have played significant roles in my journey. Veronica was a godsend, helping me think through the material, coaching me through the exercise of writing, and making countless contributions to the text. Finally, she inspired me, again and again, with the right words, articles, clips, videos, and quotes at just the right time to keep me going and to give me greater confidence in my writing.

I am grateful to my agents, Jennifer Joel and Esther Newberg. More than they probably know, I leaned upon their vast experience, trusted them, and benefited from their candor and the tough love they offered every step of the way.

I want to thank my immediate family. Their

support for this book, as for every endeavor of my life, has been relentless and unyielding. I praise my mother, Carolyn, whose love, majesty, and wisdom are present throughout this book; my brother, Cary, who is a best friend and third parent; sister Lucille and niece Zelah; brother and inspiring idealist John Taylor; sister Mati; nephew Omar; and nieces Alexa Gabrielle and Elaina.

So many people were interviewed for this book. They gave up their time and spoke from the heart; they chose to share deeply personal stories from their lives. There were a number of people who have moved on to new beginnings, yet they courageously shared details of their past lives and activities. I am grateful for their willingness to share their stories.

I am grateful to Timothy Horne and Jimmy Wright, who were critical in bringing together so many people from the Brick Towers community. A number of chapters in this book were strengthened by that enduring community. From our annual reunions to the continuing friendships, people came forward eager to help me with this project. I want to thank my friends and former neighbors, in particular Reginald Swiney, Tony Stratford, Alonzo Lamar, Emma Dorsey, Earl Dorsey, Jean Wright, Jace Bradley, James Robinson, William Robinson, Brenda Cushberry, Ms. Doris Garrett, Doris Blanchard, Jacqueline Hinkson, Cyndy Moore, Charlton Holliday, Kyle Wright, Qadia Smith, Ms.

Virginia Jones's daughters, Ruby and Bessie, Ms. Cynthia Perkins, and the entire Jacobs family.

I am grateful to those interviewed for other chapters, and those who influenced my writing through their deeds and words. Among them are: Leroy Edwards, Kendrick Isaac, Billy Valentin, Robert Boyer Jr., Hector A. Rodriguez, Alex Rodriguez, Ovidio Valentine, Robin Dougherty, Jose Negron, Elizabeth Reynoso, Keith Williams, Naimah Evans, Anthony Ambrose, Sammy DeMaio, Garry McCarthy, Richard Cammarieri, Nancy Zak, Jermaine James, Richard Whitten, Darrin Sharif, John McKeon, Richard Trenk, Susan Blum, Jimmy Blum, Mathew Blum, Victor Herlinsky, Elnardo Webster, Charlita Mays, Richard Buery, Nick Turner, Jean Strickholm, Lee Porter, Art Lesemann, Ms. Rosalie Powell, Congressman John Lewis, the Onetta Harris Community Center staff, Michelle Baird, Doug Lasdon, Ray Chambers, Bill Goode, Thomas Reddick, Pablo Fonseca, Paul Fishman, Udi Ofer, Colden and Frances Raines, Rose Doctor, Tom Sharpe, Ann Davis, Rosalie Powell, Bernice Fitzpatrick, Saidi Nguvu, Denise Cole, Debra Cole, Wilbur Cole, and, of course, one of my significant friends, inspirations, and mentors, Bill Bradley.

I want to warmly thank Natasha Laurel, who so bravely opened up about her life and became a significant part of the chapter "The High Cost of Cheap Labor." I am particularly thankful for her generosity of spirit and courageous candor.

There were a number of people who contributed to this project by serving as readers of drafts and giving me invaluable input. Each of them not only invested time but also provided critical insights, constructive critiques, and ideas that I incorporated into the work: Matt Klapper, Modia Butler, Jeff Giertz, Addisu Demissie, Drew Littman, Steve Demicco, Karen Dunn, Brad Lawrence, Kevin Griffis, Eddie S. Glaude Jr., Sean Bailey, Mark Warren, Bari Mattes, Gayle King, and Sharon Macklin.

Also, Roscoe Jones contributed substantive research to the sections about the criminal justice system. Mark Elias gave me critical legal support and, perhaps more important, wise counsel. I am deeply grateful for the invaluable and thorough fact-checking done by Cole Louison.

I am thankful to Tom Moran and Vinessa Erminio at the **Newark Star-Ledger** for their help in finding old articles not available online.

I owe an incredible debt to Henry Louis Gates Jr. and his team at Ark Media—especially Johni Cerny, Julia Marchesi, and Hazel Gurland-Pooler—as well as researchers Sandra Chappell, Judy Riffel, Phillip Smith, and Troy Wiley. I also offer affection and gratitude to members of the Brown family who, thanks to Henry Louis Gates's team, I discovered are my family, too: Dorothy and Lynne Brown, Donald Brown, and Michael Hislop.

There is a large group of friends who made invaluable contributions to this book—supporting me with encouragement and practical support, talking me down from metaphorical ledges, taking calls late at night and admonishing me to be brave and authentic, or inspiring me through their example and kindness. They loved me through the process, nurturing me and—as this process absorbed nearly all of my non-Senate waking hours—generously forgiving me for my absences in their lives. These friends are many, and some may not even realize how their kind words and gestures over the months of writing lifted me. They include Unjin Lee, Kim Pereira, Adam Zipkin, Sarah Rojas, Kevin Batts, Adam Topper, Don Katz, Christine Gentry, Ira Lit, Dean Ornish, Danielle Posa, Chris and Patches Magarro, Eugene Young, Andrew Tisch, Richard Plepler, Emily Sussman, Cliff and Robin Kulwin, Kevin Craw, Len Harlan, Lee Cho, David Shuman, Erin Schrode, Artie Rabin, Reid Hoffman, Laurie Tisch, Anne Devereux, David Mills, Michelle Thomas, Julian Neals, Vicky Klapper, Margarita Muniz, Henrique Ferreira, Casto Maldonado, Henry Amoroso, David Giordano, Anthony Santiago, John Kirtley, Rick Gerson, Bill Ackman, Bobbi Brown, Steven Plofker, Chris Cerf, Van Jones, Zoe Towns, George Helmy, Richard Grayson, Boykin Curry, Marshall Curry, Bill Budinger, Mark Hyman, Francis Greenburger, Pat and Tracey Johnston, Cynthia Ryan, Koya Webb, Menachem Gerack, John Griffin, Jimmy and Lisa Donofrio, Shmully Hecht, Wayne Pacelle, Ashley Rhinehart,

Neil Barsky, Charlie Kushner, Ellen Chube, Srinija Srinivasan, Brendan Gill, Jonathan Zimmerman, Levi Block, and of course Drew Katz, who bugged me for months to make sure his name was in the book—Drew, it is.

So many of my Senate colleagues encouraged and helped me through this process and gave me invaluable advice. I'd like to particularly thank Kirsten Gillibrand, whose advice along the way, especially as I began the process, was invaluable; Heidi Heitkamp, who was relentless in her encouragement and check-ins; Chris Coons, who stepped up to support me in the process in a way that gave me great comfort; Brian Schatz, who gave me invaluable feedback; Al Franken, whose own experiences proved very instructive (plus he tells awesome stories that lifted me, again and again); Claire McCaskill and Amy Klobuchar, who shared with me their writing experiences; and my senior senator, Robert Menendez.

There are people who were not interviewed for this book yet whose presence and influence looms large over these chapters: the teachers, staff, athletic coaches, and fellow students at two critical public schools, my elementary school, Harrington Park Elementary, and my high school, Northern Valley Regional High School at Old Tappan, who laid a foundation of learning and wisdom that I stand upon every day, and who deserve much credit for any good I might do; Jody Maxmin, who was such a significant life mentor at Stanford, as well as my other Stanford professors, my football coaches, my classmates, and the Stanford community, who collectively deserve thanks and enduring gratitude for their contributions to my life; the professors at Yale and especially the Yale Legal Clinics, who helped to shape my professional aspirations, as well as my classmates who continue to inspire and support my endeavors; my Oxford tutor, John Davis, and my many friends from Oxford who have also deeply shaped my life. I am grateful to Lynn Mertz, Bill Hoogterp, Doug Lasdon, and Ted and Nina Wells, who were so critical to my journey to Newark; Ray Chambers; Barbara Bell-Coleman, Richard Grossklaus, Doug Eakeley, Mark Gerson, Ed and Helen Nicoll, Victor Herlinsky, and Elnardo Webster, whose profound kindnesses—especially in my early years in Newark—were critical to my start in the city; Ms. Virginia Morton, who helped shape and guide me and was another one of my wise and great circle of elders in Newark; Newark's Central Ward community, where I met some of my greatest heroes and whose people collectively helped start my professional journey—thank you for embracing me as one of your own; my pastor, David Jefferson, who has been a spiritual guide to me through this writing process and for years of my life; and Phil Grate, who was heaven-sent and became part of my family. Jimmy Mitchell, whose loyalty and friendship made me a better person amid trials and triumphs, is gone but remains in my heart always. I am grateful to all the members of the Newark Municipal Council with whom I served during my time as a City Council member and as mayor, and to the city clerk and his strong staff. I also have deep appreciation for Newark's city employees, and especially my city council and mayoral staffs, whose sacrifices for Newark and for me are too immense to be described in words; my Senate staff, who in a short amount of time are creating a legacy of service that will be felt long after my tenure in Congress; and the many people who volunteered on, labored for, and contributed to my campaigns, from my 1999 city council seat to my 2014 Senate race—there is no conceivable way I can repay the work, sacrifice, and faith they afforded me.

I would like to acknowledge the memory of a number of people who are present in this book even though they are no longer present in this world. After all, death ends a life but it can't end a love. To my father, Cary Booker: I feel your love every day. I may be many things, but I am profoundly proud that I am your son. To Ms. Virginia Jones: God sought for me to have another mother, and your love was so mighty that I am only one of your thousands of children. To Frank Hutchins: I strive every day to make you proud of me, to live your lessons, to walk humbly amid God's glorious creations. To Elaine Sewell: I miss you so much, and I thank you for teaching me by your example what it means to be a leader elected by your community. To Carl Sharif: You were a profound force of wisdom, love, and essential support in my service to Newark and development as an activist. Finally, to two men who died as teenagers, Hassan Washington and Wazn Miller: Your passings shook me, the loss of you still haunts and motivates me, and I pray this book is a worthy call to the conscience of our national community to end such horrible and all too regular deaths in our nation.

Finally, I'd like to acknowledge the larger community of all people. No man is an island, and I recognize that before I took my first breath of life, millions of people's actions colluded to allow my existence and to offer the abundant opportunities I inherited. The book you hold in your hands is indeed the result of a conspiracy of love; it is also a prayer that we will continue to lead with purpose, passion, and love, so that future generations will know a nation and world far better and more united than we are now experiencing.

ABOUT THE AUTHOR

CORY BOOKER is the junior United States senator from New Jersey. He was born in Washington, D.C., and his parents, who both worked for IBM, later relocated the family to Harrington Park, New Jersey. A star high school athlete, Booker received a football scholarship to Stanford University, where he earned his bachelor's and master's degrees. While at college, Booker ran a peer-counseling center and worked with disadvantaged youth in Menlo Park. He then attended Oxford University as a Rhodes Scholar before earning his law degree from Yale University. Booker won a special election to fill the term of the late Senator Frank Lautenberg to become New Jersey's first African American senator and only the twenty-first person in American history to ascend directly from mayor to senator. Booker lives in Newark's Central Ward.

corybooker.com
Facebook.com/corybooker
@CoryBooker